AFRICAN EPISTEMOLOGY

This book investigates how knowledge is conceived and explored within the African context. Epistemology, or the theory of knowledge, has historically been dominated by the Western approach to the discourse of knowledge. This book however shines a much-needed spotlight on knowledge systems originating within the African continent.

Bringing together key voices from across the field of African philosophy, this book explores the nature of knowledge across the continent and how they are rooted in Africans' ontological sense of being and self. At a time when moves to decolonize curricula are gaining momentum, this book shows how understanding the specific ways of knowing that form part of the everyday life of the African, will play an important part in rebalancing studies of philosophy globally. Employing critical, conceptual and rigorous analyses of the nature and essence of knowledge as understood by indigenous African societies, the book ultimately asks what could pass as an African theory of knowledge.

This important guide to the connections between knowledge and being, in African philosophical thought, will be an important resource for researchers and students of philosophy and African studies.

Peter Aloysius Ikhane is Lecturer in the Department of Philosophy, University of Ibadan, Nigeria.

Isaac E. Ukpokolo is Professor in the Department of Philosophy, University of Ibadan, Nigeria

ROUTLEDGE STUDIES IN AFRICAN PHILOSOPHY

Futurism and the African Imagination
Literature and Other Arts
Edited by Dike Okoro

Critical Conversations in African Philosophy
Asixoxe – Let's Talk
Edited by Alena Rettová, Benedetta Lanfranchi and Miriam Pahl

Environmental Justice in African Philosophy
Munamato Chemhuru

Feminist African Philosophy
Women and the Politics of Difference
Abosede Priscilla Ipadeola

Kimmerle's Intercultural Philosophy and Beyond
The Ongoing Quest for Epistemic Justice
Renate Schepen

African Epistemology
Essays on Being and Knowledge
Edited by Peter Aloysius Ikhane and Isaac E. Ukpokolo

For more information about this series, please visit: https://www.routledge.com/Routledge-Studies-in-African-Philosophy/book-series/AFRPHIL

AFRICAN EPISTEMOLOGY

Essays on Being and Knowledge

Edited by Peter Aloysius Ikhane and Isaac E. Ukpokolo

LONDON AND NEW YORK

Designed cover image: Getty

First published 2023
by Routledge
4 Park Square, Milton Park, Abingdon, Oxon OX14 4RN

and by Routledge
605 Third Avenue, New York, NY 10158

Routledge is an imprint of the Taylor & Francis Group, an informa business

© 2023 selection and editorial matter, Peter Aloysius Ikhane and Isaac E. Ukpokolo; individual chapters, the contributors

The right of Peter Aloysius Ikhane and Isaac E. Ukpokolo to be identified as the authors of the editorial material, and of the authors for their individual chapters, has been asserted in accordance with sections 77 and 78 of the Copyright, Designs and Patents Act 1988.

All rights reserved. No part of this book may be reprinted or reproduced or utilised in any form or by any electronic, mechanical, or other means, now known or hereafter invented, including photocopying and recording, or in any information storage or retrieval system, without permission in writing from the publishers.

Trademark notice: Product or corporate names may be trademarks or registered trademarks, and are used only for identification and explanation without intent to infringe.

British Library Cataloguing-in-Publication Data
A catalogue record for this book is available from the British Library

ISBN: 978-1-032-02201-7 (hbk)
ISBN: 978-1-032-02200-0 (pbk)
ISBN: 978-1-003-18232-0 (ebk)

DOI: 10.4324/9781003182320

Typeset in Bembo
by Newgen Publishing UK

CONTENTS

Notes on Contributors vii
Preface and Acknowledgments xi

Introduction: On the Meaning and Discourse of
African Epistemology 1
Peter Aloysius Ikhane and Isaac E. Ukpokolo

PART I
Knowledge and Knowing in African Epistemology 17

1 African Epistemology: Knowledge Ontologised 19
   Peter Aloysius Ikhane

2 Knowledge and Truth as Interaction between the Knower and
   Being: Knowing in African Epistemology 35
   Anselm Kole Jimoh

3 Exploring the Theory of Communo-Cognition 48
   Elvis Imafidon

PART II
On the Object of Knowledge in African Epistemology 61

4 Understanding a Thing's Nature: Comparing Afro-Relational
   and Western-Individualist Ontologies 63
   Thaddeus Metz

5 Being as the Object of Knowledge in African Spaces   79
   Wilfred Lajul

6 The Ontological Foundation of African Knowledge:
   A Critical Discourse in African Communitarian Knowledge   91
   Munamato Chemhuru

PART III
Context-Discourse of African Epistemology   105

7 Truth in African (Esan) Philosophy   107
   Isaac E. Ukpokolo

8 From Ontology to Knowledge Acquisition in Africa and the
   Caribbean: What Can Be Known for Certain?   115
   Sandra McCalla

9 Elẹ́ẹ̀rí as Omọlúàbí: The Interface of Epistemic Justification
   and Virtue Ethics in an African Culture   131
   Abosede Priscilla Ipadeola

PART IV
African Epistemology in Applied Context   143

10 Onto-normative Monism in the ሐተታ (ḥāteta) of Zera
   Yaqob: Insights into Ethiopian Epistemology and Lessons
   for the Problem of Superiorism   145
   Björn Freter

11 Personalism and an African Epistemology of Personhood   159
   Philip Edema

12 Knowledge, Being, and the Case for an African Epistemology   172
   Dennis Masaka

Index   *183*

NOTES ON CONTRIBUTORS

Philip Akporduado Edema holds a PhD in philosophy from the University of Ibadan, Nigeria, and is a senior lecturer in the Department of Philosophy and Religious Studies, Augustine University, Ilara-Epe, Lagos, Nigeria. His teaching, competence and research interest cover applied ethics, metaphysics, Karol Wojtyla's personalism, philosophical anthropology, socio-political philosophy, African philosophy, logic and philosophy of peace studies. He has published several papers in reputable journals and anthologies.

Munamato Chemhuru holds a PhD in philosophy and he is an Alexander von Humboldt fellow in the Department of Philosophy and Systematic Pedagogics at the Katholische Universität Eichstätt-Ingolstadt, KU, Eichstätt, Germany (2020–2022). He teaches philosophy at Great Zimbabwe University. He is also a senior research associate at the University of Johannesburg (2018–2023). His research interests are in the area of social and political philosophy. He has edited a book, *African Environmental Ethics: A Critical Reader* (2019), published by Springer.

Björn Freter received his doctorate in 2014 from Free University, Berlin, Germany. He lives in Knoxville, TN, USA, and works as Lecturer for World Philosophy at the School of Oriental and African Studies (SOAS) at the University of London, UK. He has published on a variety of topics, including pre-Socratic philosophy, baroque and classical German literature as well as decolonization, white supremacy and veganism. His main areas of work are the desuperiorization of philosophy and at the creation of the research of 'Superaltern Studies', which investigates the superiorist traditions of the Western world and its self-representation as global moral authority.

Peter Aloysius Ikhane holds a PhD in Philosophy from the University of Ibadan, Ibadan, Nigeria, where he is also a lecturer in the Department of Philosophy. He has a number of published articles and book chapters in areas such as African epistemology and metaphysics, and applied ethics. Peter Ikhane is a recipient of the 2021/2022 African Humanities Program (AHP) Postdoctoral Fellowship Award.

Elvis Imafidon is a lecturer in the Department of Religions and Philosophies, School of History, Religions and Philosophies, School of Oriental and African Studies (SOAS), University of London, London, and a fellow of the Johannesburg Institute of Advanced Study (JIAS), University of Johannesburg, South Africa. He has several published articles and book chapters. He is the author of *African Philosophy and the Otherness of Albinism: White Skin, Black Race* (Routledge 2019), and the editor of the *Handbook of African Philosophy of Difference* (Springer 2020). His areas of specialization include African ontology and ethics, philosophy of modernity and philosophy of science.

Abosede Priscilla Ipadeola is a senior lecturer at the University of Ibadan, Nigeria, and a postdoctoral fellow, Alexander von Humboldt, at Katholische Universität, Eichstatt-Ingolstadt, Germany (2020–2023). Her research areas include African philosophy, feminist philosophy, postcolonial studies and epistemology. She has several published articles and book chapters. She is the author of *Feminist African Philosophy: Women and the Politics of Difference*. New York: Routledge, 2023.

Anselm Kole Jimoh holds a PhD in Philosophy from Ambrose Alli University, Ekpoma, Nigeria. His particular area of interest is African epistemology. He is Professor and Head of the Department of Philosophy, Major Seminary of SS. Peter and Paul, Ibadan, Nigeria (affiliated with the University of Ibadan, Nigeria). He has articles and books in epistemology, philosophy of religion and history of philosophy. He is presently completing a commissioned textbook on metaphysics. Some of his publications include "Context Dependency of Knowledge: Justification of an African Epistemology," in *WAJOPS: West African Journal of Philosophical Studies*, 1999; "Evil in the Creation of a Good God? A Philosophical Discourse," in *EPHA: Ekpoma Journal of Religious Studies*, 2003; "Knowledge and Truth in African Epistemology," in *Ekpoma Review*, 2014; and *Certitude and Doubt: A Study Guide in Epistemology*, 2013.

Wilfred Lajul is an associate professor of Philosophy and former head of Philosophy Department, in the College of Humanities and Social Sciences, Makerere University, Uganda. He obtained his PhD in 1994 (Urban University, Rome), MA Phil in 1992 (Urban University, Rome) and BA Theology in 1987 (by affiliation – Urban University, Rome). He is the author of *The Role of Man in the Dynamics of History: Reflections on Kant* (1994), *African Philosophy: Critical Dimensions* (2014), *Contemporary African Philosophers: Critical Appraisal* (2017) and several articles and book chapters.

Dennis Masaka holds a PhD in Philosophy and he is a senior lecturer in philosophy at Great Zimbabwe University, Zimbabwe. He has published papers in journals such as *South African Journal of Philosophy*, *Philosophical Papers*, *Journal of Black Studies*, *Education as Change*, *African Study Monographs*, *Journal of Negro Education*, *Theoria: A Journal of Social and Political Theory*, *Alternation Journal*, *Journal on African Philosophy* and *CODESRIA Bulletin*. His areas of interest include philosophy of liberation and African philosophy.

Sandra McCalla teaches philosophy in the Department of Language, Linguistics, and Philosophy, Faculty of Humanities and Education, University of the West Indies, Mona Campus, Kingston, Jamaica. She has published articles in learned journals. She has a strong interest in ethics and social philosophy.

Thaddeus Metz is a professor of Philosophy at the University of Pretoria in South Africa. He hails from the United States, where he received his PhD from Cornell University in 1997. Prof. Metz has published more than 300 scholarly works, including books, chapters in books and articles. Many of them take an analytic approach to the meaning of life, philosophy of religion, African morality, human rights, biomedical ethics, the proper function of a legal system, the role of a university and a range of related topics in value theory and moral-political philosophy. His recent books are *A Relational Moral Theory: African Ethics in and Beyond the Continent* (Oxford University Press 2022) and *God, Soul and the Meaning of Life* (Cambridge University Press 2019).

Isaac E. Ukpokolo is a professor of Philosophy at the University of Ibadan, Ibadan, Nigeria. He specializes in Epistemology, Metaphysics, and Philosophy of Culture. He is the author of several essays published in learned journals including *Journal of Black Studies* and *Cultura: International Journal of Philosophy of Culture and Axiology*. He is also the author and editor of a number of books, including *Themes, Issues and Problems in African Philosophy* (Palgrave 2017).

PREFACE AND ACKNOWLEDGMENTS

This volume is the product of the desire to prompt further development of African epistemology, a sub-discipline of African philosophy. Given that the present state of the discourse of African philosophy in book and journal publications is rather generalist in focus, with little attention turned to extensive discussions of sub-fields such as African epistemology, African metaphysics and African ethics, we sought to edit a volume that would begin to crystalize views on African epistemology. There is, however, a motivation for this, which came as a result of an experience during a faculty meeting in our Department of Philosophy at the University of Ibadan, Nigeria.

In that meeting, members of faculty had gathered for the purpose of reviewing the curriculum for philosophy for the undergraduate program. As the meeting progressed, we (members of faculty) agreed that it was time we included courses such as African ethics, African epistemology and African metaphysics, aside the generalist course of African philosophy which is still the only course taught in African philosophy in our, and most departments of philosophy in the country and beyond. But a colleague raised the question of the availability of course materials and texts that both students and lecturers could refer to for the courses we intended to introduce. It was then we realized that there were only a handful of such materials available which will not suffice. This experience in my department is descriptive of a wider challenge of the lack of robust resources for the study of African philosophy, particularly, in its sub-fields of epistemology, metaphysics, logic and ethics.

As we began our research for this volume, we found a number of extant literature that have examined the nature and character of knowledge in Africa. In most literature, we discovered that the predominant focus is an empirical/descriptive examination of knowledge, particularly in its sociological, archaeological and anthropological contexts. As such, we noticed the absence of a philosophical approach to the discourse of knowledge in Africa. To be sure, the contributions of philosophers to the discourse cannot be dispensed with, as such contributions focus on the conceptual and theoretical nitty-gritty of the notions and ideas that inform any analysis of knowledge. In fact, as intellectual inquiry turn almost overt attention to the social scientific examination of knowledge, it cannot put aside the normative and speculative reflections that should inform the more prevalent social scientific focus. For, as von Schelling warns,

> The fear of speculation, the ostensible rush from the theoretical to the practical, brings about the same shallowness in action that it does in knowledge. It is by studying a strictly theoretical philosophy that we become most acquainted with Ideas, and only Ideas provide action with energy and ethical significance.[1]

The foregoing informed a significant aspect of how the ideas in the chapters of the volume have been approached. To be noted here is that this volume is about the first (edited) publication substantively focused on African epistemology as a sub-field of African philosophy.[2] In taking the philosophical approach, we intend the volume to provide in-depth conceptual and critical explorations of knowledge in Africa in terms of its nature and characteristics, source(s) and justification. For clarity, we suppose that a philosophical approach to examining the subject matter of knowledge as it relates to African epistemology involves finding answers to questions such as what would distinctively represent (an) African theory of knowledge? What can be known in the given African conception of reality? Are there distinctively justifiable ways of knowing in the African contexts? If there are, what makes up for a warranted source of knowledge in the African contexts? These are essential philosophical questions about knowledge relating to African traditional and modern societies and little or no answer has been provided in existing literature in philosophy. The chapters in this volume are directed at addressing these questions.

It is expected that the edited volume will be useful to academics, researchers and students (graduates and undergraduates) of philosophy, particularly of African philosophy, Africana philosophy and Afro-Caribbean philosophy. The primary aim of the book is to bring together novel ideas on African epistemology as a developing sub-field of African philosophy. And the goal is to contribute an original piece to the few available literature on African epistemology despite the decades of research and teaching that have been dedicated to African philosophy in universities across the world. One rationale that guided the editing of the volume is the increasing global approach to the discourse of knowledge, which is necessitating the imperative to erect intercultural foundations for the discourse of knowledge. In this guise, the volume would be handy in providing insights about the systems of knowledge dominant in Africa, particularly in terms of knowledge rooted in African beliefs about being ('what is), to those interested in African thought in particular and non-Western thought in general. The chapters will serve as essential materials for this as well as stimulation for further research on the analysis of knowledge in Africa.

This work would not have become the reality it is today – a text that you are able to read now – without the efforts of many. They deserve profound appreciation. In no special order, we begin by expressing profound gratitude to our collaborating authors for their efforts in putting together their various chapters, which have made the volume a success. They have been more than wonderful collaborators, exceeding what we expected when we began the project; if we have to do this again, we would very much be pleased to have them be part of it. Also, our editors at Routledge, Helena Hurd, Rosie Anderson and Katie Stokes have been wonderful. From the time we got the book proposal across, through to the production process, their insights as regards what needs to be done to ensure that the volume is a success have been tremendous. We deeply appreciate them for their efforts, kind words and, most especially, their patience when it was taking more time than expected to conclude with the little details that make a book what it is. We also want to acknowledge the contributions of the staff of Newgen, particularly Jayashree Thirumaran, who worked to ensure the success of the book. The daily 8 am emails from Jayashree were the right kind of prompt we needed to meet set deadlines. We also appreciate the efforts of the three anonymous reviewers for the book proposal, as well as the many anonymous reviewers who worked on the chapters for the volume. To our colleagues in the Department of Philosophy, University of Ibadan, with whom we share the hope of someday having a course on African epistemology taught in not only our department of philosophy but in many parts of the world, we say a big thank you for the many times you gave us audience as we shared some of the initial ideas that got this project going in the first place. Our family and friends have been wonderful with their support and encouragement. In moments when it seemed the project was having no headway, either because workplace-related tasks were preventing us from having more time for the project or because paying attention to the needs of our families was rationing time for completing the work, it was their reassuring words that kept us going. Peter would like to appreciate the American Council of Learned Societies (ACLS) for the generous fund through the African Humanities Postdoctoral (AHP) Fellowship that allowed him time off from regular academic work to pay more attention to the completion of the book. Though the manuscript had been sent to the publisher before the fellowship was awarded, the funding from the fellowship avoided him the time to attend to the completion of the book.

Peter and Isaac

Notes

1 In 1802, during the summer semester at Jena, Friedrich Wilhelm Joseph von Schelling gave his lectures on the method of academic study. It was during the lecture he emphatically renewed, in the language of German Idealism, the concept of theory that has defined the tradition of great philosophy since its beginnings.
2 The extant volume is that edited by Bert Hamminga. 2005. *Knowledge Cultures Comparative: Western and African Epistemology*. New York: Rodopi. The volume however takes a comparative approach to examining African epistemology with the intent to elucidate African epistemology as an alternative (along side the Western approach) to the discourse of knowledge.

INTRODUCTION

On the Meaning and Discourse of African Epistemology

Peter Aloysius Ikhane and Isaac E. Ukpokolo

In this introduction, we attempt a conceptualization of African epistemology by examining its meaning and some key discourse in its development. Among others, this is to provide the reader a reference with which to engage the chapters of the book. So, what is presented here regarding the various concerns highlighted are extracts. Texts at the end of the chapter can be read for robust engagements with the relevant topics. We begin with how African epistemology is conceived, and the approach to knowledge in the extant literature on the subject matter. The historical examination of the beginnings of African epistemology takes the focus after briefly looking at the discourse of the sources and justification of knowledge. The next concern we examine are some debates on aspects of the discourse of African epistemology. This introduction closes with a look at African epistemology in the context of the global discourse of knowledge.

To begin, African epistemology is the body of thought and reflections of scholars' practising philosophy within the defined discourse of knowledge from an African point of view. It should be noted that this claim is without prejudice to the existence of autochthonous pathways to cognition in traditional Africa. Indeed, African epistemology is within African traditional belief systems, and emerges from the dynamics of integrating concrete experiences of African traditional belief systems into the analyses of concepts and ideals relating to knowledge.[1] On the basis of this, it is an analysis and interpretation of beliefs about reality, as seen from the perspective of the African (see Bedu-Addo 1985; Hallen and Sodipo 1997; Tavernaro-Haidarian 2018). To be sure, the relation of knowledge to the African belief systems about 'what is' has become a mainstay in the discourse of African

DOI: 10.4324/9781003182320-1

epistemology (see Mawere 2011; Jimoh 2017; Ikhane 2018). Thus, in describing African epistemology, Kaphagawani and Malherbe (1998) have this to say:

> ... although epistemology as the study of knowledge is universal, the ways of acquiring knowledge vary according to the socio-cultural contexts within which knowledge claims are formulated and articulated. It is from such considerations that one can sensibly talk of an *African articulation and formulation of knowledge,* and hence of an African epistemology.
>
> *259*[2]

It is instructive to note here, as did Kaphagawani and Malherbe, that the expression 'African epistemology' is deployed in "the generic sense in which the term 'African philosophy' is normally used, which does not deny that there are significant variations among the many cultures in Africa" (Kaphagawani and Malherbe 1998: 259). This is based on the sense in which the term 'African' is used in qualifying epistemology. This sense can be gleaned from the writings of Thaddeus Metz (2022) and Kwame Gyekye (1995). In his stead, Metz geographically takes 'African' to include features that have been prominent in a locale for an extensive period of time in a way that they have not been elsewhere. He identifies such a locale as Africa south of the Sahara (see Metz 2022). In a similar vein, Kwame Gyekye (1995) holds that

> in many areas of thought we can discern features of the traditional life and thought of African peoples sufficiently common to constitute a legitimate and reasonable basis for the construction (or reconstruction) of a philosophical system that may properly be called African.
>
> *191*

What makes the designation, 'African', fitting a description of epistemology as we have it in 'African epistemology' is that it refers to beliefs that have been part of the worldviews of a great many peoples indigenous to the African continent south of the Sahara for a long time, unlike many other parts of the world (see Metz 2022). It is however important to note that using 'African' as a geographical label makes it such that calling something 'African' does not mean that it is entirely unique to that part of the world. Rather, though academics have suggested that there is no sense in calling something 'African' since it can invariably be found in some places other than Africa (see Horsthemke and Enslin 2005; Metz 2022), it can be useful to employ 'African' as a geographical label that refers to features (such as beliefs, practices, values, precepts, norms, and so on) that have been prominent on the Continent over a period of time. In this vein, such features do not have to be unique to Africa, though they may be distinct in some way.

From the foregoing, the basis for so naming a discourse, 'African epistemology', is that there are discernible aspects of the lived experiences of Africans that inflect on knowledge in ways that are distinct and specific, that such ways broaden our generalist/universalist understanding of the concept of knowledge.[3] Even more important is that when asked what is meant when an African makes allusion to the possession of knowledge in the traditional context, the response is that reference is made to how such assertion about the possession of certain beliefs sits within a view (of the world) that goes beyond the commonplace physicalist understanding of the world. As such, an analysis of specific aspects of African culture, including language and social conventions, reveals the distinct view of knowledge that has come to be described as African epistemology.[4] It is so described for the reason that it derives from the African view of the world, which is the view that emphasizes a relation between knowledge and being in ways that have not been characteristically conceived in the broader discourse of knowledge in other non-African contexts.

As regards this view of knowledge in African epistemology, Nkulu-N'Sengha notes that the earliest written documents providing some inkling come from Kemet, particularly in the description of the philosopher from the Antef inscription, which is believed to have been produced around 2000–1768 BCE, the Instruction of Ptahhotep, around the 25th-century BCE, and the Instruction of Nebmare-Nakt, in the Papyrus Lansing, around the 12th-century BCE (Nkulu-N'Sengha 2005: 40). Other texts of consideration in this vein include the unidentified Instruction documented on papyrus by Chester Beatty IV, around the 12th-century BCE and the moral teaching of Amenemope (Nkulu-N'Sengha 2005: 40). According to Nkulu-N'Sengha, these texts present a vital African path to knowledge that are later expressed in Zera Yacob's *Hatata*, the Ofamfa-Matemasie epistemology of the Akan, and the Bwino epistemology of Bantu philosophy, among others. In more general consideration, the African slant to knowledge can be gleaned from oral tradition, which, according to Nkulu-N'Sengha (2005), includes various

> creation myths, folktales, and proverbs; the way of seeking truth in social, political, and religious institutions; the work of healers; the avenues for finding guilty parties in traditional justice systems; and the ways of solving family disputes and other social conflicts.
>
> 40

The body of discourse of African epistemology has also had reflections that examine the sources of knowledge and the idea of justification. As regards the sources of knowledge, Nkulu-N'Sengha asserts that African epistemology comprises four basic ways of knowing that can be separated into three categories: viz, the supernatural, the natural, and the paranormal. First, for him, is that there is a supernatural path to knowledge through which humans learn things with the aid of supernatural abilities. This cognitive path includes divination and revelation (i.e. messages revealed in dreams and visions). These two are distinguished by the involvement of supernatural beings, such as ghosts, ancestors, deceased family members, gods, and goddesses, who either directly share knowledge with humans via dreams and/or visions or indirectly do so through mediums, diviners, animals, unusual life events, or physical occurrences that call for a particular kind of interpretation. The second path to knowledge is the natural cognitive mode. In this way of knowing, it is supposed in African epistemology that humans learn by making use of their inherent talents or skills. A natural inquiry of reality using the human brain and logical ways of thinking is intuition, which combines the activity of human emotions (i.e. feeling and insight) and reason, which is one of these natural skills or abilities. Given that in Africa reason and intuition are not incompatible, the phrase *African rationality* is taken to imply some distinctive features that are not included in non-African understandings of rationality. In African epistemology, between the two polarities of the natural and supernatural means of knowing, there is a third category called extrasensory perception, which includes abilities like clairvoyance and telepathy (see Nkulu-N'Sengha 2005: 40–41).

With respect to the idea of justification in African epistemology, two broad approaches are identifiable. These are the externalist and internalist notions of justification in African epistemology (see Ogungbure 2014). While the externalist understanding of justification has been advanced by Aigbodioh (1997), Jimoh (1999), Njoku (2000), and Udefi (2009), among others, internalists about justification in relation to African epistemology include Adebayo O. Ogungbure (2014). Broadly speaking and in relation to knowledge claims, the internalists argue that the epistemic agent is either aware or can be aware of the basis on which knowledge claims are made, while, in contrast, externalists hold that an epistemic agent does not always need to have access to the basis for her knowledge claims for such to be justified. In his analysis of the externalist approach in relation to African epistemology, Ogungbure notes that supporters of the viewpoint appear to be taking the metaphysical undertone to knowledge in African thinking for granted. This is because the dominant conclusion among externalist interpretations of justification in African epistemology is that the phenomenon of human knowledge can either be explained from the *contextualist* or *neo-positivist* standpoints (Ogungbure 2014: 42). For Ogungbure, while the contextualist of externalist justification in relation to African epistemology (see Jimoh 1999 as an instance of this) holds that we should not think of knowledge, truth, and rational certainty in non-concrete terms because knowledge claims are placed within social settings, the neo-positivist of externalist justification (see Hallen and Sodipo 1986 as an example of this approach) asserts that knowledge basically depends on empirical elements like sensory perception or sense experience. According to Ogungbure, the challenge with the externalist orientation of justification in African epistemology, among others, is that it leaves out elements of the African worldview portrayed in oral traditions and existential relationships, which prevents it from providing a complete picture of how Africans generally perceive reality (Ogungbure 2014: 43).

In proffering the internalist approach, Ogungbure avers that all that is required to support a knowledge claim is to establish whether the person making the claim, for example that "Olodumare is the foundation of all being," has cognitive access to this belief and whether or not the prerequisites for such a belief are present in the knowing subject's cognition (Ogungbure 2014: 43). While noting the challenge with the sort of beliefs that are typical of African worldviews, Ogungbure avers that African metaphysical beliefs are anchored in an understanding of the experience of the cosmos in daily life, and its articulation through a process of reasoned belief formation and reflective awareness congruent with the internalist approach to acquiring knowledge. The premise that knowledge is an individual effort because it begins with the self with respect to rational cognition lies at the core of the internalist conception of justification. As such, according to the internalist conception of justification, a belief can be regarded as knowledge if a cognitive agent possessing it is aware in some way of the reasonable justifications for doing so.

In a bid to underscore his assertions about internalism in African epistemology, Ogungbure draws on the Yoruba belief system. He notes that among the Yorubas, the beliefs in the after-life and that one's success or failure has to do with the destiny one has received from Olodumare, though not based on any positivist criteria for justification, are available to the individual as these beliefs are tied to the cultural belief system of the African, even though the motivations behind them frequently have a religious bent. The basis for considering such beliefs to be knowledge is contiguous with the internalist justification standard, which states that an epistemic agent must have some justifiable grounds for considering his or her beliefs to be true and to thereby constitute knowledge and that such knowledge (acquired through intuition or introspection) must be cognitively accessible to the knower. As such, he argues that it would be futile to try to persuade the Yoruba to accept the neo-positivist stance that such beliefs cannot pass as knowledge because they lack the status of first-hand empirical authentication. Therefore, knowledge for the Yoruba transcends the physical world and includes a metaphysical understanding of reality. Knowledge cannot be restricted to the physical realm. He further corroborates this view by drawing on Washington's (2010: 6) claim that

> in traditional African world-view one's vision is not necessarily limited to the range of one's physical eyesight. Human beings can be endowed with spiritual vision. What the Yoruba refer to as ori-inu (inner eyes) and what others call the third eye is the source of spiritual vision.
>
> *Ogungbure 2014: 48*

Having examined the discourse of justification in African epistemology, attention will now be turned to a reflection of the historical beginnings of African epistemology. Historically, African epistemology is taken to have substantively emerged from the work of Leopold Sedan Senghor (1964), where he defended the existence of a unique African mode of knowing, a claim which was later supported by, especially, Innocent Onyewuenyi (1978) and Kane C. Anyanwu (1983), albeit, with varied arguments and proposals. In Senghor, African epistemology is seen to have arisen from his delineation of how Africans perceptually apprehend the world. This was in reaction to the denigration and discrimination of the forms of life of Africans associated with colonization and colonialism. Very importantly, this delineation of African epistemology, in Senghor, came with the project of Negritude, which was foremost an African political emancipatory ideology aimed at freeing Africans from racial denigration and discrimination. As such, negritude was, for Senghor and others who championed the idea, a project that affirmed the integrity of African identity, and the entirety of the cultural values of Africans south of the Sahara. As Senghor (1971) puts it, "*Negritude* is simply the recognition of being Negro and the acceptance of the fact of our destiny as Negroes, of our history and our culture" (6).

Beyond taking it as a politically emancipatory ideology, negritude, for Senghor, also represents an epistemology. As an epistemology, it embodies the African perspective of knowledge rooted in the consciousness that humans share existence ('what is') with other existents and that knowledge is subject to moral evaluation. This ontological and ethical perspective to knowledge, which holds that all things in the universe are unified in a network of relations, serves as the foundation for negritude as an epistemology. As such, it is taken that humans are involved in a web of relationships with other creatures, including animals, plants, inanimate objects, and even the environment, in this unified, unitary vision of 'what is.' As a result, the epistemology that stems from Negritude does not have a dichotomy between the subject and the object in the knowing process. This is such that the subject of knowledge knows by engaging and communicating with the object of knowledge. The method of knowing captured by Negritude is thus one of "participation and communion" (Senghor 1961: 98).

Contra widely accepted criticism against Senghor's analysis regarding the place of emotion in the African's perception of things,[5] it is argued that the goal of Senghor's approach is to illustrate how the African and European modes of perceptual awareness differ in terms of culture and methodology. As such, in placing emphasis on emotion, Senghor does not dissociate the mode of the African's perception of reality from reason; rather, his concern is to stress that with the African, reason is mediated with empathic considerations for others. That is, reason is laced with human emotions that are conducive to coexistence and well-being. As such, Senghor's Negritude as epistemology may be described as inclusive as it derives from an appreciation of the relation between reason and emotion in how we grasp the world. He sees the marriage between reason and emotion in a way that there is an interplay of both, albeit, in his analysis, he inclines towards emotion, in terms of how the African cognizes the world. As such, for Senghor, while the West's epistemological tradition displays an overt inclination to reason, the African approach facilitates reason with emotion.

In support of Senghor's analysis of knowledge, Innocent Onyewuenyi alludes to a dimension of the understanding of knowledge in African epistemology. This dimension emphasizes the imperceptible aspect of knowledge, albeit within the African context. In this regard, Onyewuenyi avers that a person is said to know or have knowledge the much such person is viewed to approach deific wisdom.[6] For him, one approaches the sort of knowledge described as deific wisdom "when one's flesh becomes less fleshy, to use Leopold Senghor's expression, that is, the older a person gets, the more wisdom he has" (Onyewuenyi 1976: 525). Importantly, deific wisdom is not to be conflated with practical wisdom. Onyewuenyi makes a distinction between two classes of human intelligence given as practical (or applied) and as habitual. Whereas practical intelligence refers to cleverness and artfulness in engaging with the contingent and physical facets of reality, habitual intelligence refers to the

> active knowledge of the nature of forces, their relationship. ... this includes how man, the being with intelligence, makes use of things and activates the forces asleep in them. This kind of wisdom is different from book knowledge, which is not regarded as wisdom in the strict traditional sense.
>
> Onyewuenyi 1976: 525

Furthermore, and also in support of Senghor's analysis of the African conception of knowledge, Anyanwu develops what has been referred to as *epistemological relativity*. In noting that culture is a "human response to experience as well as the beliefs and ideas which enable human beings to live meaningful lives" (Anyanwu 1984: 82), Anyanwu contends that as people's experiences are different so are their conceptions and understandings of reality; we see evidence of this in the differences among cultures. Anyanwu (1983) corroborates this theory of cultural relativity when he says:

> Due to the plurality of cultures and different interpretations of experience, it is impossible to look for the one Truth about the meaning of life and the world in any culture. What the history of culture shows is that experience can be understood in different ways in terms of different principles or standards of interpretation.
>
> 104

For Anyanwu, then, culture, and all that flows from it, is relative. In this vein, as culture is relative, so is philosophy, which, for him, is consequent on culture. Given that systems of knowing are the results of the engagement with culture, and that culture differs from one space and/or place to another space and/or place, and from one age to another, the ensuing theories regarding knowledge and about knowing would also vary. Indeed, the above claim of Anyanwu generates, among others, the understanding that *every culture has its own philosophy; as well as that similar cultures have similar philosophies*. This explains why there are Western philosophical traditions as well as Indian, Chinese, and African philosophical traditions. It is supposed that we can discuss African epistemology or epistemology from an African perspective by engaging with African cultures. As the African culture is not the same as those of others, so it is that African epistemology is not the same as the epistemology from other cultural traditions. There are significant conceptual, logical, and methodological differences in the assumptions on which they are grounded.

Furthermore, Anyanwu, in agreement with Senghor, contends that there are distinctions in African and Western conceptions of knowledge that should, I suppose, permit us to talk of distinct ways of knowing within these approaches. For him, while the Western perspective (particularly the Anglo-Saxon tradition) favours the analytic approach, the African tradition favours the *intuitive* approach. To be sure, Anyanwu subscribes to the intuitive construct of knowledge because it provides immediacy and has a natural predisposition towards concreteness, both of which the analytical method lacks in his opinion (Anyanwu 1983: 103). This is because intuitively (or natively) knowing something directly connects the knower with the thing known and provides the knower a sense of the thing known, as the knower participates in the being of the known as much as the known participates in the being of the knower. For Anyanwu, this improves the African's comprehension of the outside world and of life in general. It also guides the knower and prevents her from destructive engagement with the rest of nature.

For emphasis, Anyanwu's analysis diverges from that of Senghor to the extent that, in Senghor, knowledge involves feeling (emotion) and reason, while, in Anyanwu, it involves experience and reason. Indeed, a key aspect of Anyanwu's claim is that acquiring knowledge requires both experience and intuition. Knowledge, in Anyanwu's view, is a spin-off of how people interact with reality; and "[r]eality refers to objects of experience and thought" (1984: 82). With the understanding that it is reality as manifested in the African experience that informs the knowing process, Anyanwu (1984) avers that experience "is a procedure by which human beings become immediately and directly acquainted with the object of knowledge" (84). For him, therefore, we can talk of African epistemology on the basis that with different experiences come different conceptions of those experiences that, in turn, generate different perspectives on knowledge.

Having alluded to some of the early expositions of African epistemology in terms of how it has been conceived, we would now turn attention to some of the debates that have dotted the rather short history of African epistemology. Two of which will be briefly examined here are: (i) the question of the existence of a unique mode of knowing and (ii) the charge that African epistemology is epistemically authoritarian. As regards (i), by definition, the question is whether there is a unique African way of knowing; and the debate is between those who claim that there is a unique African mode of knowing, which is superior to that of the West and available only to Africans, and those who object to this claim. Whereas those who claim the existence of a unique African mode of knowing argue that its uniqueness is that it makes no distinction between the subject and the object of knowledge, those who object assert that the claim of the existence of a unique African mode of knowing is a myth and that it does not exist because what is claimed to be the unique African mode of knowing is a reproduction of what had been done in Western philosophy.

In essence, early proponents (Senghor 1964; Onyewuenyi 1978; Anyanwu 1983) of the existence of a unique African mode of knowing argue that there is a peculiar African mode of knowing that is discernible from the monism of interaction of the subject and the object of knowledge in African belief systems, rather than the dualism of both in Western epistemology (Senghor 1964: 71; Anyanwu 1983). For clarity, the objections divide into an initial reaction championed by Olu-Owolabi (1995) and Adegbindin (2008), and a latter reaction led by Felix A. Airoboman and Anthony A. Asekhauno (2012). In the initial reaction, Olu-Owolabi (1995) objects to early claims of a unique African mode of knowing made explicitly by Leopold S. Senghor (1964), and defended by Onyewuenyi (1978) and Anyanwu (1983), referring to their claims as myth, while in the latter reaction, Airoboman and Asekhauno (2012) question the existence of African epistemology as conceived in the works of both early and later proponents, such as Uduigwomen (1985/2009), P. K. Roy (1986), and Anselm Jimoh (1999; 2004). In both objections, the core of their claims is that extant conceptions of knowledge in and descriptions of African epistemology are reproductions of Western epistemology (Owolabi 1995: Airoboman and Asekhauno 2012).

With respect to (ii) – the charge of epistemic authoritarianism against African epistemology – Kwasi Wiredu (a key proponent of the charge) describing authoritarianism in his classic, *Philosophy and an African Culture*, says:

> What I mean by authoritarianism may be stated in a preliminary way as follows: Any human arrangement is authoritarian if it entails any person being made to do or suffer something against his will, or if it leads to any person being hindered in the development of his own will. This definition is likely to be felt to be too broad. It might be objected that no orderly society is possible without some sort of constituted authority which can override a refractory individual will. Anybody wishing to elaborate on this kind of objection has a rich tradition of both Western and non-Western philosophical thought to draw upon. Let me here cut the matter short by making a concession. We might now say that what is authoritarian, is the *unjustified* overriding of an individual's will … a society would be seen to be revoltingly authoritarian in as much as a person's will would usually be the result of the manipulations by others.
>
> *Wiredu 1980: 2*

Read in the context of African epistemology, Wiredu's analysis implies that epistemic authoritarianism is the imposing stance on knowledge regarding what is real, the truth, and so on, that society persuades or induces its members to hold without question to the extent that it unjustifiably overrides the individual's preferences to do otherwise.

Kwasi Wiredu and Kwame Anthony Appiah are two notable scholars who have been at the forefront in showing that authoritarianism featured greatly in African traditions (see Wiredu 1980; Appiah 1992). They aim to show by this that many of African traditional beliefs – which served as the foundation for knowledge claims, practices, and ways of life – are not held on the basis of sufficient evidence, but rather on the authority of elders, who are revered as the sources of knowledge. The grovelling reverence accorded to tradition and elders may, in part, mean a dogmatic, unthinking approval of their authorities, and their directives and ideas. (Ikuenobe 2006: 175). Didier Kaphagawani shares a similar view. He contends that while necessary, this kind of authoritarianism is a drawback to African communalism. He asserts that in African cultures, elders were revered as the ultimate arbiters of traditional customs and knowledge. Elders were given a great deal of power and authority, and they held a position where their dictates and will are accepted as representing both the community's and the supernatural deities' wills. (Ikuenobe 2006: 175).

Polycarp Ikuenobe (2006) has however raised objections to these interpretations of the African traditional epistemic system as authoritarian. His objection is that though authoritarianism was supported by African customs, it is rationally justified. He makes a distinction between irrational and rational authoritarianism and claims that critics like Wiredu, Appiah, and Kaphagawani erred by failing to recognize the rational version. He asserts that the concept of epistemic testimony, as well as the social, contextual, and pragmatic aspects of knowledge and justification, constitute the foundation of the rational form of authoritarianism. Therefore, epistemic or logical authoritarianism is neither evil nor pernicious. In fact, as Odhiambo notes, an element of epistemic authoritarianism is accepted in science as a legitimate principle (Odhiambo 2008: 1). To this, Ikuenobe adds by saying that the main reason why African traditional principles, values, and practices were not questioned was that, apparently, Africans did not feel the need to question their beliefs, particularly the fundamental beliefs that accorded their traditions and elders the status of epistemic authority. They also refrained from questioning due to their community's epistemic norms, practices, and evidence, which support an understanding of their inter-subjective, social, communal, and contextual character of inquiry and justification (Ikuenobe 2006: 209).

In a similar vein, Helen Lauer (2003) contends that the authoritarian attitude identified with African epistemology is not particular to African traditional societies, nor is it specific to traditional societies in general; rather, it is a feature of our everyday experiences, even in contemporary society. According to Lauer, it is commonly acknowledged that particular aspects of traditional parenting prevent people from articulating their own ideas and achieving their own self-set objectives. For instance, it is well known that authoritarian practices restrict freedom of expression, independent thought, and curiosity. Indeed, Lauer suggests that superstition is taken to be typical of the personality type called authoritarianism (Lauer 2003: 18–19). Having pointed out extant debates in African epistemology, we would now highlight key ideas regarding the method for doing African epistemology, sources of knowledge, and justification Indeed, Lauer suggests that superstition that are dominant in the literature on African epistemology.

Speaking in a rather futuristic sense, the discourse of African epistemology will continue to generate issues for discussion and debate. This is because African epistemology is still a developing discipline, with a handful of published work in the subject area. An issue that has begun to generate renewed critical reflections, in recent publications, is the debate on the question of method in African epistemology. Another is the question of the place of African epistemology in the global discourse of knowledge. About the debate on the question of method, for instance, while Peter Ikhane, in addressing the question of the method for doing African epistemology,[7] canvasses for a method that is essentially retrieval, Paul Irikheife argues that on the issue of framing a viable method for theorizing knowledge in African epistemology the method of wide reflective equilibrium holds more promises than the extant methods of ethno-epistemology and particularistic studies. In his stead, and with the understanding that the retrieval method (which builds on similar assumptions as that of the method of ethno-epistemology) implies the exposition of the belief systems and cultural practices of indigenous Africans through critical conversation and dialogue, Ikhane supposes that the retrieval method is to uncover the underlying patterns of epistemic reasoning and logic that ground African belief systems and practices. In this vein, he avers that what underlies indigenous African cultural practices and belief systems are assumptions and claims about knowledge and what it means to know that pass as philosophy understood as a critical and reflective discipline. In a rather contrasting view, Irikheife argues that the method of wide reflective equilibrium articulates a proper balance between philosophy and culture, a balance that is absent in the other extant methods of ethno-epistemology and pluralistic studies. His preference for the method of wide reflective equilibrium is also on the grounds that it endows a theory of knowledge with multiple sources of normativity.

In examining the debate on the question of the method for African epistemology, some insight into the crux of the debate may be gleaned from Anyanwu's analysis of the question of the existence of a theory of knowledge from an African perspective. In arguing for the existence of African epistemology, he notes that the type of knowledge practice we have in Africa now is a result of the subjugation of "African cultural facts to the assumptions, concepts, theories and world view suggested by the Western culture and developed by the Western thinkers" (Anyanwu 1984: 77). This knowledge practice involves employing Western conceptual scheme in discussing African epistemology. As a result of this, Anyanwu claims that the "knowledge arrived at with the Western principles of understanding is not the knowledge of the African cultural reality but enlightened rationalism of knowledge emancipated from the African world" (Anyanwu 1984: 77). The point here is that Western epistemic categories and notions are being imposed in some way on Africa when they are utilized to describe and understand African reality. Additionally, an epistemology produced in this manner is alien to the worldviews of the African. Anyanwu believes that in order to acquire knowledge from an African perspective, African epistemology should be the analysis and description of reality employing African concepts, conceptual frameworks, and epistemic categories. African epistemology is an approach to knowledge that one can apply to come to a reliable understanding of reality. It is a theory of knowledge fashioned from African culture.

As regards the place of African epistemology in the global discourse of knowledge, Emmanuel Ani (2013) begins by noting that any form of knowledge that does not fit into the objectified and universalized Western-oriented paradigm of knowledge is considered illogical. As a result of this, he states that a key argument in the rejection of African-oriented epistemology is that it is unscientific and delusory. He however retorts (in a way that takes 'science' broadly) by stating that it is unfortunate that mainstream epistemological discourse significantly fails to capture diverse indigenous knowledge systems that have helped individuals and cultural groups make sense of their lived world. Indeed, for him, despite the limitations arising from the posture of established scientific epistemological traditions regarding knowledge, indigenous knowledge practices continue to have a tremendous impact on people and the meaning they make of their lives. In this vein, he asserts that the African knowledge system continues to have a significant impact on the actions, attitudes, and thought processes of persons of African heritage. Ani further argues that besides the holistic approach (which includes the intuitive, religious, and mythological perspectives) to the examination of knowledge in African epistemology being justified, the outcomes of this examination deserve consideration in contemporary education systems and epistemological discourses. As such, for him any attempt to analyse knowledge solely through the prism of Western-oriented epistemology results in an unnatural and arbitrary reductionism.

In view of the global context of the discourse of knowledge in epistemology, Ani calls for the decolonization of the continent through the transformation of the mindset of Africans, so that Africans can begin to value their indigenous forms of knowledge and integrate same into education systems and epistemological discourses. This is in addition to his call for Africans to build their socio-economic and political systems so that the continent has a solid foundation from which to establish itself and its worldview. This is because, for him, "powerful nations delineate what constitutes valid knowledge worthy of pursuit and what is not" (Ani 2013: 295).

Having made some remarks about a few key concerns in the rather short history of African epistemology, we would conclude here by noting that while the foregoing discussions about African epistemology do not represent all that has been done about the subject matter, what we sought to do in this introduction is to highlight key developments in the subfield. This is with the intent to give the reader some fundamental insights to African epistemology that can be useful as the reader goes through the reminder of the book.

Notes

1 V.Y. Mudimbe's (1985) take on African philosophy is slightly different from the one taken here about African epistemology. Whereas Mudimbe supposes that, strictly speaking, African philosophy can be taken to apply to the traditional thoughts of African only in a metaphorical of historicist sense, we take African epistemology to reside within, and derive from an analysis of, the autochthonous practices of knowledge of indigenous Africans.
2 Although this claim seems to restrict African epistemology to ways of knowing, the business of African epistemology acknowledges that epistemology as a discourse includes the character, the source, the scope, and the value of knowledge, and that these aspects of the discourse of epistemology are not mutually exclusive from the understanding of African epistemology here stipulated.
3 There are those who, taking to a strong universalist line of thought, deny that there are any distinctive cognitive principles belonging only to any one group of people. Their claim is

that knowledge cannot differ from one group of people to another. If we refer to a claim as 'knowledge', then it is so for all peoples, irrespective of the social context. After all, say the universalists, aren't the criteria by which we decide the truth or falsity of a claim, like 'It's raining', the same across all cultural contexts? If this is so, then the epistemological character and structure of all cultures is essentially the same. Furthermore, they seem to assert that there may well be ways in which communities differ with regard to the institution of knowledge, but they refer to these as not epistemologically important. As such, for them, epistemology, wherever it is practised, is the same; just as one does not get a distinctively Chinese or American or African mathematics, so too there is no such thing as a distinctively African epistemology, except it might be reflections on the nature of the universalist understanding of knowledge carried out on, say, the African continent. It may however be retorted here that those who argue as the universalists do, by referring to the non-existence of such as African mathematics or African physics, aside other limitations, fail to appreciate the distinction between disciplines described as the humanities (such as those relating to language, history, culture, and religion) and those referred to as the sciences, particularly the natural sciences. The point here is that while it does seem incorrect to talk of African or American or Chinese Mathematics of physics, the same cannot be said of philosophy, history, or language.
4 Whereas features of language include sentence structures, proverbs, and other linguistic habits, the features of social convention include customary methods of resolving disputes, educating the young, learning about the outside world, and applying that information.
5 The criticism of Senghor's position concerned the task of relating an academic philosophy that is predominately rationalistic in orientation with the supposition of predominance of emotional considerations in his description of thinking in Africa. Many of Senghor's critics suppose that Negritude ultimately proved to be a less than effective attempt to achieve this because it largely confirmed and strengthened the reason/emotion split between the West and Africa. Many African intellectuals objected, arguing that critical thinking must also be a fundamental component of African philosophical systems.
6 For clarity, in Oyewuenyi, deific wisdom refers to the insight found to be possessed by those who are able to demonstrate understanding of the operations of the imperceptibles.
7 See Peter Aloysius Ikhane (2018). How not to do African epistemology. *Synthesis Philosophica: Journal of the Croatian Philosophical Society* (Special Issue on African Philosophy and Fractured Epistemology), 33(1): 225–236: doi: 10.21464/sp33114

Bibliography

Aigbodioh, J. 1997. Imperatives of human knowledge illustrated with epistemological conceptions in African thought. *Ibadan Journal of Humanistic Studies*, 7: 17–34.
Airoboman, F. A. and Asekhauno, A. A. 2012. Is there an 'African' epistemology? *Journal of Research in National Development (JORIND)*, 10(3): 13–17. ISSN 1596 – 8308. www.tran128scampus.org/journals,www.ajol.info/journls/jorind
Ani, N. C. 2013. Appraisal of African epistemology in the global system. *Alternation*, 20(1): 295–320. ISSN 1023-1757.
Anyanwu, K. C. 1983. *The African experience in the American market place: A scaring indictment of western scholars and their distortion of African culture*. New York: Exposition Press.
———. 1984. The African worldview and theory of knowledge. In E. A. Ruch and K. C. Anyanwu (eds.), *African philosophy: An introduction to the main philosophical trends in contemporary Africa*. Rome: Catholic Book Agency, pp. 77–100.

Appiah, K. A. 1992. *In my father's house: Africa in the philosophy of culture*. New York: Oxford University Press.
Bedu-Addo, J. T. 1985. On the concept of truth in Akan. In P. O. Bodunrin (ed.), *Philosophy in Africa, trends and perfectives*. Ile-Ife: University of Ife Press, pp. 68–90.
Gyekye, K. 1995. *An essay on African philosophical thought*. Rev. edn. Philadelphia: Temple University Press.
Hallen, B. 2004. Yoruba Moral Epistemology. In K. Wiredu (ed.), *A companion to African philosophy*. Malden: Blackwell Publishing, pp. 296–303.
Hallen, B. & Sodipo, J. O. 1986. *Knowledge, belief and witchcraft analytic experiments in African philosophy*. London: Ethnographica Ltd.
———. 1997. *Knowledge, belief, and witchcraft: Analytic experiments in African philosophy*. Stanford: Stanford University Press.
Horsthemke, K. & Enslin, P. 2005. Is there a distinctly and uniquely African philosophy of education? In Y. Waghid and Berte Van Wyk (eds.), *African(a) philosophy of education: Reconstructions and deconstructions*. Stellenbosch: Department of Education Policy Studies, Stellenbosch University, pp. 54–75.
Ikhane, P. A. 2018. How not to do African epistemology. *Synthesis Philosophica: Journal of the Croatian Philosophical Society* (Special Issue on African Philosophy and Fractured Epistemology), 33(1): 225–236. doi: 10.21464/sp33114
Ikuenobe, P. 2006. *Philosophical perspectives on communalism and morality in African traditions*. London: Lexington Books.
Irikefe, P. O. 2021. The prospects of the method of wide reflective equilibrium in contemporary African epistemology. *South African Journal of Philosophy*, 40(1): 64–74. doi: 10.1080/02580136.2021.1891801
Jimoh, A. K. 1999. Context-dependency of human knowledge: Justification of an African epistemology. *West African Journals of Philosophical Studies*, 2: 18–37.
———. 2004. Knowledge and truth in African epistemology. *Ekpoma Review*, 1: 66–81.
———. 2017. An African theory of knowledge. In I. E. Ukpokolo (ed.), *Themes, issues and problems of African philosophy*. Cham: Palgrave Macmillan, pp. 121–135.
Kaphagawani, D. N., & Malherbe, J. G. 1998. African epistemology. In P. H. Coetzee & A. P. J. Roux (eds.), *The African philosophy reader*. London: Routledge, pp. 259–319.
Lauer, H. 2003. *Tradition versus modernity: Reappraising a false dichotomy*. Ibadan: Hope Publications.
Mawere, M. 2011. Possibilities for cultivating African indigenous knowledge systems (IKSs): Lessons from selected cases of witchcraft in Zimbabwe. *Journal of Gender and Peace Development*, 1: 91–100.
Metz, T. 2022. *A relational moral theory: African ethics in and beyond the continent*. Oxford: Oxford University Press.
Mudimbe, V. Y. 1985. African gnosis philosophy and the order of knowledge: An introduction. *African Studies Review*, 28(2/3): 149–233.
Njoku, F. 2000. Rorty on post-philosophical culture: Shaping our culture without thoughts. *West African Journal of Philosophical Studies*, 3(1): 88–110.
Nkulu-N'Sengha, M. 2005. African epistemology. In M. K. Asante and A. Mazam (eds.), *Encyclopedia of black studies*. Thousand Oaks: Sage Publications, pp. 39–44.
Odhiambo, O. 2008. Book review: Philosophical perspectives on communalism and morality in African traditions by Polycarp Ikuenobe. Lanham: Lexington Books, 2006, 329 pp. *African Studies Quarterly*, 10(1): 1.
Ogungbure, A. O. 2014. Towards an internalist conception of justification in African epistemology. *Thought and Practice: A Journal of the Philosophical Association of Kenya (PAK) New Series*, 6(2): 39–54.

Olu-Owolabi, K. 1995. On the myth called 'Negro-African mode of knowing'. *Bodija Journal: A Philosophico-Theological Journal*, 5: 38–60.
Onyewuenyi, I. C. 1976. Is there an African philosophy? *Journal of African Studies*, 3(4): 513–528.
———. 1978. Towards an African philosophy. In O. U. Kalu (ed.), *Readings in African humanities and African cultural development*. Nsukka: University of Nigeria.
Roy, P. K. 1986. African theory of knowledge (epistemology). *The Nigerian Journal of Philosophy*, 6(1 and 2): 1–10.
Senghor, L. S. 1961. *Nationhood and the African road to socialism*. Paris: Presence Africaine.
———. 1964. *On African socialism*. Transl. by M. Cook. London: Paul Mall Press.
———. 1971. *The foundations of Africanity or negritude or Arabity*. Paris: Presence Africaine.
Tavernaro-Haidarian, L. 2018. Deliberative epistemology: Towards an Ubuntu-based epistemology that accounts for a prior knowledge and objective truth. *South African Journal of Philosophy*, 37(2): 229–242.
Udefi, A. 2009. Rorty's neopragmatism and the imperative of the discourse of African epistemology. *Human Affairs*, 19: 78–86.
Uduigwomen, F. A. 1985/2009. Philosophy and the place of African philosophy. In A. F. Uduigwomen (ed.), *From footmarks to landmarks on African philosophy* (2nd ed.). Lagos: O. O. P.
Washington, K. 2010. Zulu traditional healing, African worldview and the practice of Ubuntu: Deep though for Afrikan/Black Psychology. *Journal of Pan-African Studies*, 3(8): 24–39.
Wiredu, K. 1980. *Philosophy and an African culture*. Cambridge: Cambridge University Press.

PART I
Knowledge and Knowing in African Epistemology

1
AFRICAN EPISTEMOLOGY
Knowledge Ontologised[1]

Peter Aloysius Ikhane

Introduction

Discernible in the literature is the delineation of African epistemology as a discourse of the relation of knowledge to being, i.e. 'what is', such that knowledge is taken to derive from how being is conceived. Here are some characteristic expressions of this position:

> ... it is important that we understand the African cultural and ontological conceptions of reality to enable us to understand the African approach to knowledge.
>
> *Jimoh and Thomas 2015: 54*

> African epistemology is a discourse of the knowledge attitudes of Africans in terms of their cognitive relations with the world around them, which is influenced by their broader understanding or conception of reality.
>
> *Ikhane 2018: 225*

Notwithstanding this well-documented view of African epistemology, which includes discussions of its nature and characteristics, there has however not been an extensive elaboration of the nature of knowledge in African epistemology.[2] Put differently, an account of knowledge that may derive from the view of African epistemology as the relation between being and knowledge remains under-examined. An attempt at this is the focus of this chapter. The question that therefore drives the analysis of the chapter could be stated thus: what account of knowledge results from an epistemological system that is grounded on the relation of knowledge to being (understood as 'what is')? To address this question, and similar ones, I attempt a portrayal of the nature of knowledge in African epistemology, which, for want

DOI: 10.4324/9781003182320-3

of better designation, I dub 'Ontologised knowledge'.[3] In taking this approach to elaborate on knowledge in African epistemology, I countenance the idea that the philosophical understanding of knowledge about African belief system(s) cannot be fully understood without reference to views about reality that are widely held by members of the given society in Africa (see Ellis and Haar 2007). And since the prevalent view of reality in Africa assumes a structural wholeness of the visible or material world and the invisible or immaterial world, the distinctive mode of acquiring knowledge about the world is characteristically a holistic approach, in which the sacred and non-sacred, the material and the immaterial are held to constitute one organic reality (Ilesanmi 1995: 54; Ellis and Haar 2007: 386).

To achieve my aim in this chapter, I begin, in the section following the present one, with a presentation of the assumptions that I consider central to my analysis. The first of these concerns the conception of being (i.e. 'what is') that is taken to be the foundational belief about 'what is', and to which knowledge is seen to bear relation in 'Ontologised knowledge'. The section examines the senses of 'Africa' that drives how African epistemology is understood in the chapter. After examining these assumptions, I turn attention, in the section following the one clarifying these assumptions, to examining what I refer to as the universe-of-harmony belief. For clarity, it is this belief that I take to be foundational to the conception of being dominant among Africans. In examining the universe-of-harmony belief, aside from expounding on the nature of the belief, I also examine the ontological commitment arising from taking to such beliefs about 'what is'. Having examined these concerns and the ones in the section on the assumptions of the chapter, I turn attention to developing the Ontologised epistemology account of knowledge.

Preliminary Considerations

Foundational to my portrayal of knowledge is the assumption of a conception of being, upon which the portrayal epistemically depicts the nature of knowledge. To a significant extent, this is in keeping with the delineation of African epistemology as the relation of knowledge and being. Straightforwardly, this is to say that the conception of knowledge in African epistemology presented here derives from widely held views about the universe among Africans. To be noted, however, is that views regarding the universe are central to in the belief systems and practices of various African cultural groups. Taken as such, the belief that serves the purposes for my analysis of knowledge in African epistemology is the belief about the nature of the cosmos. For clarity, the widely held belief about the cosmos can be roughly stated as the belief that the universe is an organic whole of material and immateriality components, composed of a hierarchy of existents. As such, by Ontologised knowledge, I show how knowledge derives from the African belief in a universe of organic wholeness or harmony of the corporeal and the incorporeal. For ease, I will refer to this belief as universe-of-harmony belief.[4] This belief describes the conception of being that I take to be foundational to the conceptualisation of knowledge in African epistemology. I take this belief to be a reductive description of what being signifies in Africa for two reasons: (i) its widespread occurrence in the various cultures that are inclusive of the senses I take Africa and (ii) its foregroundness in the cultures that are represented, also, in the sense I take Africa. Before explicating on these reasons, let me expound on the senses in which I take Africa in the chapter.

In expounding the senses in which I take 'Africa', I begin by stating that aside how the senses are relevant to substantiating my claim that the universe-of-harmony belief is foundational, what I say about the senses in which I take Africa is also an explication of the assumptions that help improve the comprehension of how I explicate knowledge in African epistemology. The first of the senses of 'Africa' refers to cultural nationalities whose belief systems or cultural practices provide for the ontological grounds for what I say about knowledge; and the second is in terms of the period I draw on to reflect the knowledge practice constitutive of African epistemology. As it would become evident, the senses in which I take Africa are not exclusive; for, while the first sense indicates the geo-cultural context of Africa, the second sense specifies the timeframe or period to which reference is made with respect to the geo-cultural context in the first sense.

As regards the former sense, I take 'Africa' to delineate the belief systems and customs of cultural nationalities south of the Sahara. Geographically, this would include cultural enclaves such as the

> Zulu and Xhosa peoples in South Africa, the Basotho in Lesotho, the Shona in Zimbabwe, the Batswana in Botswana, the Nso' in Cameroon, the Gikuyu and the Luo in Kenya, the Oromo and Maasai in Ethiopia, the Acoli in Uganda, the Chewa in Malawi, the Dinka in Sudan, the Baluba in the Congo, the Bemba in Zambia, the Yoruba, Igbo, Tiv, and Hausa in Nigeria, and the Akan in Ghana.
>
> *Metz 2022: vi*

To be noted is that this sense of 'Africa' is much informed by the contiguity of cultures founded on, among others, geographical proximity. I however by no means imply that these cultures are homogeneous in their belief systems or cultural practices; rather, my supposition is that beyond the details in ceremonial and ritual practices, that is, beyond the differences in the material aspects of their belief systems and cultural practices, these cultural nationalities possess beliefs and cultural practices that are comparable in their formal aspects (see Metz 2022). In the latter sense, 'Africa' refers to the pre-colonial life-forms of Africans south of the Sahara. This is the timeframe or period to which reference is made in the second sense of Africa. In other words, 'Africa', here, speaks to the belief systems and cultural practices of the ethnic nationalities south of the Sahara before the subjugating encounters with the cultures of countries mainly domiciled in the geographical region of Western Europe. I do not however here allude to any claim of the assertion that the Africa south of the Sahara of pre-colonial subjugation no longer exists. Rather, with not a few writers who affirm its existence,[5] I contend that it persists; it persists side by side the life-form inaugurated by colonial encounters. In fact, it is the persistence of the pre-colonial life-form that continues to fund the reference made in expressions such as "African values are different from Western values."[6] Having clarified the senses of Africa in my analysis, I turn to an explication of the two reasons why I take the universe-of-harmony belief to be a reductive description of being in Africa.

As regards the first reason, I take the universe-of-harmony belief to be a reductive description of how 'what is' is conceived in Africa because of its widespread acceptation in the various cultures of Africa south of the Sahara. Some instances here will suffice. Among the Akans of Ghana, there is the belief in the triad of Nyame, Nyankopon, and Odumankoma as the rulers of the universe. Roughly translated and understood, Nyame represents matter, Nyankopon the vital force or life, and Odumankoma consciousness or intellect. This triad understanding of nature in Akan culture can also be gleaned from the work of Philip F.W. Bartle, who lived among the Kwawu people and studied their way of life as an ethnographer. In his analysis, he showed the difference in the perception of reality of the Akan from that which is dominant in societies in western Europe. He writes of his coming to understand this difference thus:

> What I came to realize was that my own [Western] way of seeing things was 'either-or', based on Socratic logic and reflected in the bipartite structural models of Levi-Strauss. In learning to think Akan, I began seeing things as 'both-and' as well as the previous 'either-or'. Instead of classifying things as 'profane-sacred', for example, I discovered that there were two kinds of sacred: 'sacred/white' and 'sacred/black'. Then what I had thought of as 'profane' later became, in a sense, 'sacred/red'.
>
> *Bartle 1983: 88*

He further noted that his exposure to the worldview of the Akan revealed the conception of the universe as having three elements, two of which contrasted the Western understanding of the binary differences connoted in the relations of down-up, or left-right. The third of the elements, according to Bartle, sometimes went beyond this binary of difference but was also sometimes parallel or equivalent to the binary, yet different from the first two represented by such as "down-up or "left-right". In his words,

> I saw that the concept of the human individual, too, had this three-fold nature, and reflected the concept of the universe. ... At each step, I saw the latter a higher level of abstraction of the former. Armed with this tripartite model of the threefold individual at three levels, and the threefold universe at three levels, I could understand the tripartite structure of society and culture.
>
> *Bartle 1983: 88*

With respect to the second reason, the belief can be seen to permeate the life-forms of the African cultures within which it occurs. For instance, among the Bambui of Cameroon, the practice of propitiating dead family members through celebrations and sacrifices is indispensable to the survival and future prosperity of the family. This is such that the failure to propitiate the dead is believed to result in misfortune, which can sometimes retard the future prosperity of the family. Indeed, for the Bambui people, families must be so attached to their ancestors to the extent that they believe that if they do not venerate them, they will be punished. The practice of the Bambui regarding the belief in propitiating dead family members can be seen to be foregrounded by what I have described as the universe-of-harmony belief. That is, propitiating dead family members indicates a belief in a universe of existents where the living is linked with other existents, such as the living-dead.

As a way of corroborating the foregoing, Fubah (2014) notes in his research and participation in some of the ceremonies for the dead and sacrifices in the Bambui Kingdom, through which he eventually discovered that apart from the natural family relationship, that rituals are also performed to strengthen the bond between the dead and their living kinsmen before they are buried. One of such rituals reported by Fubah (2014), in his study, is the ritual of placing on the deceased a drinking horn or cup and a flat stone on his or her forehead in order to transfer his or her power before burial to the drinking horn or cup (see Fubah 2014). This is meant to create a link between the deceased and his or her living kinsmen through the drinking horn and the stone when they are eventually handed to the deceased's successor as tools for pouring libation to him or her and other family ancestors represented by the objects or those who preceded the last ancestor. The Bambui people use the horn or cup in communicating with their ancestors, especially in times of crisis, such as severe illnesses in the family, or in times of extreme joy, such as the giving of a daughter's hand in marriage (Fubah 2014: 633). In another instance to show how the universe-of-harmony belief permeates the life-forms of the African cultures where it occurs, a study by Matuire on the *Mbira dzavadzimu*'s space within the Shona cosmology reveals that it is a common belief among the Zezuru, like most African ethnic group south of the Sahara, that death is not the end of life but a breakthrough into a totally new world of the invisible (Matuire 2011: 29). Indeed, for the Zezuru, the progeny-progenitor relationship depicts an everlasting relationship between the living and the dead and it ultimately acts as the basis of the Shona way of life. In the same vein of showing that the universe-of-harmony belief permeates the life-forms of Africans, among the Ga of south-eastern Ghana, the act of libation is performed in a variety of situations. It forms an integral part of every *kpele* rite,[7] every life crisis rite, every traditional and modern political ceremony, and it is used to confirm secular transactions and agreements (see Kilson 1969). Though the intention and content of libation differ according to the situation or context, the form is essentially the same in every rite and ceremony, and it depicts a belief in the connection between the living and their ancestors.

The foregoing analyses of Bartle, Fubah and Matuire, which indicate how widely spread and accepted the universe-of-harmony belief is, as well as how the belief pervades and foregrounds the belief systems in various cultures in Africa south of the Sahara, it, can be taken to reinforce the claim that the belief foundationally represent the African worldview about 'what is'.

The Universe-of-Harmony Belief and Its Ontological Commitment

In the previous section of the chapter, I expounded on the universe-of-harmony belief as the belief foundational to the ontological worldview of the 'Africa' of my analysis of African epistemology. The point of doing this was to indicate how we may begin to conceive knowledge in African epistemology. But before I take up the task of presenting an analysis of knowledge derivable from this view about being (what is) in Africa, I will consider the sort of commitment to ontology that the universe-of-harmony belief makes of the African. This is because the assumptions of ontology to which the African belief system commits us may be taken to relay the nature of knowledge in African epistemology. The point here is that as we 'see' the world through our worldviews, which are inclusive of our thoughts, beliefs, ideas, notions, and language, there are certain assumptions of being that undergird such worldviews. As such, as worldviews, which are a product of, and integral to, culture, are a means by which we categorise reality into different representations, though the contents of those representations change from culture to culture (Bartle 1983: 87), they commit us to certain assumptions regarding the nature of being (i.e. what is).

Given what has been said so far regarding the senses of Africa and the reasons for which the universe-of-harmony belief is represented as a reductive description of the ontological worldview of the African, it can safely be said that the African belief in a harmonious universe represents the foundational belief of the African regarding *what is*, that is, regarding being. As such, the universe-of-harmony belief envisions the universe as an organic whole with a hierarchy of existents. Taken as foundational in the African belief system, it foregrounds and organises the conceptual and practical life of the African; it permeates the social, ethical, religious, and political life of the African. It yields what may be referred to as methodological ontologism – the view that the organising category of human thought and social relations derives from our ontological commitments (that is, the beliefs we hold about the nature of reality or what is). For further elucidation, the universe-of-harmony belief may be stated thus:

The universe is an organic (harmonious) whole made of a hierarchy of existents. (φ)

From (φ), it can be taken that irrespective of how the universe-of-harmony belief is expressed or what is believed to make up the hierarchy of existents, the belief asserts the existence of certain entities. This is what is taken to represent the existential claims of the universe-of-harmony belief. And since we can know what ontology people endorse by finding out what existential claims or assertions they make or are prepared to make or accept, it is by establishing what a belief says *there is* that we understand the ontological commitment of such belief. More precisely, since beliefs are inert and cannot themselves make claims, we should ask what existential claims or assertions would be made by someone who asserts a belief of what *there is*. It is important to note that an utterer's ontological commitment depends on whether the utterer believes that the content of the utterances of the kind made are ontologically significant. In this regard, for the African, statements of the kind of (φ) are utterances that are ontologically significant given the disposition of the African to the content of (φ). This, indeed, is why believe in (φ) can be seen to calibrate the life of the African in terms of what she does, believes, and says – the things that matter and those that do not. Talks about the ontological significance of beliefs or statements are talks about what it means to exist. So the discourse of the ontological significance of beliefs presupposes the discourse about ontological commitment, which examines what it means to posit the existence of something.

The discourse of ontological commitment is widely taken to have been brought to the fore in the 1939 work – "A Logical Approach to the Ontological Problem" – of the American philosopher William von Orman Quine. In his discussion, Quine proposed a thesis intended to redefine and restrict the meaning of 'existence'. This is because his definition of existence was meant to allow targeted contents of systematic theories to be treated as actually describing the world, while avoiding the apparently insoluble problems involved in formulating an all-encompassing theory of existence (Hallen 2021: 3). The discourse of ontological commitment originally relates to the problem of universals. The problem of universals has to do with how to address the question of whether universals are as real as the so-called particular material objects, in the sense, that they also exist independently of their use in everyday conversations. While my goal is not to rehearse the history of the discourse of ontological commitment, which bothers on the problem of universals, I will pay some attention to Quine's analysis of the concept 'exist'. To this end, the crux of Quine's analysis regarding the question of "what is" was what it *means* to affirm the existence of an entity, rather than what *things* exist. As such, the product of Quine's investigation was not "a catalogue of what exists, but a construal of *what it is to exist*, which is the core of a 'concept of existence' and an important part of a broader 'doctrine of being'" (Durante 2018:). This is how Quine (1966) puts it:

> Note that we can use the word 'roundness' without acknowledging any such entity. We can maintain that the word is syncategorematic, like prepositions, conjunctions, articles, commas, etc.: that though it occurs as an essential part of various meaningful sentences it is not a name of anything. To ask whether there is such an entity as roundness is thus not to question the meaningfulness of 'roundness'; it amounts rather to asking whether this word is a name or a syncategorematic expression.

64

From the above, Quine can be read to make a distinction between understanding the notion of existence as *meaningfulness* and as a *reference* (that is, a name or a syncategorematic expression).[8] For clarity, relating existence with meaningfulness or significance seems a good way of linking with idealistic or phenomenalistic notions of existence, or even with a deflationism about ontology, while connecting being with reference, by contrast, seems a reasonable path towards ontological realism. Quine however rejects associating existence with *meaningfulness* or *significance*; he instead approves of associating existence with *reference*. The two ways of *significance* and *reference* by which existence may be conceived, according to Quine, may be seen to be radically different in terms of the relation between concepts and the contents of concepts.

Resulting from Quine's analysis, the examination of the nature of the ontological commitment of the African worldview about the universe bothers not on whether the wholly harmonious universe made of gods and deities and ancestors exists, but on what it means *to say* (or believe) that the world is an organic whole or that deities and gods exist. The distinction here is that whereas the former demands *an explication of the catalogue of evidence* that the universe is an organic whole or how it is that gods and deities and ancestors exist, the latter requires an appraisal of *what it means* for a harmonious universe with a hierarchy of gods and deities and ancestors to exist. In examining the ontological commitment arising from (φ), I will attempt a construal of *what it means* for such a universe to exist, which, according to Daniel Durante, is "the core of a 'concept of existence' and an important part of a broader 'doctrine of being'" (Durante 2018:). Before doing this, I will pay some attention to specifying the ontological commitments of the universe-of-harmony belief in relation to the two concepts of existence identified by Quine. This is with the intent to indicate the requirements of both, as well as to specify which best apprehends the route to construing the epistemic attitude of the African in relation to being. This will help to elucidate my choice of paying attention to *what it means*, rather than *an explication of the catalogue of evidence*, for such a universe to exist.

In specifying the ontological commitments of the two concepts of *meaningfulness* and *reference* regarding 'existence', let us recall (φ): *The universe is an organic (harmonious) whole made of a hierarchy of existents*. The phrase, '*an organic whole made of a hierarchy of existents*', is a meaningful term of the sentence (φ). According to the doctrine which associates being with significance or meaningfulness, it is plausible to impute the existence of '*an organic whole made of a hierarchy of existents*' to anyone who sanctions a sentence or an assertion wherein it portrays a *significant* association with being. That is, if meaningfulness assures existence, then (φ) expresses an ontological commitment with the belief in the existence of '*an organic whole made of a hierarchy of existents*'. According to Quine's preferred doctrine which relates being with reference, however, it is only legitimate to impute the supposition that '*an organic whole made of a hierarchy of existents*' exists to anyone who sanctions (φ) if '*an organic whole made of a hierarchy of existents*,' works as a vehicle for reference (a role usually occupied by names), even if '*an organic whole made of a hierarchy of existents*' is a syncategorematic expression which, though contributing to the meaning of the sentence, does not name any entity.

An important question that arises from the foregoing is what ontological commitments arise for an African who holds (φ) – that is, the belief in the existence of a harmonious universe with a hierarchy of gods and deities and ancestors? Does it commit her to ontological realism about the entities of the belief? Or does it commit her to a kind of meaning-making about the universe? In the first instance, the African faces the daunting task of evidential justification (very likely in the positivist/empiricist sense of this) if the belief commits her to ontological realism (particularly the hard version) regarding the existents to which reference is made in the belief. This is because reference to entities of the immaterial world of gods and ancestors would only be meaningful if such reference had referents that are perceptually accessible. But since no sense-dependent reference that evidentially justifies the existence of the entities of the African belief is readily available, it seems safe to say that commitments to the ontology of the claims of the African belief do not require those of realism. The challenge with this, however, is that the indigenous or autochthonous African believes in the 'real' existence of the entities of her belief in a wholly harmonious universe. This implies that since the African believes in real existence of gods and ancestors, even though she is not able to evidential justify her belief, the ontological commitment of the African belief in a wholly harmonious universe of gods and deities requires the specification of the *reference* version of ontological commitment.

Given this new challenge, I will pay attention to examining the ontological commitment of (φ) in terms of the requirement of specifying its reference. This is because I suppose that in addressing the ontological commitment arising from the reference specification of what existence implies, I would be addressing myself to how it is that the African conceives the reality of the universe of the gods and ancestors. That is, the reference version of the ontological commitment of what existence implies seems to better describe the dispositional attitude of the African regarding the immaterial entities of the belief regarding the universe. My examination of the ontological commitment of (φ) in terms of specifying its reference draws on the idea of 'abduction' or 'inference to the best explanation'. This is because on a review of 'evidential justification' – one that takes its understanding beyond those of the positivists – it is possible to provide some justification.

The idea of abduction or inference to the best explanation is that when faced with a set of alternative hypotheses – all of which cover the data – to explain a phenomenon, we are likely to accept the hypothesis that we, somehow, judge to be superior to the others (see Vahid 2005: 181).[9] In this sense, the chosen hypothesis, in comparison with others, entails a better explanation of the phenomenon in question (see Metz 2022). To be sure, abduction has been taken as a useful mechanism in belief formation. As a belief-forming mechanism, we sort of begin, in one instance, by putting up hypotheses to (possibly) explain a certain phenomenon. We then continue to make observations to determine which hypothesis best explains the phenomenon. Informed by what scientists describe as the doctrine of the accumulation of knowledge, we may eventually settle for a hypothesis that sort of provides an expansive explanation when compared with others.

Relating this to the belief of the African in the real existence of gods and ancestors, a rational ground for the belief may be provided by recourse to inference to the best explanation. In this vein, one may rhetorically ask whether the disbelief of an African in the reality of gods and ancestors in the face of certain experiences such as, say, the abiku/ogbanje phenomenon, and episodes that indicate 'more than' natural human display would not have posed more explanatory inconsistencies.[10] Put differently, how is the African to explain phenomena occurrences as that of abiku/ogbanje without postulating the existence of the immaterial entities she alludes to as explanatory model for such phenomena?[11] And so, in the sense in which inference to the best explanation is understood historically as explanatory reasoning in generating hypotheses, it may be taken to have undergirded the allusions indigenous Africans made in referring to the existence of forces as explanation for occurrences as abiku/Ogbanje.

It would however be noted that in instances of abduction, "the connection between the evidence and the hypothesis is non-demonstrative or inductive" (Lipton 2000: 184). This implies that though the hypothesis has been inferred on the basis of what is observed of the phenomenon, it remains possible that the hypothesis is false even though the observed phenomenon is what it is. As such, while abduction or inference to the best explanation seems a rather fair mechanism of belief formation in areas such as common sense, science, and philosophy, it is also the source of a great many puzzles. The main question that it raises concerns the nature of the inferential mechanism that is thought to underlie these cases of belief formation. Put differently, this raises the challenge of the basing relation in terms of alluding to the existence of imperceptibles as a reason for abiku/ogbanje-like events by recourse to inference to the best explanation. Specifically, it is whether the inferential mechanism in such cases is thought to be a necessary, even though not sufficient, condition for the belief in the existence of imperceptible being justified. I will however not address this question here for want of space. Suffice it to say that the discourse of counterfactuals holds.

African Epistemology: Knowledge Ontologised

Having examined and developed key ideas – especially the senses of 'Africa' in African epistemology and the ontological commitment following from the universe-of-harmony belief – I would now turn to the account of knowledge I label 'Ontologised knowledge'. As a first stab, this account of knowledge aggregates from preceding discussions on the senses of Africa and the universe-of-harmony belief. In this vein, Ontologised knowledge describes what is cognisable and eventually cognised by an acceptation of *what is*, according to the worldviews of African cultures south of the Sahara. To be noted, however, is that though the account of knowledge is analysed to derive from the worldviews of African cultures south of the Sahara, it is not exclusive to it.[12] To reiterate, *what is*, in the context of Africa south of the Sahara, is understood to constitute an organic whole in the sense of a connection of the immaterial and the material. As such, to comprehend the events and happenings of her existence, the African derives explanation from the nexus of the material and the immaterial. In practical terms, therefore, not everything is to be understood by recourse to only physicalist principles or to only spiritualist ones. Rather, her framework for engaging the world is one that draws on the principles of these aspects of the world as the event or happening demands; no principles are, ab initio, excluded. In this vein, for the African, the world or universe is a continuum that encompasses the experiential, rational, religious, intuitive, symbolic, mythological, and emotional aspects of reality. Indeed, the African notion of continuum implies the existence of spiritual components of the world that interfaces with the physical constituent of human experience.

From the foregoing, Ontologised knowledge, as an epistemic framework, is the view that to truly cognise a thing, it should be viewed from how it relates to an interdependent whole (e.g. Hamminga 2005).[13] Put differently, it is the view that knowledge, for an epistemic agent, results from social interactions and systems (see Goldman and O'Connor 2021), as well as interactions of the material with the immaterial. As such, it is knowledge relating to a variety of entities that are all richly interconnected including imperceptible entities. In this sense, African epistemology is realised in the tradition of social epistemology.[14] More specifically, it realises itself as an instance of communitarian epistemology. As an instance of social epistemology, the focus of African epistemology is how the epistemic agent achieves knowledge through interactions in/with the environment, not simply as an individual, but as an individual in a community of epistemic agents. In this vein, the nature of knowledge in African epistemology is not radically distinct from, say, the more dominant views about knowledge in mainstream epistemology.[15] The rather distinguishing mark is that in African epistemology, the nature of knowledge is characterised by how the knowing process includes assumptions that go beyond the physical or material aspect of reality, while in mainstream epistemology, assumptions are predominantly restricted to what are largely empirically demonstrable. For instance, in the traditional account where knowledge is characterised as a belief that is true and justified (the JTB account), justificatory tests for knowledge, to a significant degree, only allow for empirical-based forms of justification, because what is usually stated as the content of the justification assumes what is empirically available. But with respect to African epistemology and the account of knowledge given as Ontologised knowledge, a claim passes as knowledge if there are deducible or inferential circumstances and events that may warrant the claim in question. In some instances, if not many, such circumstances may be accepted to be warrant-granting to claims made in this regard on the grounds of prudence. And so, the nature of knowledge in African epistemology – as an epistemology that is grounded on the relation of being and knowledge – can be gleaned from an explication of, say, the epistemic of (φ). But to talk about this is to indicate how epistemic claims in the Ontologised knowledge account is achieved or justified. Explicating this however exceeds the focus in this chapter, as the focus in the chapter is to identify the nature and character of knowledge in African epistemology, which has been given as 'Ontologised knowledge'.[16]

In brief, however, talking about the epistemic of (φ) is quite similar to talking about the epistemological value of (φ). This is on the grounds that since the epistemic of (φ) requires a specification of what makes (φ) worthy of rational acceptation, the epistemological value concerns the purpose(s) the belief serves. That is, given that African epistemology is an instance of social epistemology, the basis for why (φ) is worthy of rational acceptation is as a result of the purpose(s) (φ) serves. And so, the epistemological of (φ) – what makes (φ) rational – is not simply that it conduces to the truth according to some view of the epistemological conception of truth, but that it achieves pragmatic/prudential purposes in organising social life (of the African). Put differently, the epistemological value of (φ) is prudential, where its acceptance serves for dealing with human experiences. To this end, the epistemic value of (φ) (and similar African beliefs) is derivable from its significance/usefulness and not from its correctness; that is, its epistemic worth is not to be judged by the correctness of its belief content, but by usefulness of its belief content for organising social life.[17] Following from this, I do not by any means imply that the only basis of knowledge in the context of African epistemology is the prudential value of, say, (φ). Rather, I assume, in this regard, that if, with respect to the basing relation between a reason and a belief, a reason possessed by an epistemic agent is distinguished by the contribution it makes to the personal justification of a given belief though such reason may not contain empirical evidence, in the instance of African epistemology where knowledge serves, among others, the purposes of social cohesion and comprehension of the complimentarity of the material and immaterial aspects of reality, prudential reason(s) suffice for holding the beliefs that are characteristics of the African worldview.

Conclusion

In concluding this chapter, I would like to make a few remarks regarding the distinctiveness in the approach to knowledge in African epistemology that this chapter has attempted to portray. The distinctive feature of the relation of knowledge to being ('what is') in the context of African epistemology emphasises rather different concerns from that in, say, the traditional account of knowledge, if, in any case, the traditional account is read to imply this relation. Whereas, 'what is' from the African perspective includes a belief in immaterial realities as deities, spirits, and the relation and interaction of these with the material world, the understanding and delimitations regarding 'what is' in the traditional account implies what is materially observable. This, to a significant degree, inflects the sort of justification that is usually accepted to render a claim in the traditional account justified. So, in brief, while a discourse of knowledge in African epistemology assumes 'what is' to straddle the immaterial and the material aspects of 'what is' (being), mainstream (Western) epistemology takes 'what is' to denote that which is empirically discernible.

The above distinction made may not be said to provide African epistemology – a distillation of the way Africans cognise the world – with a unique mode of knowing. This is because the assumptions of organic wholeness about 'what is' that is said to undergird the way of knowing that is dominant among African cultures south of the Sahara is available to others of non-African extraction. The distinctiveness about African epistemology and its conception of knowledge derives from the emphasis regarding knowledge and knowing as against the emphasis in other contexts, such as in the Western approach to knowledge and knowing. While in the African approach knowledge is conceived in the context of an ontology that does not separate the immaterial from the material, in the traditional account, knowledge derives from a view of ontology that is largely materialistic. What this means is that no one account of knowledge is the comprehensive view about knowledge; rather, the various views about knowledge are grounded on certain preferences about the nature of what can be known and how it can be known.

Notes

1 For clarity, while I take 'Knowledge ontologised' to describe the distinctive character of African epistemology, I take 'Ontologised knowledge' to refer to an account of knowledge I construe in relation to African epistemology.
2 Though the linkage of knowledge and being within the broader discourse of epistemology has not been overtly examined, it can be read to have been implied. For instance, in the traditional account where knowledge is defined as justified true belief (JTB), it is noted that an epistemic agent, S, cannot be said to have a proposition, p, that is false. Put differently, only propositions that are true can be known. One implication of this in the context of the present chapter is that only what can be affirmed as the case can be known. And in the context of the study of being (ontology), what is affirmed as the case denotes 'what is'. That is, a proposition, p, can be said to affirm ϕ, as in the expression, "I know that ϕ," where ϕ ultimately implies being. In this sense, therefore, claims to knowledge are claims about 'what is'. So it can be argued that in the traditional account of knowledge – the JTB account – a relation to being (i.e. modes of being) is implied, though not explicitly.
3 I am not the first to use this coinage. For instance, see Chimakonam and Ogbonnaya. 2021. *African Metaphysics, Epistemology, and a New Logic: A Decolonial Approach to Philosophy*. Cham, Switzerland: Palgrave Macmillan. But in the way I have explicated it here differs from how it has been conceived in other works.
4 By the universe-of-harmony belief is understood the African belief about the relation that exists among entities in the world. I have done some extensive work on this in another article where I examined the use of 'Relationality' in Thaddeus Metz's African moral theory. In brief, I take 'harmony' in the universe-of-harmony to refer to relations, though in the African understanding it does include relations beyond what is supposed in Aristotle's understanding of relations as explicated in his categories of being.
5 Peter Ekeh beautifully writes in an all-important article for understanding post-colonial Africa, "Colonialism and the Two Publics in Africa: A Theoretical Statement" (1975), that Post-colonial Africa is a world signalling the existence of two different civilities;

one which was introduced by her colonial masters, the other, the remnant of life-forms extending back to autochthonous Africa.

6 The point here is that the life-form of pre-colonial Africa is what our (African) collective memory recalls to be African. That is, it is not that what we so refer to as African is uniquely an experience of Africans; rather, what we refer to as African worldview and reality today is what our collective memory/consciousness recalls as African. So irrespective of the colonial incursion, which distorted the configuration of the African identity, leaving in its wake an altered self of the African, we make recourse to the life-form of pre-colonial Africa, which persists side-by-side post-colonial life-form, as African.

7 Underlying *kpele* ritual is a system of ideas concerning the nature of the universe. At the core of this cosmology is the conception of a hierarchy of beings which comprises five classes: a Supreme Being, gods, human beings, animals, and plants (See Kilson 1969).

8 Taking existence as a syncategorematic expression implies that though the notion is taken to lack a denotation, it can nonetheless affect the denotation of a larger expression that contains it. Syncategorematic expressions are contrasted with categorematic expressions, which have their own denotations.

9 I would like to note here that how I approach providing explanation for the allusion to the existence of gods and ancestors in the African worldview by recourse to abduction or inference to the best explanation is not novel. Indeed, inference to the best explanation has informed the views of many theorists in areas as diverse as metaphysics, epistemology, and science, particularly in relation to immaterial or abstract entities in these areas. Armstrong's defence of universals (Armstrong 1978), is an instance of this. The existence of God is inferred to as the best explanation of the existence and order of the universe.

10 For an elaborate read on the phenomenon of abiku/ogbanje, see Maduka Chidi T. "African Religious Beliefs in Literary Imagination: Ogbanje and Abiku in Chinua Achebe, J.P. Clark and Wole Soyinka." *Journal of Commonwealth Literature*, 22.1 (1987): 17–25; Timothy Mobolade, "The Concept of Abiku," *African Arts*, Vol. 7, No. 1 (1973): 62–64. Some may suggest non-belief, i.e. withholding belief rather than positing belief in imperceptibles. But this would have inevitably generated its own challenges for the African; it would have, for instance, generated similar challenges as that of experiencing the phenomenon itself.

11 There is no pretense here to deny the knowledge of the causal relation medical science has made between certain illnesses, such as sickle cell, and child mortality, in explaining some of the cases that where hitherto supposed to have be caused by the existence of abiku/ogbanje. Irrespective of this, the phenomenon of abiku (Yoruba)/ogbanje (Igbo) remains a viable explanatory framework, even though its scope may have been shown to be narrow as it is not explanatory of all such phenomena. Indeed, what can be said then is that science (medical science) has shown that not all child mortality can be connected to the phenomenon of abiku.

12 It is not exclusive because the view about 'what is' is available to other cultural settings; but it is only emphasised by African cultures south of the Sahara.

13 As Nisbett shows in *The Geography of Thought*, people think about and even see the world differently because of differing ecologies, social structures, philosophies, and educational systems that date back to ancient Greece and China.

14 I take African epistemology to fall within social epistemology rather than being a unique sort of epistemology. If the traditions of epistemology, particularly in terms of the approach to knowing, that have developed are roughly categorised, at least, three broad approaches are discernible. These are: (i) the Traditional/Classical account that gives the process of knowing to be the necessary and sufficient combination of belief, truth, and justification – and hence, defines knowledge as the necessary and sufficient combination of Justification, Truth, and Belief (the JTB account); (ii) the Knowledge-first account

championed by Timothy Williams, where he argues that knowledge is not first realisable into justification, truth, and belief; and (iii) the Reason-first account championed by Eva Schmidt.
15 By mainstream epistemology, I refer to traditions of epistemology that have developed since sixteenth-century Western Europe, particularly following the rise of Modern science.
16 An explication of the claim made here is a major part of a forthcoming article: Epistemology ontologised..
17 My position here – that we understand knowledge in African epistemology in relation to epistemic prudence – suggests that in the debate of whether beliefs aim at truth/correctness or whether the pragmatic aim supersedes the truth/correctness aim, I aver that the pragmatic aim holds pride of place.

Bibliography

Bartle, P.F.W. 1983. The universe has three souls. Notes on translating Akan culture. *Journal of Religion in Africa*, 14(2): 85–114.
Danquah, J.B. 1952. The culture of Akan. *Africa: Journal of the International African Institute*, 22(4): 360–366. doi: 10.1080/18125980.2011.631291
Durante, D. 2018. Ontological commitment. *Al-Mukhatabat Journal*, 27: 177–223.
Ekeh, P.P. 1975. Colonialism and the two publics in Africa: a theoretical statement. *Comparative Studies in Society and History*, 17(1): 91–112.
Ellis, S. and Haar, G.T. 2007. Religion and politics: taking African epistemologies seriously. *Journal of Modern African Studies*, 45(3): 385–401.
Fubah, M.A. 2014. Title cups and ancestral presence in the Bambui fondom, Cameroon grassfields. *Anthropos*, Bd. 109, H. 2: 633–640.
Goldman, A. and O'Connor, C. 2021. Social epistemology. *The Stanford Encyclopaedia of Philosophy* (Winter 2021 Edition), Edward N. Zalta (ed.). https://plato.stanford.edu/archives/win2021/entries/epistemology-social
Hallen, B. 2021. *Reading Wiredu*. Bloomington, IN: Indiana University Press.
Hamminga, B. 2005. *Knowledge Cultures Comparative: Western and African Epistemology*. Amsterdam, Netherlands: Rodopi.
Ikhane, P.A. 2018. How not to do African epistemology. *Synthesis Philosophica: Journal of the Croatian Philosophical Society* (Special Issue on African Philosophy and Fractured Epistemology), 33(1): 225–236: doi: 10.21464/sp33114
Ilesanmi, S. 1995. Inculturation and liberation: Christian social ethics and the African theology project. *The Annual of the Society of Christian Ethics*. Baltimore, MD: Georgetown University Press, 49–73.
Jimoh, A. and Thomas, J. 2015. An African epistemological approach to epistemic certitude and scepticism. *Research on Humanities and Social Sciences*, 5(11): 54–61. www.iiste.org. ISSN (Paper)2224-5766 ISSN (Online) 2225-0484 (Online).
Kilson, M. 1969. Libation in Ga ritual. *Journal of Religion in Africa*, 2(2): 161–178.
Lipton, P. 2000. Inference to the best explanation. In *A Companion to the Philosophy of Science*. W.H. Newton-Smith (ed.). Oxford: Blackwell, 184–193.
Maduka, C.T. 1987. African religious beliefs in literary imagination: ogbanje and abiku in Chinua Achebe, J.P. Clark and Wole Soyinka. *Journal of Commonwealth Literature*, 22(1): 17–25.
Matiure, P. 2011. *Mbira dzavadzimu* and its space within the Shona cosmology: tracing *mbira* from *bira* to the spiritual world. *Muziki*, 8(2): 29–49.

Metz, T. 2022. *A Relational Moral Theory African Ethics in and beyond the Continent*. Oxford: Oxford University Press.
Meyerowitz, E.L.R. 1951. *The Sacred State of the Akan*. London: Faber and Faber.
Mobolade, T. 1973. The concept of abiku. *African Arts*, 7(1): 62–64.
Quine, W.V.O. 1939. A logical approach to the ontological problem. *Journal of Unified Science = Erkenntnis*, 9: 84–89.
Quine, W.V.O. 1966. A logistical approach to the ontological problem. In *The Ways of Paradox: and Other Essays*. New York: Random, pp. 64–69.
Schmidt, E. 2021. The explanatory merits of reasons-first epistemology. In *Concepts in Thought, Action, and Emotion New Essays*, Christoph Demmerling, Dirk Schröder (eds). London: Routledge, pp. 75–91.
Vahid, H. 2005. *Epistemic Justification and the Sceptical Challenge*. London: Palgrave Macmillan.

2
KNOWLEDGE AND TRUTH AS INTERACTION BETWEEN THE KNOWER AND BEING

Knowing in African Epistemology

Anselm Kole Jimoh

Introduction

Within the context of African communitarian epistemology (ACE), this chapter investigates the interaction between the knower and the known in knowledge practice. The aim is to establish that knowledge and truth are derived from the interaction between the knower and reality. ACE is premised on African ontology that understands reality as a continuum encompassing the experiential, rational, religious, intuitive, symbolic, mythical and emotional in a unitive whole. In this wise, African ontology grounds a communitarian epistemology in which knowledge is derived from a collaborative enterprise through the synthesis of individual rational insights and community rationalisation. Community rationalisation refers to the collective understanding of reality inferred from the individual inputs of members of a cognitive community. ACE emphasises the interrelatedness and interdependence of phenomena in the acquisition of this collective understanding of reality through the intertwining of the theoretical and the empirical in a cognitive process. Based on this process of cognition, I argue that knowledge is the knower's reconstructed mental picture of reality generated from the interaction between herself and reality. Although, the mental reconstruction is essentially an activity of the knower, in her capacity as a rational being, she is guided by the ontological worldview of the community in determining what is sensible and reasonable of, and applicable to, reality. The implication here is that knowledge is essentially derived from the knower's rational activity, since whatever is known does not know itself, but is known by the one who knows it. This further implies that truth in ACE is that which the knower, through community rationalisation, understands as most appropriately applicable, in and to reality.

Theorising Knowledge and Truth

The issues of interest in theorising knowledge and truth include: (i) the meaning and nature of knowledge and (ii) the meaning and nature of truth. Knowledge and truth are interwoven such that the former implies the latter in the sense that it is not possible to know that p when p is not true. This implies that knowledge is not independent of truth, since we can only be said to know when what is known is true. Truth, however, does not imply knowledge, since p can be true without S knowing that p is true. In other words, even though knowledge is not independent of truth, truth can be independent of knowledge. Nonetheless, the essential relationship between knowledge and truth often necessitates the concurrent discussion of both concepts: this does not however mean we should take both concepts to imply the same thing.

Traditional Western epistemology has considerably been concerned with clarifying knowledge as a derivative of the conjunction of truth, belief and justification, associated in a relationship of individual necessity and collective sufficiency (Ichikawa and Steup 2018, 3). This understanding fundamentally makes knowledge an objective and independent existent, thereby disassociating its derivation from human, social and environmental factors. It characterises knowledge as *that* which we acquire, given the appropriate requisite conditions, and explains knowledge as intimately bringing the concepts of epistemic evaluation together. For example, knowledge implies truth, and since truth is taken to be factive, knowledge, therefore, requires justification since we cannot know a truth without having evidence to believe that it is true. The history of Western epistemology is replete with the concerns to delineate these concepts and establish their interconnectedness so as to clarify what we know and how we know them. This approach has not yielded a satisfactory account of knowledge.

Plato's analysis of how we arrive at knowledge in the *Meno* and *Theaetetus* provided the grounds for the definition of knowledge as justified true belief. Ever since, from the Cartesian failed attempt to establish indubitable foundation for knowledge in pure reason, to the phenomenological project of Edmund Husserl, Western epistemological enterprise unsuccessfully tried to establish that knowledge consists in the mind's accurate representation of reality (see Rorty 1979, 171). Within the equation of the debate which was mainly between rationalist's and empiricist's conceptions of knowledge, the role of social, cultural, environmental and human factors in knowledge practice was trivialised and dismissed as distortive to a correct conceptualisation of knowledge.

Kant's (1965) epistemological project attempted to bridge the empiricist's and rationalist's theories of knowledge, but it became a victim of the scepticism it wanted to resolve by driving a wedge between the *noumena* and the *phenomena* in his analysis of the synthetic a priori. The project, nonetheless, made some vital analysis about how we understand reality. Contrary to the general assumption that our minds conform to the objects of cognition, Kant provokes our thought to assume that the objects of cognition, instead, conform to our minds. He argues that knowing can, and only, takes place within the ability and capacity of the knower to cognise. Take the analogy of a container and its content. The container is not reshaped by its content in order to hold the latter. In like manner, reality does not impose itself on human consciousness and/or cognition. Instead, reality is understood and known according to the ability and capacity of the human mind that interacts with it. In other words, we come to know phenomena only as our minds are enabled and allowed to know them; we do not and cannot transcend the bounds of our mind in acquiring knowledge of the world. This implies that the human mind is not a passive receptor in the process of knowing; it is active and it imposes its structures on things through what Kant describes as the categories of the mind (or understanding).

After centuries of theorising without providing a satisfactory account of knowledge and truth, some contemporary epistemologists have argued that the failure of traditional Western epistemology to provide a satisfactory account of knowledge is the result of a misconstrued investigation. For example, Mark Kaplan (1985) argued that Edmund Gettier's (1963) ground-breaking disagreement with the collective sufficiency of justification, truth and belief, for knowledge as upheld by the traditional definition of knowledge, is irrelevant. According to Kaplan, Gettier misconstrued the traditional definition of knowledge to be about propositional knowledge, when indeed, it is a definition inferred from the Platonic analysis of non-propositional knowledge. Therefore, both Gettier's intervention and the attempts to provide an un-Gettiered definition of knowledge, consequent upon Gettier's position, is not important to the central question about when and how we know that we know. Also, Timothy Williamson (2000) championed the project of 'knowledge first' in his argument that knowledge is a factive mental operator stative and, therefore, cannot be analysed. For him, the project to define knowledge by factorising it is misguided, and that is why it has not yielded dividends in terms of resolving the controversy about the meaning and nature of knowledge.

On Knowledge Derivation

In knowledge derivation, there are two vital agents: (i) the object that is known and (ii) the agent (knower) that knows. The role of (i) – the object of knowledge – is that it is there; if it is not there, it cannot be known, and for it to be known, it has to be perceived, not by itself because it cannot perceive itself. It is to be perceived by the subject of knowledge, which is (ii) above. Therefore, (i) is usually passive in the process of knowing. On the other hand, (ii) – the knower – is the active agent whose mind gains awareness and understanding of *that* which it perceives or becomes aware of. The mind's understanding of (i) above is subject to various factors that impact upon how the mind perceives. These factors include social relations, environmental and cultural influences as well as the human disposition of the knower. Contemporary social epistemology tries to investigate and determine how and what role these factors play in knowledge derivation (Goldman and O'Connor 2021, 1).

Knowledge is a universal concept that does not vary in meaning from place to place. However, the process of deriving knowledge "varies from one social [and cultural] environment to another because of the natural proclivity of human beings to interpret things differently by their backgrounds" (Jimoh 2018, 14). Knowing is about awareness through observation (empirical), inquiry or information and rationalisation (rational). The knower, and not the known, is the agent that performs these functions of observation, inquiry and rationalisation. Therefore, knowledge is derived from the process of knowing in which the knower is the active agent.

What does the activity or process of knowing entail? In other words, what exactly occurs in knowing that convinces the knower that she knows? Based on the Western objectivistic model, when the knower has evidence(s) to believe that a proposition is true, the knower can be said to know. This notion is contestable and has been criticised in the works of some Western epistemologists. For example, Orman Quine (1969), Thomas Kuhn (1970), Richard Rorty (1979) and Paul Moser (1993) disagree with the objectivist theory of knowledge that "knowledge of things … does not depend on one's conceiving them" (Moser 1993, vii). Also, Edmund Gettier's counter-cases (1963), Mark Kaplan's repudiation of knowledge (1985), and Timothy Williamson's unanalysability of knowledge (2000) question the possibility, plausibility and veracity of knowledge being a product of the conjunction of truth, belief and justification.

And so, discourse in social epistemology attempts to redirect epistemology from objectivist evaluative paradigms to a consideration of the role of social interaction in knowledge practice. If knowledge is about how we come to understand reality (Jimoh 2017, 121), then we cannot dismiss the factors that shape our understanding from the equation of knowledge as intrusive and distortive. ACE recognises and incorporates this in its approach to knowledge. This approach conceives knowledge derivation as a social, cultural and communitarian process in which the knower, through interaction with the external world, gains understanding and knowledge of the latter. It espouses the connectivity between knowledge, wisdom and action, and sees knowledge as demonstrative and teleological – directed towards a purpose. In the context of this understanding, truth is the agreement between our claim (belief/proposition) and the state of affairs that it describes.

African Communitarian Epistemology

In Western political philosophy, communitarianism challenges classical liberalism, criticising and opposing the latter as ontologically and epistemologically incoherent. It places emphasis on the idea that the community shapes and defines the individual (see Avineri and de-Shalit 1992). Martin Kusch draws on this latter aspect of the notion of communitarianism to advocate its application to epistemic practice by describing communitarian epistemology as "the claim that *communities* rather than *individuals* are the primary bearers of knowledge" (Kusch 2002, 335). Based on Kusch's theorisation, Anselm Jimoh argued that "African indigenous epistemology is a distinctively … epistemic system; a social and communitarian epistemology that espouses a cultural and situated position of knowledge firmly established on the ontological notion of a continuum" (Jimoh 201814). ACE should not be mistaken as/or for traditional African knowledge. The common mistake is to describe African thought pattern as traditional, implying by that, some form of derogation. For instance, we often talk about traditional African knowledge in the sense of a primitive and unrefined, alogical and unanalytical way of knowing prior to so-called African civilisation through colonisation, which implies that colonisation is the dawn of civilisation in Africa. ACE is not traditional African knowledge in this sense; rather, it is African indigenous knowledge.

Anna Hunter, as cited by Wilfred Lajul, made a lucid distinction between traditional knowledge and indigenous knowledge. While the former refers to "knowledge developed over time in any society or culture, [the latter] … is grounded in an indigenous worldview" (Lajul 2018, 59); where 'indigenous' means native, that is, *that* which occurs naturally in a particular place. According to Hunter (2007), indigenous knowledge consists of a set of pre-suppositions, beliefs and value system through which an individual understands and interprets the world. Gloria Emeagwali presents a more articulated notion of indigenous knowledge as "the cumulative body of strategies, practices, techniques, tools, intellectual resources, explanations, beliefs, and values accumulated over time in a particular locality, without the interference and impositions of external hegemonic forces" (Emeagwali 2014, 1). This definition implies the communitarianism that characterises African ontology (Jimoh 2018, 7).

If knowledge is about having an understanding of particular states of affairs, an epistemology that theorises knowledge derivation within social and cultural context, as African indigenous knowledge does, is communitarian. To be communitarian epistemologically is to centralise the role of society in knowledge practice – to emphasise the connection between the individual and the community, especially the role of the community in shaping the individual's understanding. This is typical of African epistemology that is firmly established on African ontology.

The debate between Ifeanyi Menkiti and Kwame Gyekye on African communitarianism would help us to understanding the notion of communitarianism in African thought. Whereas Menkiti enunciated the African communitarian ethos in defence of a radical communitarianism (RC), Gyekye tried to balance perspectives between RC and individualism by maintaining the position of moderate communitarianism (MC). The overall thrust of the debate is whether the individual stands alone independent of the community, as espoused in Western ontology, or she is naturally embedded in the social relations of the community as claimed by African ontology. For Menkiti, in African thought, the community takes priority over the individual. Here, he leans on John Mbiti's "I am because we are; and since we are, therefore I am" (1969, 108–109), to argue that "as far as Africans are concerned, the reality of the communal world takes precedence over the reality of individual life histories" (Menkiti 1984, 171). Therefore, the communal ethos takes both ontological and epistemological priority. Menkiti disagrees with the Western idea of community as an aggregation of separated individuals. He argues that the community is "a thoroughly fused collective we," not just a mere additive "we" (1984, 179).

This is a radical notion of African communitarianism which can be extended easily to logically imply that the individual is subjugated to community rationalisation without the freedom of exercising her personal rationality.

Many protagonists of African communitarianism do not agree that communitarianism necessarily subjugates individuality. For example, Ellen Corin argued that individuals are not always overshadowed by societies as certain modalities in the practice of communitarianism allow individual particularisation and expression of the self against possible collectivisation of clan image (1980, 146). Obiora Ike and Ndidi Edozien provide insight into how these modalities operate, by referring to the structure of the Igbo community. According to them, to ensure that the system guarantees the individual's freedom of speech, movement and action, the social structure of an Igbo clan consists of smaller communities, within which various groups in the villages hold power. This ensures that there are checks and balances to maintain social balance (2001, 115). David Lutz argues, in a similar vein, when he claims that communitarianism does not restrict individuality because the individual pursues her own good through pursuing the common good (2009, 314). These claims strengthen Gyekye's account of MC, which is a lucid presentation of how the African retains her individuality in a communitarian system.

Gyekye argues that individuality is not suppressed or compromised in communitarianism. He thinks that Menkiti's RC is misleading because it overstates the communitarian claims. Relying on the Akan proverb that 'one tree does not make a forest,' Gyekye argues that individuals exist prior to the community and that the community is essentially a derivate of individuals and the relationships that exist between them (1997, 38). He supports his argument with the following proverbs: 'A clan is like a cluster of trees which, when seen from afar, appear huddled together, but which would seem to stand individually when closely approached'; 'One does not fan [the hot food] that another may eat'; and 'The lizard does not eat pepper for the frog to sweat'. These proverbs undergird his claim that individuals have and maintain their particular attributes and exercise them within, and at times, in contrast to the community. Thus, for Gyekye, the individual has her separate identity and she is "separately rooted and is not completely absorbed by the cluster … [the] community does not obliterate or squeeze out individuality" (1992, 32). For him, radical communitarians like Menkiti exaggerate how history and communal structures impact on individual autonomy.

We may argue that to strengthen individuality in African communitarianism is to concede to Western values. This argument is misplaced because the genuineness of inquiry ensures that the inquiry is free of biases and accepts truth wherever it is found; no tradition is to be universalised and none is to be objectified. The argument also lacks merit because individuality is not the prerogative of Western ontology; besides, Western tradition supports communitarian perspectives, which does not imply that they are giving concession to African values. Whether RC or MC, the notion of communitarianism in African thought accentuates the intricate relationship between the individual and the community and emphasises that the individual's cognitive success is predicated on the collective rationalisation of the community.

Based on the foregoing, we understand ACE as an African theory of knowledge that explains how knowledge and truth are socially, culturally and collectively generated. It is the view that the individual's knowledge is justified in and by the community. It emphasises the "dialectics, cooperation, and togetherness, which makes knowledge a derivative of a chain relationship" (Jimoh 2018, 16), and, therefore, a holistic and integrative grasp of phenomena. The cognition of any aspect of reality is interrelated with the knowledge of the other aspects of reality; hence, Innocent Onyewuenyi opines that the African theory of knowledge is closely associated with African ontology (1976, 525).

A people's ontology delineates their distinctive worldview and differentiates them from other peoples; it informs their particular mode of perception. As a theory that emphasises the continuum of being, African ontology "implies the presence of spiritual components of nature that influence human experience and perception" (Jimoh 2018, 14), because they possess awareness of nature which enables them to respond to perceptions just like humans do. Consequently, African ontology does not fractionise reality into the rational, empirical and mystical. Instead, it conceives reality as a unity and harmony of all there is. It provides a vision of totality where every aspect or mode of being makes meaning in relation to other aspects or modes of being. The rational, empirical and mystical are considered as parts of the same whole, and together, they provide the unitive and holistic understanding of being. In this wise, we understand the claim of Léopold Senghor that the African does not merely analyse the object of cognition as if it is independent and separated from her being, she feels, touches and smells it (1964, 72). The knower and the known enter into an organic and dynamic relationship that provides the knower a comprehensive and profound understanding of the known. In other words, "the self of the subject and [the] objective world outside the self are united as one in a relationship in which the self of the subject vivifies and animates the objective world" (Jimoh 2017, 127). As a theory of knowledge grounded on her ontology, ACE is "the symbiotic harmonious relationship within an individual, between an individual and society, and between an individual and nature and the spiritual world of their ancestors and their gods" (Lajul 2018, 55). This characterisation of ACE highlights the different levels of interaction in the cognitive process.

The first level of interaction is a process within the individual which is essentially rational. At this level, the individual makes a mental abstraction on the basis of the object perceived in association with the ideas already in her mind. The second is between the individual and society; here, social interactions, societal practices and cultural beliefs inform her assimilation and comprehension of her direct perception of the object of knowledge. The third is between the individual and nature, as well as the mystical and spiritual world. At this level, the harmony between the individual and non-empirical realities that implicate her perception is established. According to Lee Brown, even though this aspect of reality is not empirically accessible, it is nonetheless a fact. Brown claims that "one can acquire an understanding of natural phenomena by appealing to experiences whose characterisations are not empirically confirmable but are nonetheless warrantably assertible" (2004, 160). ACE recognises that "there are spiritual components of nature that influence human experience and perception ... [such that] when a phenomenon is not readily explainable by empirical verification, it can be explained by the causal efficacy of the spiritual components of nature" (Jimoh 2017, 122). Lajul's and Brown's assertions represent the African ontological and cultural view of reality and how the latter provides grounds for the African epistemic practice.

The symbiotic connection between the individual and society in the process of knowing is what makes African epistemology communitarian. In this symbiotic connection, the society plays an essential role in the determination of what the individual knows. It is mistaken and erroneous to assume that because society plays an essential role in knowledge derivation, it implies that the individual's rationality is relegated or subjugated to the communitarian enterprise. If this is the case, it means the society infringes on the individual's rational ability to grasp reality since the individual cannot know by herself, but only knows what the society permits her to know. Such an assumption is a hangover from the Western epistemological view that for one to genuinely know, one must transcend personal, environmental, social and cultural 'interferences' and achieve a phenomenological grasp of what is known. According to this view, to transcend the so-called interferences ensures that one's cognitive process is not distorted. Existing literature on this subject, however, shows that even contemporary Western epistemology does not support this position any longer; contemporary social epistemology is built on the claim that knowledge and truth are socially constructed.

Knowledge and Truth in African Communitarian Epistemology

Knowledge in ACE is teleological. In other words, it is understood in terms of the purpose it serves and not necessarily by what causes it. This does not suggest that the sources of knowledge are irrelevant to ACE; rather, it is an emphasis on the goal or telos of knowledge as the operative factor in determining what is knowledge and what is not knowledge in ACE. Knowledge, in ACE, is possessing true information about being; a false or mistaken information about a given state of affairs is not and cannot be knowledge.

A teleological idea of knowledge implies that a claim is knowledge if and only if what the claim asserts is demonstrated to be such; otherwise, it is considered mistaken. To prove that a knowledge claim is the case warrants an empirical or theoretical demonstration to establish that it is the case. Demonstration affirms the truth of the content of a knowledge claim and, therefore, justifies that the agent actually knows. Take for instance: Suppose I claim to *know* that "going to bed early, irrespective of any other circumstances, would make me wake up early the following day" – Q. And on the basis of Q, I went to bed early claiming that Q. Suppose I wake up early the following day, can my claim that Q be contested as knowledge? The answer is 'No', because my waking up early the following day validates and justifies my claim that Q. Therefore, I know that Q because the state of affairs that Q asserts is the case. On the other hand, suppose I fail to wake up early the following day, despite going to bed early the day before, then it means I do not know that Q since the state of affairs that Q asserts is not the case. The latter invalidates and shows that Q is mistaken.

Knowledge does not exist independent of the knower; it is the property of the knower, because there is no knowledge without a knowing subject who knows it. Objects of knowledge do not cognise themselves as long as they are the objects of another agent's knowledge. And an object of knowledge, which is a state of affairs, is not knowledge until it is cognised. For instance, "a bottle of water on the table" is a state of affairs; it becomes knowledge when a cognitive agent becomes aware and claims that it is the case or not the case that "there is a bottle of water on the table." Knowledge is not the bottle of water on the table; it is the cognition and subsequent declaration that the bottle of water is on the table that is knowledge. A cognitive agent cannot truly make the claim that "there is a bottle of water on the table" without a prior interaction with the state of affairs of a bottle of water being on the table. The interaction between the knower and what is known can be empirical or rational depending on the nature of the subject matter of the knowledge in question. It is empirical when the subject matter is about the physical and contingent world and rational when the subject matter is about mental and metaphysical realities. The nature, manner and form of interaction is determined by the empirical or rational nature of the subject matter.

Although knowledge and truth are not interchangeable because they do not mean the same thing, they are, however, intrinsically related. We cannot have knowledge that is not true, and the way by which we adjudge a claim to be knowledge is by testing its truth content. A claim that is false is a mistaken representation of the state of affairs it describes and, therefore, not knowledge. This is the point where we need an analysis of truth in ACE.

The general philosophical interest about truth is to establish what we mean when we predicate truth to a statement. In other words, what are the conditions under which what is said to be true can be true? Aristotle, in his *Metaphysics*, claims that "to say of what is that it is, or of what is not, that it is not, is true" (1011b, 26). In other words, 'P is true, if and only if P', when it is not P, then it is not true. In this regard, Bertrand Russell articulates the conditions for truth thus, any account of truth: (i) must allow for the possibility of falsehood or error, (ii) truth and falsehood must be properties that belong to conscious beings – truth bears and (iii) truth bearers must be true in relation to something else, other than themselves – facts (2001, 18–19). Since these conditions are widely accepted as reasonable attempts to clarify the nature of truth, Western epistemologists try to establish the nature of truth by developing various robust and deflational theories of truth like the correspondence, coherence, pragmatic, redundancy and performatory theories. None of these theories successfully explained the meaning and nature of truth.

To delineate and defend the objectivity of truth, Western epistemological tradition theorised truth beyond our intellectual and cognitive abilities. It takes truth out of the social conversations of its usage and shrouds it in impersonal, abstract and transcendental language beyond human comprehension. Thus, one wonders if truth is no longer supposed to describe the human experience of reality. Contrary to this very abstractive description of truth, Adegboyega Orangun avers that

> truth is the property of human experience and a link between the perceiver's thought and the reality of the state of affairs or events of the external world ... truth is not [an] exclusive property or claim of propositions but the relations of personal experience.
>
> *2001, 71*

If Orangun's claim is correct, it means that truth is not as enigmatic in African thought as it is in Western thought.

Even though Africa is a multiplex of cultures and languages, there is a common notion of truth across sub-Sahara African cultures as indicated in the words and phrases that denote truth in different African languages. Take the three dominant cultures in Nigeria, for instance; among the Igbo, truth is designated with the compound word *ezi-okwu*, which means the right word or correct sentence. It is right or correct because it agrees with the facts or states of affairs. We find the same idea among the Yoruba, who describe truth as *otitọ*, and the Hausas, who refer to truth as *gaskiya*. By far, one of the most articulated accounts of truth in African thought is Kwasi Wiredu's analysis of truth in Akan language. Wiredu disagreed with the traditional view that truth is a consensus of opinion by dismissing the idea that "consensus is an essential aspect of truth for the African" (see Jimoh 2004, 78). According to him, it is an epistemological aberration to claim that "cognitive truth consists in agreement among the members of a community [as] there is a sharp awareness of the disparity between the cognitive capabilities of the wise persons of the community and the populace" (Wiredu 1998, 234). Nonetheless, he does not totally remove the element of consensus from the truth equation. Rather, he emphasises that communal agreement is not the primary essence of truth. At the end of a conscientious effort to articulate the Akan notion of truth, through a detailed analysis of the various words that could be used to depict truth, he concludes that for P to be true, it means that P is so. This implies that truth is what agrees with the state of affairs to which the truth is predicated.

Didier Kaphagawani's analysis of the Chewa notion of truth does not differ much from Wiredu's submission. According to Kaphagawani, "what is true among the Chewa is what is seen. And since seeing is experiencing visually, it follows that what is true is what is experienced" (1998, 241). This notion of truth seems to eliminate the non-experiential (the rational) as candidate for truth. If this is the case, how do the Chewa explain non-empirical concepts like wizardry, witchcraft and sorcery, which are part of their linguistic scheme? Kaphagawani acknowledges these concepts as part of the Chewa linguistic scheme, but he does not provide a categorical response to how they feature in the truth notion of the Chewa. Rather, he posits that the word *zoona* from which the Chewa notion of truth is derived equally connotes perception, which allows its extension to include that which is not seen, but nonetheless, cognised as truth.

Wiredu's and Kaphagawani's analyses of truth in Akan and Chewa cultures are attempts to explain under what conditions, in African thought, we can say a statement is true. In an earlier analysis of truth in Azande culture, Peter Winch (1958) argues that the truth or falsity of a statement is dependent on the meaning of the statement. The meaning of the statement itself depends on how it is used – how it functions as part of the form of life it belongs to (see Jarvie 1972, 44). Wiredu's and Kaphagawani's analyses, therefore, testify in support with Winch's position that truth is culture dependent. This is indicative of some form of epistemological relativism. The relativism here does not imply that there are no standards or criteria for determining the truth; rather, it emphasises that there are no independent standards or criteria of truth applicable to all cultures. This should not be interpreted to mean that there are no standards or paradigms for truth, but that there are no universal standards, independent of contexts that make truth impersonal, abstract and mystified as Western analytic epistemology conceives it (Jimoh 2004, 79). Like knowledge, truth does not exist on its own; it exists as a property of that which is true. Truth is always about a state of affairs, and states of affairs are always within given contexts. The context of the particular state of affairs determines the truth of the claim that is in reference to it. Therefore, truth in ACE implies consistency and correspondence with states of affairs. A statement is true if and only if it agrees with a set of beliefs and accepted facts.

Conclusion

The cognitive process of knowing involves an interaction between the knower, situated within a community, and the object (being) that the knower knows. This interaction which is, most times, described as perception could be rational, empirical or mystical. To be in interaction is to have a mutual relationship of intercourse between two agents – in this case, the knower and what is known; and this always takes place within a given context (e.g. a particular culture). The absence of such mutual interactive relationship nullifies the possibility of knowing, which implies the absence of knowledge. When the knower comes in contact with the external world, she interacts with the external world and gains awareness of how things are in the external world. The awareness, which is informed by the interaction between the knower's consciousness and reality, constitutes knowledge. For awareness to pass as knowledge it has to be in concord with the object of awareness (the state of affairs) – that it is the case or it is not the case. For example, if S is aware that P, where P is 'a bottle of water on the table', it must be the case that there is 'a bottle of water on the table'. The interaction between the knower and the known enables the knower to reconstruct a mental picture of that which she has interacted with. The process of mental reconstruction involves the interpretation of input data which is guided by the knower's worldview (ontology) and it is essentially an activity of the knower in her capacity as a rational being. The knower's ontological worldview informs her understanding of what is sensible, reasonable, true and applicable to reality. Knowledge and truth are interwoven such that we cannot know that which is not true. Therefore, knowledge and truth are products of the interaction between the knower and being (reality).

Bibliography

Aristotle. *Metaphysics*. Harvard: Harvard University Press, 1993.

Avineri, S. and de-Shalit, A. *Communitarianism and Individualism*. Oxford: Oxford University Press, 1992.

Brown, L. M. "Understanding and Ontology in African Traditional Thought." In *African Philosophy: New and Traditional Perspectives*, edited by Lee M. Brown, 158–178. Oxford: Oxford University Press, 2004.

Corin, E. "Vers une réappropriation de la dimension individuelle en psychologie Africaine." *Revue canadienne des études africaines* 14, no. 1 (1980): 135–156.

Emeagwali, G. "Intersections between Africa's Indigenous Knowledge Systems and History." In *African Indigenous Knowledge and the Disciplines. Anti-Colonial Educational Perspectives for Transformative Change*, edited by G. Emeagwali and G.J.S. Dei, 1–17. Rotterdam: Sense Publishers, 2014. https://doi.org/10.1007/978-94-6209-770-4_1

Gettier, Edmund L. "Is Justified True Belief Knowledge?" *Analysis* 23, no. 6 (1963): 121–123.

Goldman, A. and O'Connor, C. (2021). "Social Epistemology," *The Stanford Encyclopedia of Philosophy* (Spring 2021 Edition), edited by Edward N. Zalta, https://plato.stanford.edu/archives/spri2021/entries/epistemologysocial. Accessed 17/4/2021.

Gyekye, K. "Person and Community in African Thought." In *Person and Community: Ghanian Philosophical Studies I*, edited by Kwasi Wiredu and Kwame Gyekye, 101–122. Washington: Council for Research in Values and Philosophy, 1992.

———. *Tradition and Modernity: Philosophical Reflections on the African Experience*. New York: Oxford University Press, 1997.

Hunter, A. *Traditional and Western System of Knowledge*. Rovanieni: University of the Arctic, 2007.

Ichikawa, J. J. and Steup, M. (2018). "The Analysis of Knowledge." *The Stanford Encyclopedia of Philosophy* (Summer 2018 Edition), edited by Edward N. Zalta, https://plato.stanford.edu/archives/sum2018/entries/analysis. Accessed 17/4/2021.

Ike, O. F. and Edozien, N. N. *Understanding African Traditional Legal Reasoning, Reasoning, Jurisprudence and Justice in Igbo Land*. Enugu: CIDJAP Publications, 2001.

Jarvie, C. *Concepts and Society*. London: Routledge and Kegan Paul, 1972.

Jimoh, A. "Knowledge and Truth in African Epistemology." *Ekpoma Review* 1(2004): 66–81.

———. "An African Theory of Knowledge." In *Theme, Issues and Problems in African Philosophy*, edited by Isaac E. Ukpokolo, 121–136. New York: Palgrave Macmillan, 2017.

———. "Reconstructing a Fractured Indigenous Knowledge System." *Synthesis Philosophica* 33, no. 1 (2018): 5–22.

Kant, I. *Critique of Pure Reason*, translated by Norman Kemp Smith. New York: St. Martins, 1965.

Kaphagawani, D. "Themes in a Chewa Epistemology." In *The African Philosophy Reader*, edited by P. H. Coetzee and A. P. J. Roux, 240–239. London: Routledge, 1998.

Kaplan, M. "It's Not What You Know that Counts." *Journal of Philosophy* 82, no. 7 (1985): 350–363.

Kuhn, T. *The Structure of Scientific Revolution*. Chicago, IL: Chicago University Press, 1970.

Kusch, M. "Testimony in Communitarian Epistemology." *Studies in History and Philosophy of Science* 33 (2002): 335–354.

Lajul, W. "Reconstructing African Fractured Epistemologies for African Development." *Synthesis Philosophica* 33, no. 1 (2018): 55–76.

Lutz, D. "African Ubuntu Philosophy and Global Management." *Journal of Business Ethics* 84 (2009): 313–328.

Mbiti, J. *African Religions and Philosophy*. London: Heinemann Publishers, 1969.

Menkiti, I. A. "Person and Community in African Traditional Thought." In *African Philosophy: An Introduction*, edited by Richard Wright, 171–182. Lanham, MD: University Press of America, 1984.

Moser, P. *Philosophy after Objectivity: Making Sense in Perspective*. New York, NY: Oxford University Press, 1993.

Onyewuenyi, I. "Is there and African Philosophy?" *Journal of African Studies*, 3, no. 4 (1976): 513–528.

Orangun, A. *Epistemological Relativism: An Enquiry into the Possibility of Universal Knowledge*. Ibadan: African Odyssey Publisher, 2001.

Quine, W. V. O. *Ontological Relativity and Other Essays*. New York, NY: Columbia University Press, 1969.

Rorty, R. *Philosophy and the Mirror of Nature*. Princeton, NJ: Princeton University Press, 1979.

Russell, B. "Truth and Falsehood." In *The Nature of Truth: Classic and Contemporary Perspective*, edited by Michael P. Lynch, 17–24. Cambridge, MA: MIT Press, 2001.

Senghor, L. S. *On African Socialism*. London: Frederick A. Praeger Publishers, 1964.

Williamson, T. *Knowledge and Its Limits*. Oxford: Oxford University Press, 2000.

Winch, P. The Idea of a Social Science and Its Relation to Philosophy, Second Edition. Atlantic Highlands, NJ: Routledge and Kegan Paul, 1958.

Wiredu, K. "The Concept of Truth in the Akan Language." In *The African Philosophy Reader*, edited by P. H. Coetzee and A. P. J. Roux, 234–239. London: Routledge, 1998.

―――. "Our Problem of Knowledge: Brief Reflections on Knowledge and Development in Africa." In *African Philosophy as Cultural Inquiry*, edited by Ivan Karp and D. A. Masolo, 181–186. Bloomington, IN: Indiana University Press, 2000.

3
EXPLORING THE THEORY OF COMMUNO-COGNITION

Elvis Imafidon

Introduction

The study and analysis of cognition in epistemology, philosophy of mind and the cognitive sciences in the West has been dominated by how the subject or conscious self independently or solitarily cognises. Rene Descartes' *cogito ergo sum* (I think, therefore I am [and by extension, therefore I know or cognise]) laid the foundation and cemented the platform for the study and analysis of cognition as one essentially concerned with mental states, processes and features for acquiring, learning, understanding, remembering and recollecting knowledge and information. Cognitive sciences such as psychology, computational neurosciences and epigenesis is thus the scientific study of the mind, or more aptly, of brain processes and its computation of information. Friedenberg and Silverman (2006: 2–3) defines cognitive science as:

> the scientific interdisciplinary study of the mind. Its primary methodology is the scientific method, although as we will see, many other methodologies also contribute. A hallmark of cognitive science is its interdisciplinary approach. It results from the efforts of researchers working in a wide array of fields. These include philosophy, psychology, linguistics, artificial intelligence, robotics, and neuroscience. Each field brings with it a unique set of tools and perspectives … its theoretical perspective on the mind is … the idea of computation, which may alternatively be called information processing. Cognitive scientists view the mind as an information processor.

But philosophy may arguably not fit into the scope of cognitive sciences as it does not itself depend largely on the scientific method. Philosophy is rather the analysis of cognition, of the thinking subject (*cogito*) Descartes spoke about, including emotions, reason, sensuality, thought processes, memory, perception and any form of activity that might be implicated in the subject's internal cognitive processes. Such cognitive processes are in philosophical discourses not always characterised as brain processes or solely information computation, which is why cognitive science can be quite limited in associating philosophy within its interdisciplinarity. More so, there is a philosophy and philosophers of the cognitive sciences, which consists of a rigorous analysis of the methods of the cognitive sciences, its metaphysical assumptions, epistemological frameworks, ethical principles and moral implications of its research and activities (Sprevak 2017). But the scientific study of cognitive processes (as in cognitive sciences) and the philosophical analysis of cognition (as in philosophy in general and epistemology in particular) as rooted in the Western tradition of scholarship are at least united on the perspective that the object of study in cognition are internal to the subject and individuated, although there is much contention about what really is/are internal and how such individuation happens. Thus, although within the Western philosophy of cognition and cognitive sciences (see Sprevak 2016), there is growing recognition of the importance of the environment or external factors or states in cognitive processes as we find, for example in epigenesis (Waddington 1957), biocognition (Martinez 2001) and extended cognition (Clark and Chalmers 1998; Sprevak 2009, 2019), there is minimal resistance against the fundamental thesis that actual cognition happens internally and subjectively. This thesis is aptly captured by Gerken's (2014: 127) idea of outsourced cognition which states that "the cognitive states and processes of the individual are substantially and explanatorily distinct from the relevant external states and processes. In consequence, the individual remains a cognitive unit that is both central and indispensable in the explanations of cognitive science."

But the Western episteme or normative conditions guiding how cognition can be discussed no longer stands alone in the dancing arena of human inquiry. In the continually decolonising and deconstructed post-Western dominated and colonised episteme, what de Sousa Santos (2018) calls the end of the (Western) cognitive empire, we enjoy the richness of epistemological cum philosophical traditions globally and what they bring to the philosophical table on all forms of inquiries and discourses including those concerning cognition. From *prama* – knowledge episode and true cognition in Indian philosophy (Mohanty 2001), to Lao Tzu's theory of *wu wei* (inaction and not striving to cognise) in Taoist philosophy (Lin 1977), and to knowledge and cognition as a collective and relational project in African philosophy (Hamminga 2005), there is a growing and robust non-Western literature to draw from in enriching conversations about knowledge and cognition, crystalising into an intensely rich ecology of knowledge, which acknowledges and promotes epistemological diversity and renounces any colonial, hegemonic and universalist epistemology (de Sousa Santos 2007). In this chapter, I explore and critically examine the African theory of cognition as communo-cognition. I begin by conceptualising what I mean by a communo-cognitive process that dominates the African episteme and show how it connects and disconnects from quite similar concepts in recent developments in Western cognitive studies such as extended cognition and biocognition; In doing this, I explain the power of orality, collective authorship, collective relational minds, collective relational perception and collective relational memory, hinging on the theoretical framework of Ubuntu. I then proceed to examine how communo-cognition challenges and enriches the individualistic, subjective and internalist approach to, and understanding of, cognition in the dominant literature, allowing for the flourishing of difference and situatedness in the cognitive process, thereby rehumanising the discourse of cognition. I then examine some major challenges that a communo-cognitive approach may face such as deeply rooting falsehood and ignorance and the impeding of individual autonomy. I conclude by highlighting how communo-cognition is a human cognitive episteme that should be given proper scholarly attention in cognitive sciences and interdisciplinary studies.

Communo-Cognition, Ubuntu and Relational Minds

African epistemology as the African account or theory of knowledge consists of inherited indigenous orality and literature and contemporary discourses and critical analyses of the nature, theories, processes and sources of knowledge in African places. It seeks to answer important epistemological questions from the African point of view. In the growing literature on African epistemology in the last seven decades or so, there has been strong concerns in extrapolating and deducing theories of knowledge from African philosophical thoughts, resulting in at least three African theories of knowledge: (i.) knowledge as first-hand information (Hallen 2004), (ii.) knowledge as consistency with established beliefs (Appiah 2005), and the more popular narrative, (iii.) knowledge as shared or collectively held beliefs (Hamminga 2005). The first is a very important form of virtue epistemology which requires virtues such as trust, honesty, integrity, communicative competence and truthfulness as well as elements of corroboration to flourish in an African place; the second depends largely on collective corroboration and consistency with ontological commitments in an African place for knowledge to emerge. The third encompasses the first and the second and provides a more grounding theory of knowledge that permeates African societies where to claim to know something in an African place is to claim to have shared and collectively held knowledge, to know what others know as well. African communitarian epistemology is the most popular and defended African theory of knowledge due to its felt presence in many African communities. The knower is not an individual agent but a collective agent, the community. Knowledge is not attained through some solitary process of reason or sense experiences; it is collectively attained – I know because the group knows. It emphasises the social and collective dimension of knowledge. (Imafidon 2019; Hamminga 2005). It is this collective process of knowing that defines African accounts of knowledge as a core theme in the cognitive studies that is the focal point of my discourse in this chapter.

Communo-cognition holds that the process of knowing in African traditions and the related cognitive features such as learning and remembering is essentially a community-centred process, collectively achieved by group agency and controlled by the community and its structures. This is precisely why knowledge is seen as shared, collective knowledge since the process of accessing, acquiring and remembering such knowledge is done collectively and determined by institutions and ontologies constructed and controlled by the community (Imafidon 2019). It is usually assumed in Western cognitive sciences that cognition happens individually and solitarily, that the individual solitarily perceives, senses, reasons, acquires, stores, remembers and understands knowledge claims. Even aspects of Western cognitive sciences that acknowledge in some way the importance of environments, cultures and languages in cognitive processes still stick to the subjective nature of cognition as these external factors are at best objects for cognition or tools aiding in the process of subjective cognition. Biocognition, for example, merges three key elements, cognition, biology and culture, in explaining how cognition happens. Its goal is to show that:

> (1) cognition begins in infancy with perception of undifferentiated personal space and time (i.e., undefined boundaries between self and surroundings without time discernment), (2) emotions evolve from sensations of comfort vs. discomfort and security vs. insecurity and, (3) language evolves from primordial sounds that express sensations related to undifferentiated internal and external stimuli. Bioinformation is defined as the cognitive, biological, and historical culture that individuals contextually share in their communication.
>
> *Martinez 2001: 408*

Extended cognition also emphasises the ability of the individual mind to spill itself into objects such as in the way what an individual cognises can be penned down in a paper or stored in smartphone applications such as calendars or to-do-lists. In the words of Sprevak (2020, par. 1):

> Extended cognition takes the idea that your mind is 'on' your smartphone literally. It says that human cognitive states and processes sometimes spill outside our heads and into objects in our environment. Alleged examples include not just smartphones, but also use of simpler technology (pencil and paper to perform a calculation), our own body (ticking off our fingers when we count), and other people (our spouse who remembers appointments so we don't have to).

In both cases, there is a clear prioritisation of the individual over collective, relational, cooperative cognition. In biocognition, although there is glaring evidence of the acknowledgement of human culture in shaping language and in turn cognition, there is still lots of emphasis on the individual biological role in, and features for, cognition to happen. Extended cognition explicitly prioritises the individual's cognition and how she/he spills such cognition into objects and perhaps, other subjects. But communo-cognition is essentially the claim that cognition as can be deduced from the African place is codependent, relational, shared and collectively achieved. I will instantiate this in three aspects: collective, relational minds, collective, relational perception and collective, relational memory.

In sub-Saharan African places, there is no doubt that there are individual minds cooperating, co-depending and interacting together to grasp realities as well as a collective, relational, group mind. The core principle of community in African philosophy 'I am because we are' (Mbiti 1969) aptly captures this. It can be formulated with regard to cognition as 'I cognise, because we cognise together.' In gatherings in African communities, there is a lot of emphasis on 'we know that' rather than on 'I know that'. Statements such as 'It is a taboo not to bury the dead properly', 'a good name is better than wealth', or 'colonization has destroyed Africa' will not usually begin with 'I know that …' but rather with 'We know that …'. The emphasis is on collective authorship and knowledge production. What is cognised and the knowledge produced are collectively attained and passed down from generation to generation through orality, symbolism and art, more than they are through writing. Writing is often used to portray epistemic and intellectual legitimacy of Western tradition as it is seen as the best way to preserve what has been cognised through individual authorship, serving as legitimation and corroboration of the epistemic legacy in the history of thought. In fact, writing and individual authorship has been the basis for a rejection of African philosophy by the West as the game has often been 'If you have a philosophy, show me what you wrote.' But the richness of orally and culturally preserved African philosophical thoughts and body of knowledges passed down from generations to generations and providing a basis for contemporary African philosophical history clearly indicates that writing is only one way of presenting, representing, preserving and storing what has been cognised either individually – as in extended cognition – or collectively as in communo-cognition.

More so, orally preserved African intellectual history is a self-servicing machine that corroborates and justifies its legitimacy on the basis that it survives, keeps thriving, remains deeply rooted in community and sustains a coherent body of information even though its authorship is deindividualised. This is perhaps because of the interpersonal mental activities and processes that go into the production of knowledge in African thought. Africans reason, sense, acquire and store information and knowledge claims collectively, relationally and interpersonally to the extent that the information emerging from this process cannot be individually held. Consider, for example how a strange phenomenon might be cognised in a village square meeting in an African community through the art of deliberation, a well-crafted art of reciprocal conversation, compromise, non-competitive and deindividualised forms of deliberation, which is now being explored for theorising deliberative and consensual democracy (Bujo 1998; Wiredu 1996). In such a scenario, community members will explore matters together, perceive together, think together, reason together, sense together, bringing in different individual angles based on individual expertise and understanding, and then come to a decision or knowledge claim about the phenomena by agreement and compromise that incorporates both majority and minority viewpoints (Tavernaro-Haidarian 2020). Thus, no single individual member can claim to have cognised alone or independently, thereby claiming individual ownership or authorship. Rather, the group has collaborated and collectively engaged in the cognitive process, resulting in a communal rather than individualistic understanding of a given situation. Here, there is a co-dependency process of knowledge production, where each individual mind is in a web of relationship with other minds, cooperating to produce the best body of knowledge possible, one that is mutually binding on all parties.

With these relational minds therefore, there is a collective relational perception at play. To perceive in this web of interlocked perceivers is not merely to individually, subjectively and independently see, here, feel, sense, think; rather, it is to intersubjectively perceive and acknowledge the multidimensional nature of perception, where what A perceives may be quite different but not better or less important from what B perceives. Collective, relational and intersubjective perception is thus akin to the sunlight's spectrum of colours or the parts of the human body. All colours in the spectrum or parts of the body interrelate and co-depend to form a whole true and meaningful picture. Collective relational perception thus indicates that we depend on others for meaningful, comprehensive and complete perception of the world we live in. It is the acknowledgement of complementary cognition, recognising that we never completely cognise things independently and that a robust and more comprehensive cognition emerges from the interwovenness of perceivers. Similarly, there is also a collective relational memory at work in communo-cognition. As Africans, we store, recollect and remember together. No one wants to know it all; there is satisfaction in storing some and living some for others to store since at the point of remembering, we can draw from the storage of others and they can draw from ours; more so since we cognise, perceive, experience, sense and reason together, we remember together. It explains why I can recollect knowledges I did not participate in producing because such participation is collective, relational, generic and transgenerational; and the epistemic institutions of the community brought them forward for future generations, not through writing but through orality. As Africans, we are able to remember what our ancestors went through, for example with slavery and colonisation, even though we were not physically there to cognise the situation. In fact, we contribute to our ancestor's perception of the events that happened in our absence.

Collective relational minds as evident in perception and memory reiterates the African Ubuntu principle: a person is a person through other persons. Ubuntu emits a relational cognitive principle; a person cognises through other persons. In the words of Desmond Tutu (2004),

> A person is a person through other persons. None of us comes into the world fully formed. We would not know how to think, or walk, or speak, or behave [or cognise] as human beings unless we learned it from other human beings. We need other human beings in order to be human [to be able to cognise fully].

Augustine Shutte (2001) adds that "Our deepest moral obligation is to become more fully human. And this means entering more and more deeply into community with others." Ubuntu thus emphasises the inevitability of depending on others in finding meaning and fulfilment, to be able to cognise the world (Imafidon 2022). The key idea is that we do not cognise alone; we cognise with others.

Communo-Cognition, Difference and Rehumanisation

Communo-cognition as theorised above as a collective relational project de-objectifies and de-subjectifies cognition. It de-objectifies cognition in so far as what is cognisable is no longer an object that is in front of us phenomenologically, at least in the classical Husserlian sense, and that we have all the capacity as individuals to sense, hear, see, perceive and cognise, but one that we are part of, attached to and depend on, one that always slips away, materialises and disappears all at the same time. It de-subjectifies cognition in so far as cognition becomes a human, relational and collective project, where subjects interact and contribute to the cognition process. Each subject provides a different perspective, and the multitude of perspectives achieve two things: build into a rich and diverse understanding of what is being cognised and allow for the fallibility of cognition, the unending process of enriching already available information. Again, this reiterates the theoretical strengths of Ubuntu. Ubuntu has embedded in it the inclusivity of difference principle because:

> The assertion, 'a person is a person through other persons' encoded into the concept of Ubuntu is first and foremost the acknowledgement and recognition of differences, uniqueness and diversity, and then, the acknowledgement and recognition of the need to bring together these manifold differences to create an intensely rich and diverse potpourri of social and human nourishment that every individual can benefit from. I am a person with my capabilities, weaknesses, likes, dislikes and so on that are similar, different or unique from yours. So I find meaning by depending on you where I lack and you on me where you lack. Hence, this communion of beings, in general, and of humans, in particular, is in no way a suppression of differences or the quest for sameness; it is rather an important approach to inclusivity that encourages all to bring their differences on board not the service of self, but of humanity.
> *Imafidon 2022: 10*

With particular reference to cognition, it entails enriching the cognition process by allowing the flourishing of inter-subjective perspectives. When I cognise a boat in the river, I do not cognise alone – cognising alone would result in a very limited perception. I cognise with others where A perceives the sturdiness, B the beauty, C the flaws, D the surroundings, E the river and so on and so forth. None of these perceptions are on their own complete and rich unless in conversation and in relationship with others.

The recognition of difference in the cognitive process as well as the acknowledgement that cognition is a human and not merely a mental, brain process activity rehumanises it. Cognition as conventionally theorised particularly in Western spaces is a purely mental process executed by dehumanised, biological, physiological mental gadgets such as the senses, brain processes and the rational faculty. To rehumanise, therefore, is not only to take seriously the human points of view or more aptly in the case of African philosophy, the relational, codependent human point of view, but also to acknowledge the differences in the human points of view. I do not wish to confuse the 'human' in the human point of view here with the very general and universalist idea of the totality of human and what they think at some point in time (Stroud 2020) – an obvious impossibility as humans in general never truly share such completely universal perspectives, and at best, it would be one group of humans imposing their perspectives on others. I am referring instead to what a group of humans within a particular context and situatedness collectively achieve in terms of how they view the world, knowledge, existence and things in general, something akin to perspectivism, but what I might rather call relational perspectivism, considering the collective, codependent and relational way in which such a perspective is achieved. Nietzsche is one who beautifully theorises epistemic perspectivism, the sense in which I use the human point of view. Hales (2020: 25) provides an apt summary of Nietzsche's perspective thus:

> Instead of absolute truths and impartially objective knowledge of a supra-empirical world, Nietzsche offers a vision of partial, fragmentary, perspectival knowledge. His regular praise of Heraclitus's acceptance of flux and becoming instead of the Platonic longing for an unchanging invisible world suggests the epistemology Nietzsche supports. We are not prevented from ideal cognition by our this-worldly empirical limitations; Nietzsche wants to abolish the apparent world/ real world dichotomy altogether. Rather, the very nature of truth, and therefore our knowledge of those truths, is in some way dependent on perspective. Nothing is true outside or independent of perspectives; the idea of extra-perspectival knowledge is too redolent of those Kantian or Platonic epistemologies that Nietzsche has already dismissed.

Hales (2020: 26) adds that "Perspectives … have something to do with centres of interest, or attitudes organized around a common concern … Perspectives are both local and abstract … best characterized as ways of knowing, or doxastic practices." This is precisely why, at least, with reference to African epistemic thought, it seems more apt to call the human point of view relational perspectivism – it is a communally and collectively held epistemic perspective and it is a human perspective that is fluid, fallible and limited. It thrives on difference and it is a call for the acknowledgement of difference. The perspective itself is relational perspectivism which thrives on difference because the perspective or human point of view emerges from a coming together of individual and different perspectives in ways that interweave and intertwine. What is an African communo-cognition perspective of a tree? It would include what the carpenter who uses the wood, the herbalist who uses the roots, stems and leaves, the chef who cooks with the fruits or leaves, all in the community who eat from its fruitage, the inherited ancestral knowledge about the tree and so on. These manifold ways of perception marked by different perspectives and knowledges of the tree result in the collective and relational cognition or perspective of the tree. And since human concrete experiences vary from place to place and context to context, perspectives from different places may be similar to or different from others on the same object of cognition.

Communo-Cognition: Two Charges

In this section, I look at two key charges that could be brought against a communo-cognitive process as deduced from African philosophical thought: collectively produced ignorance, falsehood and ideologies as socially necessary false illusions and impediment to individual autonomy. Concerning the first, one of the many lessons that human history has thought us is that a group can collectively fail to know, not understand or mis-understand (Schwenkenbecher 2021), collectively and deliberately turn a blind eye to the truth and to knowledge and collectively produce falsehood and ideologies for teleological reasons and the same group can effectively sustain such ignorance and falsehood to the extent that members of the group including future members accept them uncritically and as truths. This is certainly true in African contexts with regard, for example to collectively sustained falsehood about disability (Imafidon 2017, 2019). By implication, we can collectively cognise and still be wrong. But isn't this the very strength of communo-cognition, the fact that our perspective is human, always incomplete, could be wrong, always needing improvement and never to be taken as a sacrosanct, god's eye perspective? It is the objectification and universalisation of humanly produced incomplete perspectives that impede revisions to our body of knowledges, not the very process of producing them. The collective and relational process of producing knowledges and cognising the world remains vital even in questioning what has already been produced and improving on them. Thus, collectively failing to know and collectively sustaining falsehood implies the need to collectively go back to the drawing board particularly in the face of obvious challenges to previously held knowledge claims; it does not imply rejecting the collective knowing process and attempting to know alone. In fact, rejecting a particular group and its cognitive processes does not necessarily imply independently cognising; in most cases, it implies merely shifting base and accepting the cognitive processes of another group. So the goal is not to reject communo-cognition but to use the same system to revise and continually question collectively held knowledge.

Concerning the second, the question of individual autonomy often comes up in discussions about Afro-communitarian philosophy, be it in relation to ontology, personhood, ethics, knowledge and, in this case, cognition. The question is often about how much the emphasis on community and relational existence infringed on individual rights, freedom and autonomy. But this question is often raised from a very liberal, Western perspectival understanding of personhood with its emphasis on autonomy, agency and rights and less emphasis on other-regarding duties (Molefe 2017). There is a very rich literature on the debate on how much African philosophical theory on community impedes/does not impede individual will and autonomy, resulting in the radical and moderate communitarianism debate (Mbiti 1969; Gyekye 1992; Menkiti 2004; Wiredu 2008). What is obvious from this protracted and heated debate at least from the African perspective is that individual autonomy does not prohibit or prevent a person's exercise of their autonomy as long as such autonomy is exercised in ways that recognises the duties toward others. Motsamai Molefe (2017: 14) aptly captures this thus:

> I can only realize my true humanity by discharging my other-regarding duties to others. My personal goal of moral perfection and other-regarding duties are married in this idea of personhood. What is beginning to emerge is that the idea of personhood entails a pure other-regarding morality, wherein a moral agent understands herself to have duties to promote others' welfare in her quest to achieve the ideal of her leading a truly human life.

In essence, it is the human way of being to be conscious of others; we are only human through other persons and there is no self-sufficient, independently complete human. A radical, Western understanding of individual autonomy is in fact not plausible. More so, Afro-communitarianism as expressed in Ubuntu (a person is a person through other persons), and communo-cognition in particular, is a recognition of individual will, autonomy and independent contribution to the community. This is because while no individual perspective is complete or enough, each individual perspective is important and contributes to a richer perspective. The key difference with the Western understanding of autonomy, and why from the Western perspective the relational understanding of cognition could threaten individual autonomy, is due to the emphasis in the Western understanding on self-recognition, individual authorship and praise for the self, all of which dissolves into the collective whole in the African understanding. Basically, the individual autonomy to contribute to the cognitive process is crucial to cognition and cherished, but the idea of individual autonomy as independence from others and as sole cognition is not plausible. While we may individually contribute to the cognitive process, we cannot individually lay claim to the full outcome of the cognitive process.

Concluding Thoughts: The Humanness of Relational Cognition

While in the last few pages, I may have presented communo-cognition, collective cognition or relational cognition as a prominent indigenous sub-Saharan African mode of cognition, there are glaring evidences that in all spaces of human dwelling, people collectively cognise; they collectively learn, memorise, perceive, remember, sense and engage in other cognitive activities. Around the globe, in education settings, familial settings, business corporations, associations, protest, politics, religion, cultures and all forms of human coexistence, there is co-dependency, cooperation and solidarity in knowing the world around us. This collectiveness and relationality is in many cases denied, suppressed and not acknowledged due to deeply entrenched politics of cognition in spaces of human dwelling where a few with the louder voice and the institutional power to proclaim (such as the power to publish in writing in books or to air in media) what has been cognised seize ownership and authorship. To be sure, there are excellent manifestations of individual cognition in which the cogniser deserves credit for an excellent contribution to the cognitive process, but even such cognition would not come to be without the support from a wider community of cognisers. But the dominant understanding of cognition blinds us to this salient fact of solidarity in cognition, always shifting our gaze to the objective and individual rather than to the intersubjective and communal. Thus, mainstream cognitive sciences such as psychology, the philosophy of mind, neuroscience, artificial intelligence, computer science and linguistics need to explore more fully the relational dimension to cognition. What communo-cognition may look like and imply for specific areas of cognitive sciences including how relationality impacts on seemingly private mental states are important questions worth pursuing in this regard.

References

Appiah, K. A. (2005). African Studies and the Concept of Knowledge. In Bert Hamminga (Ed.), *Knowledge Cultures: Comparative Western and African Epistemology*. Amsterdam: Rodopi. 23–56.

Bujo, B. (1998). *The Ethical Dimension of Community: The African Model and the Dialogue between North and South*. Nairobi: Paulines Publications.

Clark A. and Chalmers, D. J. (1998). The Extended Mind. *Analysis*, 58: 7–19.

De Sousa Santos, B. (2007). Beyond abyssal thinking: From global lines to ecologies of knowledges. *Review* (Fernand Braudel Center), 30.1: 45–89.

De Sousa Santos, B. (2018). *The End of the Cognitive Empire: The Coming of Age of Epistemologies of the South*. Durham: Duke University Press.

Friedenberg, J. and Silverman, G. (2006). *Cognitive Science: An Introduction to the Study of Mind*. California: Sage.

Gerken, M. (2014). Outsourced Cognition. *Philosophical Issues*, 24.1: 127–158.

Gyekye, K. (1992). Person and Community in African Thought. In Kwasi Wiredu and Kwame Gyekye (Eds.), *Person and Community: Ghanaian Philosophical Studies*. Washington, DC: The Council for Research in Values and Philosophy. 101–122.

Hales, S. D. (2020). Nietzsche's Epistemic Perspectivism. In A Cretu and M. Massimi (Eds.), *Knowledge from a Human Point of View*. Cham: Springer. 19–36.

Hallen, B. (2004). Yoruba Moral Epistemology. In Kwasi Wiredu (Ed.), *A Companion to African Philosophy*. Malden, MA: Blackwell. 296–304.

Hamminga, B. (2005). Epistemology from the African Point of View. In Bert Hamminga (Ed.), *Knowledge Cultures: Comparative Western and African Epistemology*. Amsterdam: Rodopi. 57–84.

Imafidon, E. (2017). Dealing with the Other between the Ethical and the Moral: Albinism on the African Continent. *Theoretical Medicine and Bioethics*, 38.2: 163–177.

Imafidon, E. (2019). *African Philosophy and the Otherness of Albinism: White Skin, Black Race*. London: Routledge.
Imafidon, E. (2022). Exploring African Relational Ethic of Ubuntu for Inclusion and Solidarity in the Humanitarian Field. *Europe Talks Solidarity*. https://www.salto-youth.net/downloads/4-17-4259/17-Elvis_Imafidon-Ubuntu.pdf
Lin, P. J. (1977). *A Translation of Lao-tzu's Tao Te Ching and Wang Pi's Commentary*. Michigan: University of Michigan Press.
Martinez, Mario E. (2001). The process of knowing: A biocognitive epistemology. *The Journal of Mind and Behaviour*, 22.4: 407–426.
Mbiti, J. S. (1969). *African Religion and Philosophy*. London: Heinemann.
Menkiti, I. A. (2004). On the Normative Conception of a Person. In K. Wiredu (Ed.), *A Companion to African Philosophy*. Malden, MA: Blackwell. 324–331.
Mohanty, J. N. (2001). A Fragment of the Indian Philosophical Tradition: Theory of Pramana. In Roy W. Perrett (Ed.), *Epistemology*. New York: Routledge. 1–11.
Molefe, M. (2017). Critical Comments on Afro-communitarianism: The Community versus Individual. *Filosofia Theoretica: Journal of African Philosophy, Culture and Religion*, 6.1: 1–22.
Schwenkenbecher, A. (2021). How we Fail to Know: Group-Based Ignorance and Collective Epistemic Obligations. *Political Studies*, Online first: https://doi.org/10.1177/00323217211000926
Shutte, A. (2001). *Ubuntu: An Ethic for the New South Africa*. Cape Town, South Africa: Cluster Publications.
Sprevak, M. (2009). Extended Cognition and Functionalism. *Journal of Philosophy*, 106: 503–527.
Sprevak, M. (2016). Philosophy of the Psychological and Cognitive Sciences. In P. Humphreys (Ed.), *Oxford Handbook for the Philosophy of Science*. Oxford: Oxford University Press. 92–114.
Sprevak, M. (2019). Extended Cognition. In T. Crane (Ed.), *The Routledge Encyclopaedia of Philosophy* (Online). London: Routledge. https://doi.org/10.4324/9780415249126-V049-1
Sprevak, M., Anderson, M., and Garrett, P. (2020). *Distributed Cognition from Victorian Culture to Modernism*. Edinburgh: Edinburgh University Press.
Sprevak, M., Copeland, J., Bowen, J., and Wilson, R. (2017). *The Turing Guide: Life, Work, Legacy*. Oxford: Oxford University Press.
Stroud, B. (2020). Knowledge from a Human Point of View. In A Cretu and M. Massimi (Eds.), *Knowledge from a Human Point of View*. Cham: Springer. 141–148.
Tavernaro-Haidarian, L. (2020). Deliberative Theory and African Philosophy: The Future of Deliberation in Transitional Societies. *Journal of Deliberative Democracy*, 16.1: 20–26.
Tutu, D. (2004). *God Has a Dream: A Vision of Hope for Our Time*. New York: Doubleday Religion.
Waddington, C. H. (1957). *The Strategy of the Genes*. London: Allen & Unwin.
Wiredu, K. (1996). *Cultural Universals and Particulars: An African Perspective*. Bloomington: Indiana University Press.
Wiredu, K. (2008). Social Philosophy in Postcolonial Africa: Some Preliminaries Concerning Communalism and Communitarianism. *South African Journal of Philosophy*, 27: 332–339.

PART II
On the Object of Knowledge in African Epistemology

4
UNDERSTANDING A THING'S NATURE

Comparing Afro-Relational and Western-Individualist Ontologies

Thaddeus Metz

Introducing African Relationality

African ethics is characteristically relational in certain ways, roughly deeming ways of interacting between people either to merit pursuit as a final end or to be essential means towards some other important good. For instance, a certain kind of communitarianism (probably best called "communalism") is salient when discussing topics in interpersonal morality or institutional justice. A broadly similar approach is found in African metaphysics and epistemology. When it comes to knowledge, for example, it is common to encounter the view that in order to truly understand something, one must view it in terms of how it relates to an interdependent whole (e.g. Hamminga 2005; cf. Nisbett 2003). And, then, in terms of what exists, a recurrent theme is that a thing's nature is constituted by such a contextualization, viz., by how it relates to a variety of forces, including imperceptible agents that are all richly interconnected.

This chapter focuses on just one aspect of this conception of what is real, specifically, the appeal to certain relational properties when seeking to apprehend the essence of representative natural objects. Specifically, this chapter's aims are to articulate a characteristically African approach to understanding the essence of a concrete, natural thing, roughly a spatio-temporal object that is not an artefact,[1] in terms of its relationships with more care than has been done before, to illustrate the Afro-relational approach with the examples of the self and of water, to contrast these examples with a typically Anglo-American, and more generally Western, approach to them in terms of their intrinsic properties and, finally, to provide some defence of the Afro-relational approach, both by responding to objections facing it and by providing new, positive reasons to take it seriously.

In pursuing these aims, this chapter does not pursue others. For example it presumes, for the sake of argument, that some concrete, natural things have an

DOI: 10.4324/9781003182320-7

essence, roughly a nature that persists in all possible worlds in which they exist. It also assumes that not all of a thing's properties make up its essence, i.e. that some of a thing's properties are accidental or that things can survive change (or that you *can* step in the same river twice).

Furthermore, this chapter addresses only one view commonly espoused by African metaphysicians and epistemologists, regarding the respect in which a thing's nature cannot be understood without appeal to its relational properties, and it sets aside other views. So, amongst other things, it does not consider the claims that reality is an interdependent whole, that it is ultimately composed of forces, and that these include imperceptible agents such as God and ancestors. This author does not believe that it is necessary to accept these claims in order to make good sense of a relational approach to understanding the natures of things that are not artefacts. If they are defensible, then that it is to be shown elsewhere.

The rest of the essay continues, in the next section, by providing some definitions of key terms, especially what is meant by "intrinsic" as opposed to "relational" properties, as well as what is meant by the claim that an appeal to the latter as essential to a thing is "African" as opposed to "Western". In the section following the one on the definition of key terms, it advances the hypothesis, meant to refine suggestions from African philosophers, that apprehending the essence of a natural object is identical at least in part to grasping its relational properties. It then illustrates this claim with the examples of the self and of water, contrasting Afro-relational understandings of their natures with standard Western, intrinsic understandings of them, and it also provides arguments in favour of the former, in the section following the one that examines Afro-relational hypothesis. Next, the chapter responds to some objections that would be natural to raise to Afro-relationalism, and contends that they do not provide enough reason at this stage to reject it. Although the chapter does not conclude that relational understandings of the essence of the self or of water are correct, it does submit that they are worth taking seriously by philosophers around the world as rivals to the intrinsic views so prominent in the West, in the conclusion.

Definitions of Key Terms

The point of this section is to clarify the central terms of the hypothesis that understanding the essence of a natural object is not exhausted by coming to know its intrinsic properties, but also invariably includes awareness of its relational ones, where the latter view is aptly described as "African". The hypothesis itself, as well as illustrations of and defences of it, are discussed only in the following sections.

First off, by an "essence" of an object is meant those features of a thing without which it would not exist. A thing's essence is those properties it would have in any possible world in which it exists. Such a fundamentally ontological, and specifically modal, construal of "essence" differs from other, more epistemological ones, for example that an essence is to be identified as whatever plays a certain explanatory role of best accounting for a thing's surface properties (e.g. Nozick 2001: 126, 347). By the present account, if a property of a thing best explained a wide array of its other properties, then that would be strong *evidence* that it is a thing's essence, but it would not necessarily be so (as, roughly, our explanations might not be good enough or could even be incorrect).

It is difficult to define properties that count as "intrinsic" as opposed to "relational" without controversy; the literature is contested and intricate, and, furthermore, sometimes the way these terms are defined in contemporary English-speaking metaphysics begs the question from the perspective of a more relational tradition such as the African.[2] There are occasions when Anglo-American metaphysicians analyse intrinsic properties explicitly as essential properties, or invoke examples of intrinsic properties that are contentious in the context of cross-cultural debate. For one example, consider that the *Stanford Encyclopedia of Philosophy* entry on the intrinsic/extrinsic distinction (Weatherson and Marshall 2012) uses being Obama as a purportedly clear example of an intrinsic property, while the entry on it in the Blackwell *Companion to Metaphysics* similarly uses being identical to Nixon (Garrett 2009: 258). However, one major aim of this chapter is to argue that there are strong reasons to think that being a particular person such as Obama or Nixon is, at least in large part, a relational property.

The strategy this chapter uses to understand the meaning of "intrinsic" is not to provide a set of necessary and sufficient conditions or an analysis approximating that, since motivating one account as preferable to others would detract from achieving the essay's central aim and is, in any event, unnecessary to achieve it. Instead, this essay appeals to comparatively uncontested examples used in other fields and draws analogies with them. For example in ethics, intuitively intrinsic properties grounding moral status, i.e. the ability of a thing to be wronged, include having a soul, having the capacity for rational decision-making, being able to feel pleasure, exhibiting human DNA and being a living organism. These are individualist, as frequently distinguished from collectivist, features, in that they make no inherent reference to another being beyond the one with them, or do not conceptually involve interaction with another being. In epistemology and the philosophy of language, consider that properties frequently described as "internal", e.g. in relation to the content of propositional attitudes or linguistic terms, are more or less brain states. Talk of an "intrinsic" property in this essay, as it pertains to the essence of a spatio-temporal object that is not an artefact, appeals to a feature that is similar to these examples.

What counts as a "relational" property of a thing, then, will roughly be one that is not intrinsic. More specifically, it will count as a feature of a thing insofar it involves interaction, normally causally but perhaps intentionally, with other, distinct things.[3] Returning to the previous examples, in ethics, relational properties that might ground moral status are being cared for by someone, being a member of a clan or having the capacity to relate communally with others, while in epistemology and the philosophy of language, externalism in respect of content is standardly taken to be constituted by what "just ain't in the *head*" (Putnam 1975: 227), viz., the composition of things in the society and broader environment with which one's brain interacts. A relational property of the self or of water, the two cases addressed in this chapter, will be like these.

One might wonder about some of these examples. Specifically, it appears that in order to feel pleasure or exhibit brain states more generally, one has to have had a body that has been interacting with society and nature. People need to have been socialized when they were young, and brains continue to need nutrients and oxygen. Does that dependence on other things mean that these conditions are in fact best understood as relational and not intrinsic, or does it mean that this distinction is not important (cf. the example of being six feet tall in Garrett 2009: 259)?

In reply, even if the existence of another thing, Y, has brought X about or even sustains it in this world, it does not follow that there is no point to thinking of X as distinct from Y, exhibiting features that are not a function of (at least) its contingent dependence on Y. The conceptual distinctions between individualism/collectivism in ethics and between internalism/externalism in the philosophy of language and epistemology have been useful for framing long-standing and important debates. One can expect a similar distinction to be useful when thinking about metaphysics.

It would be nice to have a subtle and thorough analysis of the intrinsic/relational distinction, but that is not essential to make headway on the topic of this chapter. The examples of intrinsic and relational properties in other fields, or features similar to them there, should be enough to fix the meanings of the terms.

In addition, if one remains uncomfortable with the distinction, one could, in principle, move forward without using these particular terms. For example one could frame the debate about the essence of water simply by asking whether it is identical to a chemical composition or instead must include reference to things in an ecosystem with which it interacts. One could then, when seeking to generalize from the case of water to other natural objects, appeal to properties that are like a chemical composition or are like ecological interaction with other things. This author believes that it is easiest to speak of the former properties as "intrinsic" and the latter as "relational" and that it is revealing to do so given parallels with debates in other fields, and therefore invokes this terminology in what follows.

Below it is suggested that an appeal to relational properties to understand a natural thing's essence is "African", whereas it is "Western" to appeal merely to its intrinsic properties. What are these geographical labels meant to signify? By "African" and similar words such as "Western" are meant features salient in a locale that differentiate it from many other locales.[4] They are properties that have been recurrent over a large range of space and a long span of time in an area and that have not been in many other areas. This use of geographical labels therefore is consistent with the idea that something sensibly characterized as "African" might be encountered outside of Africa and that it also might not be found everywhere inside of Africa.

So, when calling relational accounts of natural essences "African", the claim is that they are salient in philosophies that have been expounded for a long time throughout much of Africa. At the very least, they have been common in post-independence English-speaking works described as "African philosophy", which are well known for being informed by indigenous views held by many black peoples south of the Sahara Desert. Relational accounts are not "Western" insofar they have not been prominently held by philosophers from Europe, the United Kingdom and North America. Instead, what has been salient in their views are intrinsic accounts, even if there have been some exceptions (mentioned in what follows).

An Afro-Relational Hypothesis about the Essence of a Natural Object

This section begins with some quotations from African metaphysicians about how they understand the fundamental nature of reality, sometimes specifically the nature of the self, where it is presumed that they are reflecting the sub-Saharan cultures in which they have been reared or otherwise come to know intimately. The quotations do not always focus exclusively on the notion that relational properties are essential to a thing's existence, but only those remarks in particular are drawn on, with the aim of advancing a clear and circumscribed thesis about the essence of a natural object.

Consider the following passages from African metaphysicians suggesting a relational approach to a thing's nature, particularly that of the self.[5]

> In traditional life, the individual does not and cannot exist alone except corporately. He owes his existence to other people, including those of past generations and his contemporaries. He is simply part of the whole .... Only in terms of other people does the individual become conscious of his own being, his own duties .... The individual can only say: 'I am because we are; and since we are, therefore I am'. This is a cardinal point in the understanding of the African view of man.
>
> *Mbiti 1990: 106*

This passage, from the magisterial historian of African religions and philosophies from Kenya, John Mbiti, is one of the most frequently cited in African philosophy. One way to read Mbiti's point is weak, as merely pointing out that, for many traditional African peoples, an individual needs to be socialized in order to become a responsible adult. However, another reading is stronger, as contending that, for them, who an individual essentially is, i.e. roughly what makes her one person as numerically distinct from others, is a function of who has socialized her and how. The claim is apparently not merely that an individual can be produced only by a society, but that a society necessarily helps constitute the identity of an individual.

> African metaphysics or theory of reality differs significantly from that of Aristotle, for instance, with its individuated, discrete existences – "substances" he called them – existing in and by themselves, separated from others ....
> (T)he essence of the African's cosmic vision is that the universe is not something discrete but a series of interactions and interconnections. This is equally

> the category of understanding self .... It is the community which makes the individual to the extent that without the community, the individual has no existence .... Our summary view of self in African Philosophy is essentially social. The African is not just a being but a being-with-others. Self, or "I" as we have seen above, is defined in terms of "we-existence" .... Self in African philosophy ... is almost totally viewed from the "outside", in relation to other, and not from the "inside" in relation to itself.
>
> *Okolo 2003: 251, 252*

This passage is from the Nigerian Chukwudum Okolo in a paper titled "Self as a Problem in African Philosophy" that was reprinted in *The African Philosophy Reader*. He most clearly draws the contrast between different metaphysical approaches that this chapter addresses. As Okolo points out, it is not just the self that is characteristically understood relationally by African philosophers, but also everything in the universe. At one point in this essay, Okolo approvingly quotes two other philosophers working in the African tradition[6] who say, "To exist means more than just 'being there.' It means standing in a particular relationship with all there is both visible and invisible" (Okolo 2003: 249). While Okolo does not provide reason to favour this relational approach that he presents as characteristically African, this chapter aims to do so below.

> In African thinking the starting-point is social relations – selfhood is seen and accounted for from this relational perspective. Kuckertz (1996:62) puts it like this: "African thought and philosophy on personhood and selfhood is that the 'I' belongs to the I-You-correspondence as a stream of lived experience without which it could not be thought and would not exist."
>
> *Teffo and Roux 2003: 204*

This final passage is from two South African philosophers Lesiba Teffo and Abraham Roux in an essay titled "Themes in African Metaphysics". In it they approvingly cite Heinz Kuckertz, who was an anthropologist based in South Africa and who for several years studied the Mpondo people from that country. That people's view, according to Kuckertz – and which Teffo and Roux deem to be representative of many other sub-Saharan peoples – is that relationships with others are essential to who one is.

Abstracting from the appeals to holism and an imperceptible realm of agents, here is a circumscribed hypothesis: *the essence of any concrete, natural object is, at least in part, necessarily constituted by its relationships with elements of the world beyond the thing's intrinsic properties; one cannot fully understand a thing's nature without grasping its relational properties.*

Clarifying the proposal, note that it does not say that nothing exists except relationships. Instead, it implies there are relata, things that are related to each other, and suggests that part of what makes something a particular relatum, one distinct from others, are the ways it relates to other things. In addition, note that the hypothesis is not that a thing's essence is solely a function of its relational properties and none of its intrinsic ones. Instead, it is consistent with the idea that part of what constitutes a thing's nature are its intrinsic properties, at bottom denying that these alone are sufficient for its identity.[7] While this hypothesis focuses on what it is to be a particular thing, it would be natural to extend it to apply to what it is to be a certain kind of thing, and that is sometimes done below. For instance, instead of just indicating what it is to be a particular self as one that is numerically distinct from others or as one that is numerically the same over time, it could be applied to selfhood, i.e., what it is to be a self in general.

Both the hypothesis and its potential extension contrast sharply with the dominant views of analytic, and more generally Western, philosophers, according to which the essence of a concrete, natural thing (or type of thing as something inclusive of tokens) is merely its intrinsic properties, representative examples of which are discussed in the next two sections. Traditionally, the idea has been that these inherent and static features could be captured by a set of necessary and sufficient conditions. However, even cluster or family resemblance models of what a thing is typically suppose that it can (and must) be captured solely by properties intrinsic to it.

Before considering what there is to be said in favour of an Afro-relational approach to ontology, it is worth pointing out how it differs from one of the better known relational approaches advanced by a Western philosopher, namely, Richard Rorty's (1999) view. Rorty famously rejects the existence of essences on the ground that there are no intrinsic properties and that there are instead only relational properties. Interestingly, he – like his opponents – supposes that an essence is to be identified with intrinsic properties. In contrast, the hypothesis advanced here supposes that essences exist but is the view that they are at least partially to be identified with relational properties.[8]

Motivating the Afro-Relational Approach

This section applies the hypothesis about the relational essence of non-artefactual objects to the two cases of the self and water, providing some detail about how plausibly to understand their essences. One aim is to illustrate the hypothesis, while another is to begin to defend it by providing some reason to think that the self and water are indeed relational in nature. Objections to the hypothesis are considered only in the following section.

A Relational Account of the Self

In the Anglo-American, and more broadly Western, philosophical tradition, the self or person is usually identified with something internal, either a soul that contains mental states, a brain that contains mental states or, most common these days, a chain of mental states themselves, some of which are self-aware. It is not just philosophers who think of the self in this way, but Western people more generally, some evidence for which is the fact that such a conception of the self is dominant in the field of English-speaking psychology (as pointed out by Markus, Kitayama and Heiman 1996).

The African psychologist Elias Mpofu (2002) and others[9] have complained that Western psychological research has presumed a contested, atomist perspective about the self's nature. As noted above, the self as typically construed by African philosophers is at least substantially relational, largely constituted by interaction with other persons (and the environment). This view, however, is broad, admitting of at least three distinct variants. This author has not encountered the following conceptions in the literature, but presents them as meriting consideration.

According to the **Origination Version**, a person is essentially who she is at least in part by virtue of the *initial* relationships she had. Person X is numerically identical to person Y only if, and at last partially in virtue of the fact that, Y has the same initial relationships as X had. The initial relationships might have been ones of genetic bequeathal, gestation, care or sense of togetherness.

By the **Contemporary Version**, a person is essentially who she is at least in part by virtue of the relationships she is in *now*. Person X is numerically identical to person Y only if, and partially in virtue of the fact that, Y is presently in the same relationships as X. These relationships might be cognitive, emotive and volitional, e.g. how one thinks about others and how they think of one, what one's attitudes are about others and what others' attitudes are about one, as well as how one's decisions affect others and how their decisions affect one.

The **Historical Version** is the view that a person is essentially who she is at least in part by virtue of the relationships *she has been in over time* until now. Person X is numerically identical to person Y only if, and partially in virtue of the fact that, Y has been in the same relationships as X. The relationships, here, are plausibly the same as those intuitively relevant to the Contemporary Version.

These three views admit of a further, orthogonal distinction that grounds six possible views. Above all three were characterized *descriptively*, in terms of what the relationships have in fact been. However, there are those in the African tradition (one of whom is discussed below) who would instead (or also) opt for a *prescriptive* account. By this approach, who one essentially is in part is a function of how one *ought* to relate to others and how they ought to relate to one. Any of the above three versions could take a prescriptive form.

African philosophers are likely to find the prescriptive form appealing, if they believe that part of what makes up our identity is a destiny, roughly understood as a purpose towards which one is aptly disposed to pursue. When the Nigerian philosopher Segun Gbadegesin remarks, "Persons are what they are in virtue of what they are destined to be, their character and the communal influence on them" (1991: 58), he is plausibly understood as including normative-relational elements in his understanding of personal identity with mention of "destiny"; for he also remarks that "destiny is construed as the meaning of a person – the purpose for which the individual exists" where "the purpose of individual existence is intricately linked with the purpose of social existence, and cannot be adequately grasped outside it" (1991: 58; see also Abraham 1962: 52, 59–60).

This chapter will not do the work of choosing between the various interpretations of the relational self, a fascinating project that merits systematic enquiry elsewhere. However, it will note that the Contemporary Version in its descriptive guise is probably the least plausible of the six options distinguished above. The Contemporary Version does have some things going for it. For one, it can make sense of the idea that changes of name are appropriate upon major changes in relationship, e.g. upon getting married, converting to a new religion, getting a gender change, joining a society with a new language. For another, it captures "the Eastern conviction that one is a different person when interacting with different people" (Nisbett 2003: 53), an intuition that many readers (including this author) lack, but that Africans steeped in their indigenous cultures might share. Consider:

> European culture has taught us to see the self as something private, hidden *within* our bodies ....The African image is very different: the self is *outside* the body, present and open to all. This is because the self is the result and expression of all the forces acting upon us. It is not a thing, but the sum total of all the interacting forces .... (T)hese relationships are what it is.
>
> Shutte 2001: 22, 23

Even so, the Contemporary Version, at least in its descriptive form, risks being vulnerable to counterexamples when it comes to ascribing liability, which of course famously motivated John Locke's reflections on personal identity. It seems that you could avoid blame by killing off all parties related to you, for the Contemporary Version entails that you, the killer, would no longer exist by virtue of your relationships having radically changed. Having killed off everyone you knew, the adherent to the Contemporary Version appears committed to thinking that the present "you" is not one and the same as the past "you"; for there is, by that theory, now a new person in virtue of completely new relationships having been formed.

In reply, one might suggest the possibility that one would continue to be related to those whom one had killed. Traditionally speaking, African peoples tend to believe that one can survive the death of one's body, in the form of the "living-dead" (on which see, e.g. Mbiti 1975: 70–73). In addition, it is intuitive to think that one continues to be related to one's departed grandfather, even on the supposition that there is no afterlife in which he has survived the death of his body.[10]

However, this chapter seeks to abstract from reliance on other facets of African metaphysics, and so does not invoke the idea of an imperceptible realm of persons without bodies. And as for the suggestion that one is still related to those who are dead (which does not include the living-dead), the implication would appear to be that one's relationships with others never end (and can only be added), which does not square well with the idea that the nature of the self varies as its relationships vary. Furthermore, the sense in which one is plausibly "related" to the dead, presumably principally by sharing some genetic material and by remembering them, appears to differ from the suggestion that the self is a function of the forces acting upon us.

In any event, to keep things simple, this chapter works with the (descriptive) Origination and Historical Versions in what follows. If arguments can be provided to take at least those views seriously, reason will have been provided to doubt an intrinsic view such as a Lockean/Parfitian appeal to chain of mental states.

Why believe the Origination or Historical Versions? Why think that in order to understand who a person is as numerically distinct from other persons, one must appeal to such relational features of her? No one of the following considerations is decisive, but as a package they provide some support for Afro-relationalism.

First off, if a being spontaneously arose in a chemical-rich bog and happened to have a copy of my genetic make-up and of the content of my memories, experiences, desires and beliefs, it would not be me. It would be exactly like me, i.e. would be qualitatively me, but not numerically one and the same as me. I am essentially one who was given birth to by a particular woman and reared in a particular family. Swamp-Metz would not have the same relational history as this Metz, which is one (not the only) plausible explanation of why it would not be me.

Second, recall Thomas Nagel's powerful objection to the Lockean/Parfitian stream of consciousness view, namely, that intuitively one could have been the same person and yet had substantially different mental content than one did. Of himself Nagel remarks, "This would have happened, for example, if I had been adopted at birth and brought up in Argentina" (1986: 38). Nagel's brain theory of personal identity is one, intrinsic account of how it would be possible for a given person to have had radically different awarenesses throughout his life (1986: 40–41). However, an appeal to relational history is another plausible explanation: I am identical to the one who, at least in large part, had a certain historical relationship with those who created me and gave birth to me.

Third, it is common to accept that one would not have existed had one's gamete donors or their donations have been different (somewhat ironically here, given the discussion of water below, see Kripke 1980; less ironically, see especially Losonsky 1987a: 258). I would not have existed, had the sperm or egg from which I was generated been different. A broader way to capture this intuition is by appeal to relational history.

Fourth, and finally for now, consider an analogy with theories of mind. Many theorists of the mind's nature accept multiple realizability and reject the identity theory that a mind is one and the same thing as a specific brain, even if it is, in this world, constituted by one. Similarly, a functionalist account of mind, according to which a mind is characteristically caused by certain things and in turn characteristically causes certain effects, remains a live option. Now, what goes for a mind plausibly goes for a self—*perhaps* because a self *just is* a mind. A self is plausibly not to be identified with any particular substance composed of certain intrinsic properties (whether physical or spiritual), and instead is identical, at least in part, to certain historical-causal influences on it and by it.

A Relational Account of Water

This section extends the African approach to the self to natural objects more generally, using the example of water, famously prominent in the metaphysical discussions of Hilary Putnam and Saul Kripke. For them, and a very large majority of Anglo-American and more broadly Western philosophers, water is identified entirely as a substance and as something intrinsic, specifically, the chemical composition H_2O. This section articulates and defends a contrasting view of water as something that is at least substantially (if not purely) relational and that cannot be adequately understood in terms of its intrinsic properties alone.

This author is not aware of any African philosopher who has previously discussed the nature of water, let alone construed it as essentially relational. The following discussion is meant to apply the sort of account of the self that African philosophers have discussed to a case that they have not, one that invites interesting cross-cultural debate with Western philosophers.

From an Afro-relational perspective, then, water is largely constituted necessarily by interaction with other things in an environment. In particular, consider that water might be essentially what it is at least in part by virtue of the causal relationships it has with persons, animals, plants, rocks, gasses and other liquids. By this account, a certain kind of stuff X is identical to water only if, and partially in virtue of the fact that, X has the same effects on other things in the environment and they have the same effects on it.

Here are two major arguments for a relational account of water, using some familiar thought experiments. First, consider a version of twin earth, in which two things that are chemically different are arguably the same sort of things, in virtue of playing the same role in an environmental system. Imagine that XYZ on another planet acts in precisely the same way that H_2O does here on earth, viz., it supports life, flows downhill, evaporates and so on. It would be reasonable to say that water on this other planet is composed of XYZ, because the relational features of H_2O are identical. If earthlings landed on XYZ, it would be sensible—both intelligible and pragmatically wise – for them to radio to their spaceship that they have encountered water on the planet.

Of course, Putnam (1975: 223–235; cf. 1990: 59) and Kripke (1980: 124, 128) have a famously opposing intuition. They would contend that, upon reflection, the earthlings should instead say that they found something water-like and not actual water. However, it is not merely those in the African tradition who would question their intuition; there are some in the Western tradition who have questioned it, too (e.g. Salmon 1981: 95; Nozick 2001: 130, 346–347), where an appeal to relational essence is a plausible, theoretical way to capture their dissent about this particular case.

The second thought experiment is the inverse of the first; now consider a version of not-so-twin earth in which two things that are chemically the same are arguably different sorts of things, in virtue of playing different roles in an environmental system. So imagine H_2O acted radically differently on another planet, e.g. did not support life, did not flow downhill, did not evaporate, etc. It would be plausible for us earthlings to say, upon landing on not-so-twin earth, that water does not exist on this planet, because the relational features of H_2O have dramatically changed. It would be sensible – again, both intelligible and pragmatically wise – for people to report that humans should not move there since there is no water.

In one of his mid-to-late stage works, Putnam considers a similar case, and has a different intuition or, rather, the purported lack of an intuition altogether:

> Perhaps one could tell a story about a world in which H_2O exists .... but the laws are slightly different in such a way that what is a small difference in the *equations* produces a very large difference in the *behavior* of H_2O. Is it clear that we would call a (hypothetical) substance with quite different behavior *water* in these circumstances? I now think that the question, 'What is the necessary and sufficient condition for being water *in all possible worlds*?' makes no sense at all. And this means that I now reject 'metaphysical necessity.'
> *1990: 69–70*[11]

In reply, recall that this chapter is *supposing* that things have essences, which are best understood not only ontologically, but also in modal terms, and that it is trying to ascertain how best to understand their content. It is beyond its scope to argue that this concept of an essence applies to concrete, spatio-temporal objects that are not artefacts; rejecting the idea that this concept denotes something in the real world does not provide reason to doubt that, supposing it did denote something in the real world, it would include relational properties.

Defending the Afro-Relational Approach from Objections

Whereas the previous section provided some positive reason to believe that essences of natural objects are at least partially relational and cannot be grasped solely by appeal to their intrinsic properties, this section aims to provide a negative defence of that claim. It seeks to rebut some objections that adherents to an intrinsic approach would naturally advance.

A first, familiar objection is that relations are metaphysically composed of relata that must have an intrinsic essence in order to be able to relate. "If there were not a hard, substantial autonomous table to stand in relation to .... there would be nothing to get related and so no relations" (expressed but not accepted by Rorty 1999: 55), and "(A)n object can be related to another object only if it is already individuated. If it isn't individuated, what is it that is entering into the relation?" (expressed but not accepted by Losonsky 1987b: 194). Applied to the self, the objection would be that any relationship between selves presupposes distinct ones composed essentially of intrinsic properties alone.

In reply, unlike Rorty, this chapter does not deny that there are intrinsic properties or even that they might be *partly* constitutive of the essences of non-artefactual objects such as selves and water. The hypothesis advanced here is instead that relational properties are invariably also at least partly constitutive of such essences, which would make adequate sense of the claim that relations are composed of relata—even though an admittedly fuller statement would *also* acknowledge that relata are partly composed out of relations.[12]

Another familiar objection is that epistemically identifying a particular object is metaphysically best explained by the idea that it has an intrinsic essence alone. We usually identify relations in terms of their relata, which, so the objection goes, has to be accounted for with the idea that relata are metaphysically independent of relations. How else *could* we pick out relationships except by having some independent conception of the things that are related to each other? Applied to the self, the objection would be that in order to identify a relationship between persons, we must first pick out the persons separately, and our ability to do so is best explained by their real separateness, i.e. having essences composed solely of intrinsic properties such as different brains or chains of mental states.

As an initial reply, consider that identifying a relationship by appeal to its relata is not particularly weighty evidence that the latter are utterly metaphysically independent of the former. One might specify a dollar bill, my hand, a widget and another person's hand in order to identify a financial exchange, but it hardly follows with any strength that the dollar bill is, *qua* money, not essentially relational. Similarly, you might be able to pick a person out from a crowd knowing something special about her brain, but it does not follow that she is exhausted by such properties.

A further reply is that sometimes we identify relata in terms of their relations, not solely the other way around. To identify me, you might plausibly invoke the fact that I am the guy who was born in Atlanta to parents of largely Germanic/Austrian descent, or might appeal to the roles that I have played (or even, prescriptively, which roles I should have played, given my particular abilities). And to identify water, you might well appeal to its role in an ecosystem.[13]

A third objection is that explanatory fundamentality tracks metaphysical intrinsic essence. Some maintain that an essence is probably whatever "deep structure" best explains a wide array of "surface properties" (Putnam 1975) or which "substance" best explains "appearances" (Kripke 1980). Applied to water, H_2O best explains topical features such as being a colourless, odourless liquid that is found down streams and through taps, and is, for this reason, the best candidate for being the essence of water.

However, there are many surface properties, particularly regarding how a self or water behaves, that are plausibly not due to their intrinsic features alone, but also to how other things in the world bear on them and how they bear on other things. For example, why does water move downhill? The existence of gravity and the susceptibility of water to gravity are surely part of the explanation. Why does water not give off a taste? Part of the explanation clearly involves something about our tastebuds, and not merely the fact that water is H_2O.

The intrinsic theorist is likely to reply that it is the chemical composition of those other things, viz., of the hills and the tastebuds that best explains how water behaves (suggested by Putnam 1990: 69). However, it could be other, lawlike properties that best explain these behaviours, ones that are not reducible to a chemical composition, say, because a *different* chemical composition would ground the *same* laws. And, then, note that gravity is not composed of chemicals at all (though admittedly debate about whether it has an intrinsic nature continues amongst physicists).

Fourth, and finally for now, one might object that referential rigid designation entails an intrinsic essence. In the face of various criticisms, Putnam once remarked,

> I still believe that a linguistic community can stipulate that "water" is to designate whatever has the same chemical structure .... even if it doesn't know, at the time it makes this stipulation, exactly what that chemical structure ... is.
> *1990: 70; see also 59–60*

In reply, yes, a linguistic community *can* do that, but it does not follow that linguistic communities *always do* stipulate that "water" picks out only intrinsic properties such as chemical structures (or that intrinsic properties exhaust an essence). Given that African philosophers have so frequently appealed to relational properties when seeking to understand the nature of the self and other natural objects, it is likely that the African societies from which they have come have used the term "water" to denote relational properties.[14]

Conclusion

As the sort of cross-cultural debate about metaphysics and epistemology undertaken in this chapter has not been widespread, it is too soon to expect firm conclusions. This chapter's aims have been the weaker ones of articulating a characteristically African approach to understanding the essence of a natural object in terms of its relational features, illustrating the approach with two examples, contrasting it with standard Anglo-American approaches, noting some salient arguments that must be considered to choose between them, and providing some critical appraisal of these arguments with an eye to showing that the African view should not be dismissed. It is time to give much more of a global hearing to some underappreciated facets of African philosophy.[15]

Notes

1 An artefact is roughly something other than an organism that has been intentionally fashioned by human beings, with a table and an artwork being representative examples. (For those wanting a more fine-grained analysis of what an artefact is, see Hilpinen 2011.) For many, a relational approach is intuitively apt for the natures of artefacts, on which see Losonsky (1987a). This chapter focuses on non-artefacts, and specifically natural objects, a relational approach towards which is prima facie more difficult to establish, in the absence of the supposition that they were created by supernatural beings.
2 And also the East Asian tradition, on which see Nisbett (2003).
3 One might then usefully use the word "extrinsic" to mean something more inclusive, e.g. not only relational properties but also, say, symbolic ones, on which see Bradley (1998).

4 For a more thorough exposition, as well as some defence, see Metz (2015).
5 For similar claims, see Tempels (1959: esp. 103, 108); Shutte (2001: 22–23); Nasseem (2003: 306–307); Hamminga (2005: 62, 63, 68, 75); and Lajul (2016: 29, 31–32, 37, 43).
6 They are E. A. Ruch and K. C. Anyanwu. The latter is a Nigerian epistemologist who published largely in the 1980s and is probably best known for his essay titled "The Idea of Art in African Philosophy", while the former is a philosopher originally from Europe who had relocated to southern Africa and taught at the National University of Lesotho in the 1970s. They co-authored *African Philosophy: An Introduction to the Main Philosophical Trends in Contemporary Africa* (Rome: Catholic Book Agency, 1981), from which Okolo has taken the quotation.
7 Indeed, Okolo in a further passage denies that the self is entirely relational (2003: 253).
8 When giving a talk based on this essay, the author happened to meet a Western philosopher who has advanced a view, particularly of the identity of the self, similar to what is called "African" here, namely, Michael Losonsky. However, Losonsky's view (1987a, 1987b) is not characteristically Western (on which see the second section above).
9 It has also been characteristically East Asian to understand personal identity in relational terms, on which see the philosopher Roger Ames (1994) and the Japanese psychologist Shinobu Kitayama in Markus, Kitayama and Heiman (1996: 860, 878–879, 884).
10 Jon McGinnis is responsible for this intriguing suggestion.
11 For a similar view of metaphysical necessity, see Nozick (2001: 133–141).
12 For a bolder reply, see Losonsky (1987b: 194).
13 For yet another response, from Rorty (1999), consider that numbers probably lack intrinsic properties, but that we can distinguish them easily by different relations they have. Perhaps the same point applies to physical things.
14 The same appears true of some East Asian societies, on which see Nisbett (2003).
15 For oral comments on presentations based on ideas in this chapter, the author would like to thank participants at a colloquium organized by the University of Missouri-St. Louis Department of Philosophy and participants at the Conference on Contemporary Language, Logic, and Metaphysics: African and Western Approaches organized by the University of the Witwatersrand Department of Philosophy. This chapter has also been improved as a result of substantial written input from an anonymous referee for *Synthesis Philosophica*.

References

Abraham, William (1962): *The Mind of Africa*. Chicago, IL: University of Chicago Press.

Ames, Roger (1994): "The Focus-field Self in Classical Confucianism". In: Ames, Roger; Dissanayake, Wimal; Kasulis, Thomas (eds.): *Self as Person in Asian Theory and Practice*, pp. 187–212. Albany, NY: State University of New York Press.

Bradley, Ben (1998): "Extrinsic Value". In: *Philosophical Studies* 91 (2), 109–126. https://doi.org/10.1023/A:1004269309760

Garrett, Brian (2009): "Extrinsic/Intrinsic". In: Kim, Jaegwon; Sosa, Ernest; Rosenkrantz, Gary (eds.): *A Companion to Metaphysics*, 2nd edn, pp. 258–259. Malden, MA: Wiley-Blackwell.

Gbadegesin, Segun (1991): *African Philosophy. Traditional Yoruba Philosophy and Contemporary African Realities*. New York: Peter Lang.

Hamminga, Bert (2005): "Epistemology from the African Point of View". In: Hamminga, Bert (ed.): *Knowledge Cultures: Comparative Western and African Epistemology*, pp. 57–84. Amsterdam: Rodopi.

Hilpinen, Risto (2011): "Artifact". In: Zalta, Edward (ed.): *Stanford Encyclopedia of Philosophy*, https://plato.stanford.edu/entries/artifact/

Kripke, Saul (1980): *Naming and Necessity*, 2nd edn. Oxford: Basil Blackwell Ltd.
Lajul, Wilfred (2016): "African Metaphysics: Traditional and Modern Discussions". In: Ukpokolo, Isaac (ed.): *Themes, Issues and Problems in African Philosophy*, pp. 19–48. Cham: Palgrave Macmillan.
Losonsky, Michael (1987a): "Individual Essences". In: *American Philosophical Quarterly* 24 (3): 253–260.
Losonsky, Michael (1987b): "Individuation and the Bundle Theory". In: *Philosophical Studies* 52 (2): 191–198. https://doi.org/10.1007/BF00646455
Markus, Hazel Rose; Kitayama, Shinobu; Heiman, Rachel (1996): "Culture and 'Basic' Psychological Principles". In: Higgins, E. Tory; Kruglanski, Arie (eds.): *Social Psychology: Handbook of Basic Principles*, 1st edn, pp. 857–913. New York: Guilford Press.
Mbiti, John (1975): *Introduction to African Religion*. Oxford: Heinemann.
Mbiti, John (1990): *African Religions and Philosophy*, 2nd edn. Oxford: Heinemann.
Metz, Thaddeus (2015): "How the West Was One: The Western as Individualist, the African as Communitarian". In: *Educational Philosophy and Theory* 47 (11): 1175–1184. https://doi.org/10.1080/00131857.2014.991502
Mpofu, Elias (2002): "Psychology in Sub-Saharan Africa: Challenges, Prospects and Promises". In: *International Journal of Psychology* 37 (3): 179–186. https://doi.org/10.1080/00207590244000061
Nagel, Thomas (1986): *The View from Nowhere*. New York: Oxford University Press.
Nasseem, Subairi (2003): "African Heritage and Contemporary Life". In: Coetzee, Pieter; Roux, Abraham (eds.): *The African Philosophy Reader*, 2nd edn, pp. 304–319. London: Routledge.
Nisbett, Richard (2003): *The Geography of Thought*. New York: Free Press.
Nozick, Robert (2001): *Invariances: The Structure of the Objective World*. Cambridge, MA: Harvard University Press.
Okolo, Chukwudum (2003): "Self as a Problem in African Philosophy". In Coetzee, Pieter; Roux, Abraham (eds.): *The African Philosophy Reader*, 2nd edn, pp. 247–258. London: Routledge.
Putnam, Hilary (1975): "The Meaning of 'Meaning'". In: Putnam, Hilary (ed.): *Mind, Language and Reality*, pp. 215–271. Cambridge: Cambridge University Press.
Putnam, Hilary (1990): "Is Water Necessarily H$_2$0?". In: Putnam, Hilary (ed.): *Realism with a Human Face*, pp. 54–79. Cambridge, MA: Harvard University Press.
Rorty, Richard (1999): "A World Without Substances or Essences". In: Rorty, Richard (ed.): *Philosophy and Social Hope*, pp. 47–71. London: Penguin Books.
Salmon, Nathan (1981): *Reference and Essence*. Princeton, NJ: Princeton University Press.
Shutte, Augustine (2001): *Ubuntu: An Ethic for the New South Africa*. Cape Town: Cluster Publications.
Teffo, Lesiba; Roux, Abraham (2003): "Themes in African Metaphysics". In: Coetzee, Pieter; Roux, Abraham (eds.): *The African Philosophy Reader*, 2nd edn, pp. 161–174. London: Routledge.
Tempels, Placide (1959): *Bantu Philosophy*, 2nd edn, King, Colin (trans.). Paris: Présence Africaine.
Weatherson, Brian; Marshall, Dan (2012): "Intrinsic vs. Extrinsic Properties". In: Zalta, Edward (ed.): *Stanford Encyclopedia of Philosophy*, https://plato.stanford.edu/entries/intrinsic-extrinsic/

5
BEING AS THE OBJECT OF KNOWLEDGE IN AFRICAN SPACES

Wilfred Lajul

Introduction

In this chapter, I am investigating the nature of the object of knowledge. While there are no serious discrepancies about the subject of knowledge whose activities contribute to the creation of knowledge, what constitutes the object of knowledge is highly contested. To explain the object of knowledge, distinctions are often made between objectivism and subjectivism. By objectivism, Karpatschof, for instance, means the theory that human knowledge "reflects the object rather than the subject" (2000: 235). On the other hand, subjectivism is the theory that knowledge reflects entirely, or predominantly, the subject and not the intended object (Karpatschof 2000). In the view of Dennehy (2004), the object of knowledge is actually our concept of things other than a reflection of the material or formal objects of knowledge.

These divergent views create a problem in understanding the object of knowledge. But to claim to know is to make a claim about some entity that exists, about being, or about *what is*. This is predominantly derived from African philosophical worldview, which states that the object of knowledge is 'being'. Accordingly, the object of knowledge is not just some material or formal objects, not even the subject's concept of the known objects, but it is about 'being'; it is about *what is* and that which is known about *what is*. Attributing this view to African philosophy can be problematic, since there seems to be no unified view in Africa on this matter, given that different African peoples come from different social, cultural, and geographical spaces. These occupied spaces provide differences in the African people's philosophical worldviews. Such differences can affect the way they understand 'being' as an object of knowledge. Our task is therefore, to investigate these intricacies about human knowledge in relation to its objects.

On the Nature of the Object of Knowledge

In this section, I will review literature bothering on different views of authors on the object of knowledge. The section is divided into three: objectivism, subjectivism, and African philosophical view on the object of knowledge. I will begin by analysing the concept of objectivism.

Objectivism is the theory that human knowledge is the exact reflection of the objects they represent, other than the subject. However, there are variations in the explanations given to this theory. Määttänen (2015) distinguishes four versions of objectivism: the classical, active empiricism, pragmatism, and phenomenalism. The classical version of objectivism grew around the problem of the "external world"; that is "the problem of knowing whether our inner representations were accurate" (Rorty 1980: 139–140). In this way, Rorty defines objectivism as the theory which claims that knowledge subsists in the inner representation of the external world. When this inner representation is accurate, then we can talk of objective knowledge.

Other classic objectivists, like Descartes, maintain that the external world is material, while the internal world is immaterial. Plato identifies this immaterial world with ideas, which are forms. But for Descartes, ideas are not forms, because forms occupy space and ideas do not occupy space. In the view of Lakoff and Johnson (1999), this Cartesian conception of the immaterial world or mind is based on a container metaphor. In this metaphor, ideas are in the mind like cookies in a jar. People have privilege to access their own ideas or consciousness by introspection. These explanations created a grave epistemological problem to explicate how the internal universal ideas can be knowledge of the external particular objects (Määttänen 2015).

Active empiricism is the theory derived from Peirce Sanders. In Peirce's version of objectivism, concept of experience is taken to be broader than that of perception. Peirce maintains that in human effort to perceive reality, there must be an element of effort on the side of the subject, which gives human experience its peculiar character. Määttänen emphasizes that "To experience is to be an active agent in the world" (2015:21). In a similar manner, John Dewey criticized what he called a spectator theory of knowledge, because as living creatures we perceive and act. While in classical empiricism, perception is passive, in modern empiricism, perception is active. In classical empiricism, sense organs only receive impression from the world. Modern active empiricism acknowledges that "Internal conditions have an effect on how the world is perceived. It is a commonplace that perceptions are interpreted with meanings, concepts, beliefs, theories and so on" (Määttänen 2015: 21).

Pragmatism proposes a radical change in the notion of the object of knowledge. The goal of knowledge, for pragmatism, is not to reach the 'real', but the hidden and mind-independent world causing our perceptions. John Dewey, the key proponent of this theory, maintains that "the objects of knowledge are controlled processes of change where acting agents transform a situation into another" (Dewey 1981: 128).

He believes that the knowing subject and the performed operations belong to the object of knowledge.

For Dewey, the relation between situations is mediated by action, and this makes the knowing activity an object of knowledge. So, for the pragmatists, the object of knowledge is the objective world being actively experienced; the perceiving subject, whose activities contribute to knowledge; and the relation between the situations of knowing mediated by the knowing subject.

Phenomenalism takes the world as was and as is known. Peirce Sanders maintains that this world is real and that it is an object of perception and action. For John Dewey too, "The world as we experience it is a real world" (1984: 235). Using the example of a patient coming to see a physician, Dewey illustrates his understanding of the object of knowledge according to phenomenalism, by the physician saying, to administer treatment, that she/he needs knowledge (diagnosis) of the phenomenon, on the basis of theoretical knowledge about medicine and practical past experience. When cure takes place, then one has knowledge of how to treat that sickness (Dewey 1981: 139–140).

Analysing this example, Määttänen maintains that knowledge is based on earlier experience and theories involved. "Knowledge is adequate enough if the action performed turns out to be successful" (Määttänen 2015: 21). The underlining point is that the object of knowledge is more than the reality being perceived. To have sufficient ground for knowledge, previous knowledge is required. It is on the basis of the previous knowledge (theoretically based), in relation to the present experiences (phenomenon), that genuine knowledge is derived.

Turning to subjectivism, it (subjectivism) has been defined as the theory that knowledge is entirely, or predominantly, a reflection of the subject and not a reflection of the intended object. So the object of knowledge is our concept of things, but not the representation of the real world. Dennehy defends this theory by saying that many epistemologists fail to see that "the knower contributes more to knowing than just forming beliefs, having memories and mental states, and imposing prejudices, feelings, and expectations on, or acting as a receptacle for, epistemological data" (Dennehy 2004). Criticising objectivism, Dennehy calls objectivism representationalism, since it is derived from coherence theory of truth as advocated by the idealists. In the idealists' coherence theory of truth, it is the external object that must cohere with its internal representation. So subjectivism is exactly what idealism holds, because "all we know are our ideas and ourselves" (Dennehy 2004: 130).

Dennehy believes that in knowing, "the subject becomes the object, the known thing; and dominates and possesses the object" (Dennehy 2004: 130). Failure to acknowledge this fact has led to the loss of the knowing subject in the process of deriving knowledge. This, ironically, has created what he calls "a methodological blunder that ultimately originates in a refusal to accept the mind's immediate and certain knowledge of extra-mental things" (Dennehy 2004: 130). In saying this, Dennehy affirms that the object of knowledge is the knowing subject itself, and its dominant possession of the extra-mental things.

Object of Knowledge in African Philosophy

Though discrepancies abound on the existence of African epistemology with antagonists like Airoboman and Asekhauno (2012) denying the existence of either African philosophy and specifically African epistemology, and protagonists like Ngara (2007) maintaining the existence of both African philosophy and African epistemology, I hold that African philosophy and African epistemology exist.

Refuting the antagonists' view that African epistemology exists, Ngara underlines two points: that African epistemologies exist and that these epistemologies are grounded in the indigenous African cultural traditions. Ngara insists that though Africa is immense and diverse in terms of languages and cultures, there are distinct, consistent, and enduring epistemological commonalities in Africa transcending geographical boundaries and ethnicity. Besides, one of the most enduring communalities includes their "ways of knowing that are grounded in indigenous African cultural traditions, history and ecology" (Ngara 2007: 7).

Ani Ndubuisi also believes that "beside its holistic nature, the intuitive, religious and mythological perspectives in the consideration of African epistemology is justified and deserving to be considered in contemporary education system and epistemological discourses" (2013: 295). On the basis of these arguments, the view in this paper is that African epistemology exists (see also, Kaphagawani & Malherbe 2003: 259–270). Apart from distinguishing African from Western epistemology, Jimoh and Thomas (2015) clarifies the following: (i) in African philosophical worldview, man and nature exist concretely; (ii) man and nature are conceptually two entities, but numerically one ontological reality; (iii) man and nature are sacredly united; (iv) in this unity, both man and nature participate in the same locus without being opposites; and (v) African world is unitary as opposed to the Western analytical and pluralistic World (see also, Blachowicz 2012). Jimoh and Thomas also distinguish African epistemology from Western epistemology by methodology. Whereas Western epistemology emphasizes the scientific, rational, and mathematical methodological paradigms, African epistemology does not divide the domain of knowledge on the basis of such methodology. Instead, African epistemology takes the rational, the empirical, and the mystical as constitutive of a single mode of knowing.

Nonetheless, we have now to answer the question, if African epistemology exists, then what is its object? In response to this question, I would say, in African philosophy, the object of knowledge is basically 'being', *what is*. 'Being', as we know from Aristotelian metaphysics, has material and formal dimensions. To describe the object of knowledge as material object, as some Western thinkers do, is only to describe an aspect of the same 'being' that is known. To say, it is formal object, is again to describe another aspect of the same 'being' that is known. Besides and more importantly, to say the object of knowledge is the 'perception of things' is to describe the process used in deriving that object known as it takes place in the perceiver. The fact that knowledge is a relationship between the knowing subject and the known object, and that to know we need the involvement of the subject, has not been disputed in the literature reviewed. However, there are serious difficulties to explain what constitutes the object of knowledge. Our discussion of this concern will be divided into three: we would examine the object of knowledge as outside the subject, object of knowledge as found within the subject, and object of knowledge as 'being'.

To begin, the theory of knowledge that explains the object of knowledge as the material world existing outside the subject is named objectivism. This theory maintains that human knowledge is the exact reflection of the objects they represent. Though this is a common stand point as far as this view is concerned, there are different ways in which this theory has been explained. The classics say that the object of knowledge is the external world as the accurate inner representation of what is known (Rorty 1980). Knowledge, therefore, subsists in the inner representation of the objective world. This theory faces difficulty in explaining how this inner reality becomes the exact representation of the external objective world.

To resolve this problem, Locke used the concept of similarity to explain the relationship between these inner representations with the external world by saying that the form of this inner ideas and the form of the objective reality known are similar. But, if however, these inner ideas are a mental reality distinct from the objective reality outside, how can realities with different natures, one purely mental and the other real, be meaningfully compared? Kant calls these inner consciousness concepts and Neo-Kantians say these concepts were carved from the objective world. This too is problematic. How does the subject of knowledge carve these concepts from the objective world, and if the object succeeds in this, what is the nature of the concepts? Is what is carved purely formal, or it is also material as the source from which it is carved? Contemporary thinkers made things worse by distinguishing between intentional objects of knowledge from the external objective realities. How intentional objects are related to the external objects still remains an unanswered question.

Active empiricists disagree with classical empiricists, claiming that the subject of knowledge is not passive in the process of deriving knowledge, but active. Perceptions are interpreted with meanings, concepts, beliefs, and theories. The object of knowledge is then more than the externally perceived world; it also includes the subject's activities. In saying this, active empiricists are right, but the complication they have imported into the discussion is the question of the subject of knowledge. How is that subject of knowledge who is involved actively in processing knowledge become part of the very object it is processing? In the view of the pragmatist, since the object of knowledge is the objective world, the perceiving subject and the relation between the situations of knowing mediated by the knowing subject, they do not escape from criticism. The main problem here is not that other factors, like the situation of knowing, that affect the process of deriving knowledge are indiscernible, but how the subject processing this knowledge is equally part of the object being processed. The phenomenologists begin fairly well by observing that the object of knowledge is the real world as was and as is known. However, combining the world as it was known and it is known is more problematic. This may refer to applied knowledge other than theoretical knowledge. Must all forms of knowledge refer to what was originally known? Is this possible? Probably, this could be right when referring to applied knowledge, since one must compare what was known to what is being derived as new knowledge, but this is not possible for all forms of knowledge.

While I can agree that conceptually one can distinguish between the form and matter of reality, but as African philosophy maintains, ontologically, we cannot separate the form from matter. Likewise, epistemologically, we cannot have one object of reality as formal, while the other is material. The formal are the properties that can be conceptually distinguished from the material, but in terms of knowledge they constitute one and the same object. Actually, they constitute 'being' as the object of knowledge as it has been maintained in African epistemology.

Turning to subjectivism, it is the theory that knowledge is entirely or predominantly a reflection of the subject and not the intended object outside the subject. In this theory, the object of knowledge is our concept of things and not the representation of the real world (Dennehy 2004). In saying this, we encounter a unique epistemological problem, which is the distinction between the activity of the subject in deriving knowledge and the actual knowledge derived. If the object of knowledge is entirely or predominantly the reflection of the subject, then we are saying the object of knowledge is entirely or predominantly the subject's activity. Equally wrong is to say that the object of knowledge is the concept of things and not the representation of the real world. This concept of things must have some relations with the real world it conceives; otherwise, it cannot be human knowledge.

Dennehy, who supports the Aristotelian-Thomistic subject-object tradition, says that the object of knowledge is the mind's immediate and certain knowledge of extra-mental things. To say that the object of knowledge is the mind's immediate and certain knowledge of extra-mental things may not be a problem at first sight, but at deeper look, one discovers that there is also a problem in this way of describing the object of knowledge. That object might be immediate, but how would one establish its certitude? How sure are we that what is immediate is also certain? Knowledge takes place at different levels; what might be immediate at an empirical level might not be immediate at a reflective level. For instance, when I am moving in a bus and I look at distant trees, they are all moving backwards, while I am not moving; but at a reflective level, it is I who is moving and not the trees.

To say that knowledge is the dominant possession of extra-mental things, as the subjectivists say, makes one wonder why it must be dominant. To say it is dominant means there is a possibility of possessing such extra-mental things in a non-dominant way. If it is not dominant, will it still be knowledge? Such questions still put the explanation of subjectivists' theory into doubt. When Dennehy concludes that knowledge is then the union between the knowing subject and the known object, there is more sense in saying this, because there is a much deeper relation between the subject and the object in the process of knowing. However, this does not explain what the object of knowledge is and the nature of this union between the subject and the object, which is the interest of this paper.

James Osborn gives an interesting observation about the relation between the subject and object of knowledge by saying that while Kantian transcendentalism orients itself around a subjective principle, the counter-revolution orients itself around the objective, non-human principle (Osborn 2019). Talking about philosophy and object-oriented ontology, Osborn is saying that for speculative metaphysics, 'being' is merely 'being'. That 'being' has nature, irrespective of whether it is an object or a subject. This way of looking at ontology is an alternative to Kantian revolution that prioritizes humans over other beings that are things in themselves. This alternative draws our attention to one-sided Kantianism. This solution, however, does not solve the ontological problem, because it merely shifts our focus to the objective, rather than to the subjective as Kant did (Osborn 2019). Osborn then concludes that by making 'being' the goal of philosophy, we avoid the differentiation of nature into subject and object. This differentiation abandons 'being' to the domain of transcendental philosophy. This approach, Osborn claims, brings us away from objects because it orients us towards modes of being as they themselves are and the way nature itself is. Equally, it brings them away from the machinations of objects and subjects (2019:19).

What I like from Osborn's approach is that it brings some clarity to metaphysical discussions of the object of philosophy, by focussing on being as the principal object of philosophy in general, and of epistemology in particular. The antagonism between objectivism and subjectivism, in my view, is time wasting and a distraction from the real issues of discussion. Osborn equally dismisses, as unnecessary, the dichotomy of nature into subject and object. He equally agrees that the object of knowledge can be equated with being, because being covers both subject and object. This, however, does not solve the problem we are discussing in this paper. By identifying being with both the subject and the object of knowledge does not help explain what the object of knowledge is. Even though, both the object and the subject belong to the overall object of philosophy itself, which is 'being', to understand what constitutes this object of knowledge is still important.

In African philosophy, there is common agreement that the object of knowledge is 'being' (Ogoko 2008; Tempels 1968; Ogbonnaya 2014). However, what constitutes this 'being' as object of knowledge has not been agreed upon due to variations in African philosophical worldviews. Though in African philosophy, there has been the concern to distance the discourse of knowledge from the antagonistic debate between the subjectivists and objectivists by claiming the object of knowledge is 'being' itself, Osborn would find problem with this approach. Osborn would think that it would remain the same magnification of correlationism in philosophy. However, as most authors define knowledge as a relationship between the subject that knows and the object that is known, we cannot avoid the discussion altogether by simply refusing to distinguish between the subject and object of knowledge.

In my view, the object of knowledge remains 'being'. In saying this, I am not denying that even the subject of knowledge falls under the category of 'being'; rather, I am saying that 'being as a totality of existence' should be distinguished from 'being as a totality of particular existence'. While both subject and object belong to being as a totality of existence, they however belong to different totalities of particular existences.

'Being' in African Spaces

Apparently, we have discovered that in African epistemology, 'being' is the object of knowledge, but we also do notice that 'being' is understood differently in the diverse African spaces. We shall consider four of these conceptions of being as presented by Ogoko, Tempels, Kagame, and Ogbonnaya.

Among the Igbo of West Africa, the object of human knowledge is 'being', basically understood as constituted by material and immaterial realities, since "The primary objects of Igbo knowledge are God, spirits, ancestors and material substances" (Ogoko 2008: 17). Ogoko thinks that God is one of the objects of knowledge, though his view is that God is eternal rationality, infinite immaterial substance, and supreme in essence. This way of referring to god makes him supremely removed or distanced from mortal men, and for Ogoko, we reach him through other media. Ogoko does not detail what these other media are. To acquire knowledge of other things in the universe, "Man enters into dialectics with forces of nature" (Ogoko 2008: 17). For Ogoko, then, true knowledge is the ability to see interrelatedness in everything in the universe. "Everything is related; one thing flowing into the other" (2008: 17).

For the Igbo, to derive knowledge, according to Ogoko, reference is made to the veracity of our senses, evidence of authority, and the ontological finality of the intellect (2008: 17). What Ogoko adds here is the fact that authority is equally an important source of knowledge, besides the senses. In the same way, whatever is received from authority must be reflected upon, and whatever is reflected upon must be related to the concrete experiences of life. Equally important is the fact that whatever abstract ideas are derived from human thinking must still be verified or substantiated in the concrete.

The conclusion is that methodologically, knowledge is not purely the result of human rational thinking, but human knowledge is the result of both empirical and rational activities (Ogoko 2008: 18). This is an important submission for the purpose of this paper, as we have been trying to put across. The object of knowledge is 'being', and this understanding of 'being' is material and immaterial. But as far as the natural world is concerned, humans employ both their senses and reason to arrive at knowledge. The African conception of knowledge then appeals to the immaterial (the spiritual) together with the use of the senses and the reason. True knowledge, then, is the ability to see the relatedness of everything in the universe.

In Bantu ontology, being is denoted as "Vital Force". Tempels, the main proponent of this view, holds that African philosophy rests on African ontology. "The transcendental and universal notion of being and of its force of action, and of the relationship and reciprocal influences of beings makes up bantu philosophy" (Tempels 1968: 77). Tempels maintains that this ontology is centred on the idea of the vital force which originates from God. Tempels then places God first in the Bantu hierarchy of beings, followed by spirits of the ancestors, humans, animals, plants, and inanimate objects (Njoku 2002: 18). Authors like Aja Egbeke fully buy this concept and imports it into Igbo ontology by saying for the Igbo conception, 'being' is 'force' like Tempels posits of the Bantu. Egbeke concludes that for the Igbo, "*ife na ike ife bu otu*", i.e. "being is that which is force" (2001: 53–54). Just as Tempels (1968) holds that 'being' is dynamic, Ruch and Anyanwu posit that 'being' is defined by what it assumed 'being' can do, rather than what it is (1981: 149).

From the foregoing, it is evident that the main contribution from Tempels is not about the object of knowledge as such, but this concept of being, which has been underlined as force. Being is force and force is being, because both are dynamic. So we can articulate that the object of knowledge is 'being', as a dynamic force. The details of this dynamic force, as an object of knowledge, would be difficult to extract from Tempels. In the view of Kagame, the concept of 'being' is derived from the most basic Bantu term *ntu*. The term *ntu* is equivalent to the term 'being' or 'essence' in Western philosophy (Songolo 1981: 97). *Ntu* is the most general category of being, which is divided into four: *UMuntu*, *IKintu*, *AHantu*, and *UKuntu*, corresponding to "human being", "non-human being", "place" or "time", and "quantity", respectively. *Ntu* as a universal force never reveals itself apart from its manifestations: *muntu*, *kintu*, *hantu*, and *kuntu* (Ukwamedua 2011). *Ntu* is being itself, the cosmic universal force, which only modern rationalizing thought can abstract from its manifestations. Again here, the discussion is about the concept of being, but not necessarily on 'being' as the object of knowledge. To the question as to what is the object of knowledge, Kagame would say it is 'being' or 'essence'. And as to what this means, there would still need to be some explanation.

In his stead, Ogbonnaya believes that 'being' is relational. Where Ogbonnaya diverts from the Western concept of 'being' is that it must be understood in relation to other existing realities. Though Western metaphysics distinguishes between the essence of 'being' from its attributes, they do not see any necessity in linking one particular 'being' with the existence of other beings. Ogbonnaya writes: "Being is that which cannot exist alone. [...] It can never exist in isolation. It always exists with others. It is in this relationship of mutual complementary nature that its meaning is conveyed and affirmed" (Ogbonnaya 2014: 123). Ogbonnaya continues to argue that "outside of this mutual complementary relation, which, in turn, leads to mutual service and dependent, being does not exist. Hence, being goes beyond an isolated being to a relationship being" (2014: 123). Ogbonnaya insists that

> Being is also both static and dynamic. It is static in the sense that the nature of being is the same for all beings. It is dynamic in the sense that it always manifests itself as it continuous to relate with others.
>
> *2014: 123*

In this same, Ogbonnaya would say that the object of knowledge is relational being. In distinguishing Western from African concept of being, Ogbonnaya opines that African concept of 'being' is not quite different from the Western one. This is because 'being,' whether in the West or in Africa, connotes *that which is*; that is, *that which has existence*, and *that* which has existence has two aspects: essence, which does not change and is common to a particular mode of 'being,' and attributes, by which being is manifested (Ogbonnaya 2014).

I think that like in the West, 'being' is that which is, that which is in existence, but African philosophy does not distinguish existence, conceived as such, in terms of essential and temporal natures. From the point of view of metaphysics, these expressions are not equivalent. The totality of being is not the same as the totality of particular existences. Whereas being includes whatever is – immaterial and immaterial (totality of being), particular existences refer more to material or immaterial entities that can be enumerated. Being is the totality of existence or totality of particular existences. I surmise here that the essence of being, unlike in the view of Ogbonnaya and in the West, is not static. On the contrary, in African philosophy, the essence of beings is considered dynamic, because every being that is in existence is active, which explains why it can be perceived. It continually remits energies through its different attributes, which is constantly in process.

Conclusion

We have seen that the object of knowledge is understood differently in various philosophical worldviews. The clearest of these worldviews are the Western and African. The distinction here is that in Western philosophy, the object of knowledge can be categorized as the objective world, the subjective world, or the perceptions of the objective world by the subject. In African philosophy, the object of knowledge is being, which is what is in existence. Though in Western philosophy, there is a gradual shift in acknowledging that being is the object of knowledge, some Western thinkers, like Osborn (2019), accept that being could be the object of knowledge, but that it would still remain the same magnification of correlationism in philosophy. This is because, focussing on being as the object of knowledge is another way of focussing on what is outside the subject, since both the object and subjects of knowledge are assumed to exist outside the subject.

In taking both the subject and object as beings, African philosophy, like for Osborn, resolves the subject–object dichotomy. What differentiates African philosophy from the view of Osborn is that being as subject and object of knowledge is still objectivism, while for African philosophy, this is not true. In African philosophy, both subject and object belong to being as totality of existence, while being as object of knowledge belongs to the totality of particular existences. What remains unresolved among African thinkers is to agree on what this being as the object of knowledge is.

In my view, though there are variations in the diverse African spaces on the concept of being, this by itself is healthy in philosophical discussions. Moreover, the differences are not destructive of the concept of being as the object of knowledge.

What is not clear is what constitutes this being as the object of knowledge. Whether this being is material and immaterial (Igbo's ontology), a vital force (Tempels), an essence – *ntu* (Kagame), or relational (Ogbonnaya), these only supplement the understanding of being as a totality of particular existences. There may not be any need to try to reconcile these different views on the African concept of being, because what is important is the acceptance that the object of knowledge remains 'being'.

References

Airoboman, F.A., & Asekhauno, A.A. 2012. "Is There an African Epistemology?" *JORIND.* Vol. 10, No. 3, pp. 13–17.

Blachowicz, J. 2012. *Essential Difference: Towards a Metaphysics of Emergence.* Albany: State University of New York Press.

Dennehy, R. 2004. "The Loss of the Knowing Subject in Contemporary Epistemology". D.A. Ollivant, (ed.). *Jacques Maritain and the Many Ways of Knowing.* Washington, DC: Catholic University of America Press, pp. 128–149.

Dewey, J. 1981. "Experience and Nature". J.A. Boydston (ed.). *The Later Works of John Dewey*, Vol. 1, 1925–1953. Carbondale and Edwardsville: Southern Illinois University press.

Dewey, J. 1984. "The Quest for Certainty". J.A. Boydston, (ed.). *The Later Works of John Dewey*, Vol. 4, 1925–1953. Carbondale and Edwardsville: Southern Illinois University press.

Egbeke, A. 2001. *Metaphysics: An Introduction.* Enugu: Donze.

Jimoh, K., & Thomas, J. 2015. "An African Epistemological Approach to Epistemic Certitude and Scepticism". *Research on Humanity and Social Sciences.* Vol. 5, No. 11, pp. 54–61.

Kaphagawani, N.D. & Malherbe, G.J. 2003. "Introduction: African Epistemology". P.H. Coetzee & A.P.J. Roux (eds.). *African Philosophy Reader, 2nd Edition; A Text with Readings.* New York: Routledge, pp. 259–270.

Karpatschof, B. 2000. *Human Activity. Contributions to the Anthropological Sciences from the Perspective of Activity Theory.* Copenhagen: Dansk Psykologisk Forlag.

Lakoff, G. & Johnson, M. 1999. *Philosophy in the Flesh.* New York: Basic Books.

Määttänen, P. 2015. *Mind in Action, Studies in Applied Philosophy, Epistemology and Rational Ethics,* Vol. 18. Cham, Switzerland: Springer International Publishing.

Ndubuisi, A. 2013. "Appraisal of African Epistemology in the Global System". *Alternation.* Vol. 20, No. 1, pp. 295–320.

Ngara, C. 2007. "African Ways of Knowing and Pedagogy Revisited". *Journal of Contemporary Issues in Education.* Vol. 2, No. 2, pp. 7–20.

Njoku, F. 2002. *Essays in African Philosophy, Thought and Theology.* Owerri: Clacom Communication.

Ogbonnaya, L. 2014. "The Question of "Being" in African Philosophy". *Filosofia Theoretica: Journal of African Philosophy, Culture and Religions.* Vol. 3, No. 1, pp. 108–126.

Ogoko, A.O.M. 2008. "Igbo Theory of Knowledge: Theoretical and Methodological Considerations". *African Journal Online.* Vol. 5, pp. 13–26.

Osborn, J. 2019. "On the Difference between Being and Object". *Philosophy Today.* Vol. 63, No. 1, pp. 1–28.

Rorty, R. 1980. *Philosophy and the Mirror of Nature.* Oxford: Blackwell.

Ruch, E.A. and Anyanwu, K.C. 1981. *African Philosophy: An Introduction to the Main Philosophical Trends in Contemporary Africa.* Rome: Catholic Book Agency.

Songolo, A. 1981. "*Muntu* Reconsidered: From Tempels and Kagame to Janheinz Jahn". *Ufahamu: A Journal of African Studies.* Vol. 10, No. 3, pp. 92–100.
Tempels, P. 1968. *Bantu Philosophy*. Paris: Présence Africaine.
Ukwamedua, N.U. 2011. "A Critical Review of Alexis Kagame's Four categories of African Philosophy". *Ogirisi: A New Journal of African Studies.* Vol. 8, No. 1, pp. 248–256.

6
THE ONTOLOGICAL FOUNDATION OF AFRICAN KNOWLEDGE

A Critical Discourse in African Communitarian Knowledge

Munamato Chemhuru

Introduction

The denial of African knowledge paradigms and the scepticism surrounding their existence has a long history, which has influenced the nature and direction of African philosophy and epistemology in different ways. Non-African philosophers such as Georg Wilhelm Friedrich Hegel, David Hume and Immanuel Kant all passionately denied Africa of having a history and an epistemic tradition. For example, Hegel sees Africa, particularly sub-Saharan Africa which he looks at as

> *Africa proper* and that it has largely remained – for all purposes of connection with the rest of the world – shut up; it is the Gold-land compressed within itself – the land of childhood, which lying beyond the day of self-conscious history, enveloped in the dark mantle of night
>
> Hegel 1837/2001: 109

Kant has the same low opinion about Africa as he thinks that Africans, particularly blacks, do not have the capacity for reason. As a result, Kant comes to some fascinating conclusion about Africans' incapacity to reason based on mistaken premises like race as exemplified in the often-quoted statement: "*this fellow was quite black from head to foot, a clear proof that what he said was stupid*" (Kant, cited in Zack 2018: 15). Contrary to such perceptions, African history and its epistemic tradition seem to have always been part and parcel of African existence because no human existence is without a history and its epistemic tradition. For that reason, Paulin Hountondji sees "a contradiction in Western philosophy while thinking of itself as the most self-conscious of all intellectual disciplines and at the same time assuming that some non-Western philosophies could be self-unconscious" (2009: 124). This contradiction has serious implications on perceptions about African epistemology

DOI: 10.4324/9781003182320-9

to the extent that some may think that it does not exist, or that it is second order to Western epistemology.

In this work, I venture into the problem of African epistemology and seek to discover the ontological foundations of African knowledge. By this, I seek to analyse how conceptions of African ontology might be understood as being oriented towards their epistemic traditions. Specifically, I analyse the nature of African communitarian ontology in terms of its bearing to African knowledge traditions. I consider how conceptions of existence stretching from spiritual beings, human beings down to non-human beings could ultimately inform epistemology in African philosophy. Ultimately, I seek to satisfy the quest for "knowledge for Africa" and "knowledge by Africans" as opposed to "externally oriented [knowledge] intended first and foremost to meet the theoretical and practical needs of Northern societies" (Hountondji 2009: 121). *Knowledge of Africa* and *knowledge for Africa* are used by Hountondji here to refer to the kind of approaches to African philosophy that are not initiated, controlled and influenced by Western paradigms and approaches to Africa philosophy. I use the similar approach in considering African ontology as the basis for knowledge in Africa.

African knowledge is not necessarily limited to the individual epistemic agent like what could be loosely read from other non-African traditions such as in Western philosophy where focus is mostly put on the individual person. For example, in the Cartesian view (*I am a thinking thing, I think, therefore I am*), emphasis is so much on individualistic traits like individual human reason and consciousness in the quest for knowledge and ultimately in the understanding of the human person. While the notion of what existence is, particularly that of the person, plays a significant role in determining what knowledge is, I appeal to a different perspective in African epistemology based on its ontological conceptions as opposed to the largely individualistic conceptions predominant in Western philosophy. I argue that African knowledge is mainly anchored on its ontological view of reality (see Jimoh and Thomas 2015: 54) and communitarian structure of society, rather than on individualistic traits in the individual person.

In appealing to African ontology as the basis for African epistemology, I will take the particularist and protagonist approaches to African epistemology. This position has mainly been popularised by Innocent Onyewuenyi (1976), Kwame Gyekye (2007, 2013), Anselm Kole Jimoh (2017) and Wilfred Lajul (2018). According to Lajul, "the protagonists argue that there is African mode of knowing peculiar to Africans, context-dependent and social bound, and *superior* to other epistemologies" (2018: 58). From Lajul's view, I have put 'superior' in italics to show my caution in accepting that African epistemology could be superior to other epistemologies. I do not wish to take that position as I suspect that there are competing challenges to such claims. What I prefer to emphasise is perhaps that it is different from those epistemologies. Nonetheless, the protagonists' position is contrary to that held by antagonists who take a somewhat universal view and analytic approach to African philosophy and subjecting African epistemology to approaches and tools mostly used in Western philosophy (see Lajul 2018: 58). At the same time, I also borrow from the universalist approach as I look at African metaphysical ideas about ontology from a generalised perspective where I will work with the assumption that "fundamental ideas on the question of ontology are common to most sub-Saharan African communities" (Chemhuru 2016: 91). Of course I am cautious of the need to be mindful of particulars with regard to African ontology.

In the first section, I unpack the nature of African ontology by looking at how existence is conceived in African philosophy in general. Here, I indicate how the African hierarchy of existence is conceived as following a hierarchical pattern that stretches from spiritual beings, human beings down to non-human animals and other non-animate beings. After that, I proceed to show how each of these levels of existence influences human knowledge as I specifically focus on the role of spiritual existence, that of communitarian existence and that of the individual in the process of knowledge acquisition. Overall, from this hierarchy of beings, I demonstrate how African ontology influences a communitarian view of epistemology that does not necessarily take away the individual's ontological status as an epistemic being.

A Look at African Ontology

African ontology could loosely be taken as concerned with African metaphysical questions, though it is apt to say that questions about ontology are more specific to the question of being than metaphysical questions which look at broader questions. Roberto Poli (2010) has given a compelling distinction of the two as follows:

> ontology deals with what can be rationally understood, at least partially. Metaphysics is broader than ontology in the sense that the possibility is admitted of aspects of reality that in principle may go beyond the capacity of any rational enterprise we may happen to develop.
>
> 1

From this understanding, questions on ontology therefore specifically revolve around issues that are within the bounds of rational comprehension such as those that concern the reality or essence of *being* or *existence*. This understanding of ontology agrees with an earlier view provided by Onyewuenyi who argues that ontology "is the science of *being as such, the reality that is*" (1976: 524). It therefore makes sense to approach African epistemology specifically from such an ontological perspective because it relies on an approach that deals with what can be rationally comprehended. This approach resonates well with that taken by Jimoh and Thomas as they consider "African epistemology as that which is strongly based on African ontological conceptions of reality" (Jimoh and Thomas 2015: 54). Following such a view, ontological questions have more to do with existence, reality and the problem of knowledge, and hence my consideration of African ontology as the basis for understanding African knowledge.

By focusing on African ontology, I specifically consider African conceptions of being, existence and reality as inseparably anchored on human beings' quest for knowledge. In a similar vein, Jimoh sees the "African ontological notion of reality as a continuum in which both the subject, as the cognitive agent, and the object, as the cognized phenomenon, are part and parcel of the same reality" (2017: 121). I will therefore consider what the implications of such ontology are for African epistemology because the meaning of African life is mainly based on African ontology or conceptions of existence, being and reality. Although, knowledge might be viewed as universal to all cultures, and the themes and issues dealt with in philosophy are somewhat universal, "how each culture traces these themes, synthesises, or organises them into a totality is based on each culture's concept of life, namely the interrelationship between objects and persons and between persons and persons themselves" (Onyewuenyi 1976: 521). One implication of this view is that the synthesising of knowledge in each cultural context is based on that particular cultural ontology. Thus, African knowledge must be based on its own cultural life, reality, being or ontology which can be either different or similar to other non-African ontologies and epistemologies.

African ontology has strong implications for various spheres of life such as ethics, religion and epistemology. African ethics, religion and epistemology are products of African ontology such that the former cannot be understood without making reference to the latter. This explains why Gyekye (2010: 102) challenges us to consider how the ontological understanding of the individual and the community in Africa could be taken as the basis for understanding African normative issues. Similarly, this view resonates with the approach which I take in trying to consider the import of African ontology to its epistemology. African ontology must therefore be taken in terms of how it can possibly address questions like, what is knowledge and how can we come to know it? It can also address issues such as where such knowledge comes from, and whether and how we can ultimately attain it?

While the ethical and religious dimensions have been fairly explored in the existing literature on African philosophy by, for example Tempels (1959), Mbiti (1970), Menkiti (1984, 2004), and Gyekye (2010), little work has been done within the area of epistemology in terms of how conceptions of knowledge might be informed by the understanding of African ontology. With the exception of Tempels (1959), Onyewuenyi (1976), Dzobo (2010), Jimoh (2017) and Lajul (2018), one would expect a considerable body of literature in this area. Rather, the area of African epistemology based on its ontology is still in need of further interrogation because roughly understood, African epistemology is still fractured along the universalist/particularist perspectives (see Lajul 2018). As I take a particularist approach to African epistemology based on its ontology, I will argue that each society has a different conception of ontology and, therefore, approaches to knowledge will also differ. For Lajul, "because each society has a unique understanding of this ontology, there is deemed to be different ways of understanding these realities and using such understanding in deriving the knowledge society needs for her development" (2018: 55).

African ontology is based on the understanding of an ontological hierarchy of beings. Onyewuenyi envisages that in African ontology "there is a hierarchy of forces starting from God, spirits, founding fathers, the dead, according to the order of primogeniture; then the living according to their rank in terms of seniority. After the living men come animals, vegetables, and minerals, which are in turn categorised on their relative importance in their own classes" (1976: 524). Such ontology is not just pointing to existence of the various beings, but that it is teleologically oriented (see Teffo and Roux 1998: 139) in so far as each of the beings in such a hierarchy has some purpose for existing and influence in other being/s. This teleological orientation in each of the levels of being has some strong epistemic dimensions and implications for human beings because of the understanding that human beings do not exist in an ontological vacuum. They exist with other beings that ultimately have an effect on their conception of knowledge. According to Lajul, African epistemologies refer to "ways of knowing that flow from African ontology, which is the symbiotic harmonious relationship within an individual, between an individual and society, and between an individual and nature and the spiritual world of their ancestors and their gods" (2018: 55). Properly conceived, thus, African ontology ought to be understood in terms of the epistemic import in each of the various beings (or modes of being) within the hierarchy of existence. As I will show in the following three sections, each of these, i.e. spiritual beings, community and the individual human beings, have different roles in the process of communitarian knowledge acquisition.

Spiritual (Immaterial) Existence and African Knowledge

In this section, I consider an important component of African knowledge which is mostly attained through human beings' relationships with the spiritual (immaterial) world. Because the spiritual realm is the apex of the African hierarchy of ontology, it is also taken as the ultimate source of knowledge from which all other knowledge cascades. This view is based on the understanding that the spiritual world of the Supreme Being and other gods and ancestors is part and parcel of African ontology or reality and that such a spiritual reality can actually be known by human beings.

First, I must highlight the metaphysical premises on which my arguments are based before I venture into the nature of the knowledge of spiritual existence and how it could be attained by human beings. Because of these metaphysical reasons, such knowledge is mostly objected to on the basis that it is grounded on what cannot be empirically verified in experience like the existence of spiritual beings like god and ancestors. In order to respond to this objection, I bring in some sort of a *tu quoque* argument that appeals to the hypocrisy in Western philosophy. According to this view, for example religious knowledge about the existence of God in non-African religions like the Judeo-Christians traditions is not quickly dismissed, yet African religious knowledge about the existence of the same spiritual beings is deemed metaphysical. According to Jimoh and Thomas, "it is important to note that not all of Western religion is supported by science, yet it is not considered a metaphysical fantasy or mere superstition" (2015: 54). This therefore gives me the conviction to appeal to similar premises because human beings have always accepted metaphysical knowledge in different epistemic contexts. Nevertheless, the objection for unverifiable religious and metaphysical claims in both African and non-African traditions will always be difficult if not impossible to satisfactory responses to.

The ontological argument for spiritual knowledge based on *a priori* reasoning can be traced as far back as the medieval period in Western philosophy and it continues to characterise most contemporary views based on the acceptance of divine knowledge. African epistemology also takes the same approach that is implicit in St Anselm's view that *God is that than which nothing greater can be conceived*. Following the African hierarchy of ontology, beings or forces (see Tempels 1959: 73; Onyewuenyi 1976: 524) exist according to a hierarchy in which the spiritual being (God) is at the apex and being the most powerful force, followed by other lesser powerful beings such as deities, ancestors, human beings and other beings. According to Onyewuenyi, "God is Force; God is also wisdom in that he knows all forces, their ordering, their dependence, their potential, and their mutual interaction" (1976: 525). Following such a view, which is roughly accepted in African ontology, the human person lacks knowledge if she/he lacks the knowledge of the Supreme Being (God) because "a person is said to know or have wisdom inasmuch as he approaches divine wisdom" (Onyewuenyi 1976: 525).

From the above, a question that remains is how such divine knowledge might be attained by the individual and whether it is 'revealed' to individuals? This question is perhaps answered by Menkiti in his view of personhood according to which personhood is gradually acquired in individuals as one develops from childhood to adulthood. Although Menkiti is not explicit about divine knowledge, his view of personhood might be interpreted to mean that a person who lacks personhood also lacks some sort of 'divine wisdom' which is usually associated with age. In Onyewuenyi's view, "the older a person gets, the more wisdom he has" (1976: 525). Following a similar ontological view, it is thought that the ancestors have more wisdom, followed by the elders and then other mature human beings down to children in that order. The reason for looking at such kind of knowledge as becoming more qualitative in accordance with the hierarchy of existence is that, mature people, older people and ancestors have more exposure and experience about the world. Therefore, it might be true to say that wisdom and old age are closely knit. However, it is possible that some old folks may lack such wisdom. This view makes sense especially if such knowledge is accepted as wisdom or higher order form of knowledge as opposed to book knowledge which some children might possess while some elders might lack it.

An important aspect implicit from the above conception of knowledge about the existence of spiritual or divine knowledge is that the spiritual realm of God and ancestors is part of the African ontological reality or that it is part of African knowledge. Yet African knowledge based on the *a priori* is often objected using theories of science in Western epistemology and philosophy, especially after the linguistic turn in philosophy, "the fundamental teaching of Western culture is that science is the primary determinant of what is real and what is not real" (Jimoh 2017: 122). This view has been used as the basis on which to dismiss some forms of African knowledge such as religious knowledge and metaphysical knowledge. However, it is interesting to note that Western science itself is still to come up with satisfactory explanations about some forms of knowledge in the African epistemic traditions such as knowledge of witchcraft. For example, the view that a human person can actually harness or at least manufacture natural phenomenon such as lightning and use it to strike purported enemies is still unanswered from these scientific perspectives.

The above views confirm that from African ontology, knowledge is not only limited to empirical knowledge, or that which can be empirically verified through the senses. This is why Jimoh and Thomas contend that from African ontological conceptions of knowledge, "there is more to reality than what is within the realm of empirical inquiry" (201554; see also Jimoh 2017: 122). Accordingly, the realm of knowledge in African ontology is much broader such that even knowledge – such as that of the spiritual beings – outside the empirical framework could also be justified. According to Jimoh and Thomas, "there are spiritual components of nature that influence human experience and perception. Therefore, when a phenomenon is not readily explainable by empirical verification, it can be explained by causal efficacy of the spiritual components of nature" (2015: 54). Such kind of an ontological conception of reality accepts the realities that go beyond human comprehension. This view gives human beings the freedom to at least take as knowledge, beliefs about certain spiritual phenomenon that they see having a fundamental and practical bearing on their being and reality.

Communitarian Ontology and Knowledge

The African communitarian view of existence is one of the most defining and key ontological features of African social structures (Menkiti 1984, 2004; Gyekye 2010). Notwithstanding the fact that African communities are not homogeneous, it is a fact that communitarian existence is a basic characteristic of most of these communities. However, its implications to African epistemic traditions have never been seriously examined. In this section, I therefore analyse some of the implications that African communitarian ontology might have for an African theory of knowledge.

First, I do not wish to pretend that communitarianism is an exceptionally African philosophy as such. There also exist other variants of communitarianism in non-African traditions like in Aristotelian political philosophy as well as in Alasdair MacIntyre, Michael Sandel, Charles Taylor and Michael Walzer, especially if the latter philosophers are read in connection with their critique of Rawls' (1971) liberal theory of justice. However, within the African context, the African communitarian perspective was mainly used as a socialist ideology by most African nationalist thinkers in order to resist colonialism as a united African people in their quest for independence. Gyekye (2010) notes that

> the advocates of the ideology of African socialism, such as Nkrumah, Senghor and Nyerere, in their anxiety to find anchorage for their ideological choice in the traditional African ideas about society, argued that socialism was foreshadowed in the African traditional idea and practice of communalism (communitarianism).
>
> *104*

In the post-colonial African academy, the African communitarian view was initially *baptised* by Mbiti (1970) before it was popularised by Menkiti (1984, 2004) and Gyekye (2007, 2010). For example, John Mbiti's (1970: 141) famous dictum that "I am because we are, and since we are, therefore I am" should be interpreted as pointing to the affirmation of communal, relational and humane existence based on what it means to relate with, and exist with others in a community. This is the same perspective that is also presented in both Menkiti and Gyekye's communitarian accounts. Both Menkiti's (1984, 2004) and Gyekye's (2010) conceptions of person and community, especially their insistence that the individual person is characteristically communitarian, might be taken as generally speaking to the kind of relationships that human beings ought to have in society (Gyekye 2010: 103) based on what it means to exist and to exist with others as alluded to by Mbiti. In Menkiti's view, for example its[1] sense is not that of a person speaking on behalf of, or in reference to, another, but rather of an individual, who recognises the sources of his or her own humanity, and so realises, with internal assurance, that in the absence of others, no grounds exist for a claim regarding the individual's own standing as a person. The notion at work here is the notion of an extended self (Menkiti 2004: 324). In this rather communitarian understanding of persons, which is also later accepted by Gyekye (2007, 2010) and Kalumba (2020), Menkiti is convinced that group solidarity is the key or defining feature of African traditional life based on what he sees as *the notion of an extended self* (Menkiti 2004: 324). According to this view, the *self* is extended by virtue of one's inability to exist without others. This view is meant to emphasise the importance of the community. Hence, it would be proper to say that the individual is essentially a communitarian being. Overall, I must also emphasise that while the above ontological conception of society based on communitarianism has been popularised recently in the African academy, the African communitarian tradition is not necessarily a new tradition. It is an old-age tradition that has always been characteristically part of African epistemic traditions.

The communitarian view of society plays an integral role in African epistemology. It is not merely an arrangement that is just social; it also has some epistemic implications that ought to be critically examined. First, it must be noted that there is a close connection between African communitarian philosophy and traditional knowledge. Dzobo (2010) looks at traditional knowledge as knowledge that is passed down by word of mouth … from one person or from one generation to another [or] knowledge that is passed from parents and elders to the next generation and contained in proverbs and other forms of literature.

74

In African communitarian societies, it is easy for such traditional knowledge to be passed from one generation to the other or from the elders to the younger generation because the communitarian arrangements or structures of society make it easy for the attainment of such knowledge. Connected to this view, Ikuenobe, who does not make a distinction between communitarianism and communalism, argues that "communalism involves the idea of mutual dependence and organic relationships between community and individuals, and among individuals. For him, this relationship exemplifies relevant values and beliefs that are sustained by the informal oral methods of learning about cultural traditions" (Ikuenobe 2018: 230). These views signify the centrality of not only the community in knowledge acquisition, but also other methods that are at the centre of inculcating knowledge to individuals from generation to generation such as the oral method of imparting knowledge to individuals. This method based on the oral tradition "is an informal method of learning, acquiring, imparting, and transmitting knowledge, beliefs, traditions, and values, involves among other things, parables, myths, proverbs, artwork, and folklore" (Ikuenobe 2018: 23).

In African traditions, thus, knowledge is passed from generation to generation and especially from the community to the individuals because the community is regarded as the custodian of traditional knowledge. Such kind of an approach to knowledge, also based on some division of labour, sharing of evidence and acceptance of the community as the epistemic authority, could best be described as "epistemic communalism" (Ikuenobe 2018: 23). African ontology and its communitarian structure are dependent on this epistemic communalism. Properly understood, the African communitarian community is the epistemic community in so far as it should be seen not just as a mere community of individuals, but that it is an epistemic community or epistemic authority (Ikuenobe 2006: 195). Individuals can therefore rely on knowledge from epistemic communalism without necessarily having to labour themselves in trying to "adequately evaluate, and voluntarily accept the contents and adequacy of all the evidence … [since] some of the evidence may be too complex for us to understand and evaluate" (Ikuenobe 2006: 195). However, this view should not be taken to imply that individuals are not entitled to critical reflection and evaluation with reference to such knowledge as I will show. It is only that they readily accept it because of the intricacy of such knowledge, as well as that it would have already passed all the processes of justification and truth conditions when the community initially accepted it as knowledge.

Following the above understanding, the African court system is a typical case in point that goes to demonstrate the nature and importance of epistemic communalism in terms of how knowledge is taken and trusted when it comes from the community rather than from the individual as such. African communities, in general, are guided by traditional leaders like chiefs and village heads who preside over traditional tribunals. Contrary to modern court systems that are mostly modelled in accordance with Western styles of governance, African traditional court systems' decision processes are done by more than one individual (neither the chief nor the village head) because of the understanding that knowledge does not necessarily reside in one person. The chief or village head mostly presides over such tribunals, but in consultation with their subjects. According to Dzobo, this view is shaped by the fact that in African epistemology, "knowledge is like a baobab tree; no one can embrace it with both arms" (2010: 77). This means that no one can know everything. In this case, it is not possible that either the chief or the village head can know everything as a lone individual to the extent that she/he can preside over cases and make lone decisions on all matters. This is because knowledge is thought to be limitless (Dzobo 2010: 77) to the extent that no one can know everything. Accordingly, the approach to knowledge through epistemic communalism makes decision-making easier and objective because knowledge used to make decisions is not a product of one person.

In an African communitarian ontology, it is emphasised that the individual cannot be successfully taken as being independent of the community especially if understood in the sense in which communitarianism is not optional for the person (Gyekye 2010: 105; Kalumba 2020: 138). This means that in terms of epistemic quest, the community also plays a significant role in order for the individual persons constituting it to access knowledge. In such a scenario, it therefore becomes somewhat difficult to clearly define the individual person as an autonomous epistemic agent, or an individual that can rely on its own in terms of knowledge acquisition independent of the community such that one can be said to also have epistemic responsibility. However, if African ontology and communitarianism are read well, they do not necessarily take away the agency and responsibility of the person as I now proceed to show in the following section focusing on the role and responsibility of the individual in African ontology in acquiring knowledge.

Communitarian Knowledge and the Individual

From the preceding section, one might get the impression that African communitarian ontology is so strict that it stifles the role of the individual in the process of knowledge production. Specifically, epistemic communalism, which is at the core of such ontology, might be read as if the individual is a passive and not active receiver of knowledge. However, as opposed to a radical view of communitarianism implicit in Menkiti (1984), in a moderate communitarianism where the rights of the individual are not completely taken away (see Gyekye 2002, 2010 and Kalumba 2020), the individual person has an important role to play as an individual epistemic agent, and assumes epistemic responsibility in the process of knowledge acquisition as I show below.

African communitarians essentially accept that the community is ontologically prior to the individual (Kalumba 2020: 138). Especially read from the perspective of radical communitarian ontology, one may get two impressions: first that the individual is overshadowed to the extent that one does not have a role to play in the process of knowledge production. Second that such epistemology which is based on communitarian knowledge lacks criticality. For example, in the conception of personhood in African communitarian ontology, Menkiti infers that "it is the community which defines the person as a person, not some isolated quality of rationality, wills or memory" (1984: 72). Although, Menkiti is more focused on the idea of personhood, this view also has implications for the ontological status of the person and ultimately the question of knowledge. Its implications are that, it completely takes away not only the ontological status of the person, but also the aspects of epistemic agency such as epistemic autonomy and individual critical reflection such that one cannot know the self or at least have knowledge of the self simply because it is the community which defines him/her as a person.

Because of the limits of the radical ontological view of the community over the person and its implications to epistemology, Gyekye tries to give an answer to the question of whether there is individuality and criticality in communitarian epistemology. First, Gyekye tries to grapple with the question of whether a person has "ontological priority over the community or whether he/she is by nature a communal (communitarian) being having natural or essential relationships with others" (2002: 297). Second, Gyekye is also concerned with "the status of the rights of the individual ... [as well as] the place of duties [in terms of] how the individual sees his/her socio-ethical roles in relation to the interests and welfare of others" (2002: 297). If correctly read in terms of how he responds to these questions, Gyekye is of the view that African ontology-based communitarian knowledge does not necessarily point to communitarian beliefs or knowledge being forced on the individual such that the individual is the mere receiver of everything from the community without questioning.

The other view that accommodates individuality and criticality in African communitarian ontology is that knowledge is a product or the sum total of knowledge from individuals that would have passed processes of reflection and introspection. This view is aptly captured by Lajul (2018) as follows:

> When an idea has filtered through to us from the diffuse and indistinct unwritten traditions; it does not mean that such an idea was produced collectively. Equally, the African body of knowledge could not have been produced collectively, since ideas can only be produced by individuals and may be preserved collectively.
>
> 57

Accordingly, the individual person stands to actively work on all knowledge that one receives from the community. The community is like the source from which individuals have to search for knowledge through their individual effort; although, of course, the community is readily available to impart such knowledge. Dzobo gives the maxim that "knowledge is like a garden, if it is not cultivated it cannot be harvested" (2010: 77). This shows that although the community is fundamental in the acquisition of knowledge by the individual, still "the individual has an active part to play in the acquisition of knowledge" (Dzobo 2010: 77). For that reason, it marks the distinction between human beings and other non-human beings because at least human beings are capable of accessing knowledge and truth through active processes of receiving knowledge and reflecting. That process of knowledge acquisition is done through what Dzobo sees as deductive and contemplative processes (2010: 74). The human ability not only to acquire knowledge but also to have true knowledge makes them unique and different from other non-human beings. According to Dzobo "indigenous African societies consider knowledge and truth as the key factors in living a meaningful and satisfying life; the capacity to comprehend these has been used as the principal criterion for differentiating human beings from the lower animals" (2010: 71). This shows that despite human beings getting much of their knowledge from the community through some empirical processes, they also have an intellect that is capable of actively working on such knowledge because at the end of it all, "to be human is to know and understand things, especially the fundamental ideas and principles of life" (Dzobo 2010: 71).

One of the fundamental questions that might be asked with reference to the above conceptions of African communitarian ontology is: what is the role of the individual in the quest for knowledge considering the role of the immaterial world of deities and ancestors as well as the community in the ontological lives of individual persons? One would always be tempted, and for good reasons, to think that spiritual beings will ultimately determine the kind of knowledge that one will get from the community because of the perceived determinism in such societies based on the acceptance of the existence and influence of spiritual beings like gods and ancestors. However, despite the spiritual world having some of these strong implications on the relationships between various beings and other spiritual dimensions, at least in terms of knowledge, they play a passive role while the person is the one that actively participates in the quest for knowledge. Dzobo captures this view which is accepted in most African communities that "knowledge is not the gift of the gods" (2010: 77). Although Dzobo's 'knowledge from the gods' is not necessarily equivalent to *a priori* knowledge, his view could be understood as dismissing the possibility of all knowledge about the spiritual, together with *a priori* knowledge (knowledge attained before sense experience or inborn knowledge, for example in the Platonic sense). In African ontology, there seems not to be emphasis on *a priori* knowledge but mostly *a posteriori* knowledge, which is the kind of knowledge that community holds from their wealth of experience with the world and it is directly fed into the community by the very individuals that compose it. This is why it is believed that "man is not born with knowledge; whatever he knows is acquired through experience and through a deliberate effort on his part to know" (Dzobo 2010: 77). However, this should not be taken to mean that there is not *a priori* knowledge.

Conclusion

The discourse of African communitarian ontology could be read from various philosophical perspectives. In this chapter, I have mainly examined it from the perspective of epistemology, especially in terms of how it informs the latter. I do not wish to claim that I have been exhaustive about how to conceptualise African epistemology from an ontological perspective. However, I have tried to show what ontological communitarianism entails for African epistemology by considering the import of the African hierarchy of ontology stretching from the spiritual beings down to non-human beings. Specifically, I have shown how African communitarian existence meaningfully contributes to communitarian epistemology without necessarily taking away the ontological status of the individual person.

Acknowledgements

I would like to thank the Alexander von Humboldt Foundation for sponsoring me to do this research.

Notes

1 Used with reference to John Mbiti's dictum: *I am because we are*.
2 My emphasis.

References

Chemhuru, M. (2016). *The Import of African Ontology for Environmental Ethics*. DLitt et Phil (Philosophy). [Unpublished]: University of Johannesburg. Retrieved from: https://ujcontent.uj.ac.za/vital/access/manager/Index?site_name=Research%20Output. Date Retrieved: 5 April 2021.
Dzobo, N. K. (2010). Knowledge and Truth: Ewe and Akan Conceptions. In Kwasi Wiredu and Kwame Gyekye (Eds.) *Person and Community: Ghanaian Philosophical Studies 1*. Washington, D.C.: The Council for Research in Values and Philosophy, 71–82.
Gyekye, K. (2002). Person and Community in African Thought. In P. H Coetzee and A. P. J. Roux (Eds.) *Philosophy from Africa: A Text with Readings*. New York: Oxford University Press, 297–312.
Gyekye, K. (2007). *Tradition and Modernity: Philosophical Reflections on the African Experience*. New York: Oxford University Press.
Gyekye, K. (2010). Person and Community in the Akan Thought. In Kwasi Wiredu and Kwame Gyekye (Eds.) *Person and Community: Ghanaian Philosophical Studies 1*. Washington, D.C.: The Council for Research in Values and Philosophy, 101–122.
Gyekye, K. (2013). *Philosophy, Culture, and Vision*. Accra: Sub-Saharan Publishers.
Hegel, G. W. H. (1837/2001). *The Philosophy of History*. Kitchener: Batoche Books.
Hountondji, P. J. (2009). Knowledge of Africa, Knowledge by Africans: Two Perspectives on African Studies. *RCCS Annual Review*. 2009 (1): 121–131.
Ikuenobe, P. (2006). *Philosophical Perspectives on Communitarianism and Morality in African Traditions*. Lanham: Lexington Books.

Ikuenobe, P. (2018). Oral Tradition, Epistemic Dependence, and Knowledge in African Cultures. *Synthesis Philosophica*. 65 (1): 23–40.
Jimoh, A. K. (2017). An African Theory of Knowledge. In Isaac E. Ukpokolo (Ed.) *Themes, Issues and problems in African Philosophy*. Cham: Palgrave Macmillan, 121–136.
Jimoh, A. K. and Thomas, J. (2015). An African Epistemological Approach to Epistemic Certitude and Scepticism. *Research on Humanities and Social Sciences*. 5 (11): 54–61.
Kalumba, K. M. (2020). A Defence of Kwame Gyekye's Moderate Communitarianism. *Philosophical Papers*. 49 (1): 137–159.
Lajul, W. (2018). Reconstructing African Fractured Epistemologies for Development. *Synthesis Philosophica*. 65 (1): 51–76.
Mbiti, J. S. (1970). *African Religion and Philosophy*. London: Heinemann.
Menkiti, I. A. (1984). Person and Community in African Traditional Thought. In Richard Wright (Ed.) *African Philosophy: An Introduction*. Lanham: University Press of America, 171–181.
Menkiti, I. A. (2004). On the Normative Conception of a Person. In Kwasi Wiredu (Ed.) *A Companion to African Philosophy*. Malden: Blackwell Publishers, 324–331.
Onyewuenyi, I. (1976). Is there an African Philosophy? *Journal of African Studies*. 3 (4): 513–528.
Poli, R. (2010). Ontology: The Categorical Stance. In Roberto Poli and Hohanna Seibt (Eds.). *Theory and Applications of Ontology: Philosophical Perspectives*. New York: Springer, 1–22.
Rawls, J. (1971). *A Theory of Justice*. Cambridge: Harvard University Press.
Teffo, Lesiba J. and Roux, Abraham P. J. (1998). Metaphysical Thinking in Africa. In P. H. Coetzee and A. P. J. Roux (Eds.) *The African Philosophy Reader*. London: Routledge, 192–258.
Tempels, P. (1959). *Bantu Philosophy* (Trans. Rev. Collin King). New York, USA: HBC Publishing.
Zack, N. (2018). *Philosophy of Race: An Introduction*. Cham: Palgrave Macmillan.

PART III
Context-Discourse of African Epistemology

7
TRUTH IN AFRICAN (ESAN) PHILOSOPHY

Isaac E. Ukpokolo

Introduction

The present chapter begins with the question, "what is truth?"[1] And the approach employed as well as the content endorsed herein rest on the answer to the question and provide ground for the analysis of the notion of truth with particular reference to Esan philosophy – of the *kwa* language branch of the Niger-Congo language family, found in the Southern part of Nigeria.[2] To be sure, the desire for truth is an integral part of human nature. This is so because

> truth is not only the fundamental essence of good, it is also the 'Pole-Star' of human freedom; without it, human freedom loses its sense of direction, degenerates and becomes isolated and reduced to sterile arbitration. With it freedom is rediscovered and recognized to have been sought for our good and is expressed in action and behaviour.
>
> *Coulet 2007: 29*

These convictions inform the very importance of the place of truth as emphasized and persistently reenacted not only by individuals but also in societies – in culture, politics, religion, science and philosophy. What then is this thing called truth?

In its fundamental sense, truth may be defined as a quality or state of reality. It is the quality and property of beliefs, things, events, assertions, thoughts, sentences or propositions (Honderich 2005: 926). And so, in philosophy, the question of truth is found prominent in the areas of metaphysics, epistemology, philosophy of language and ethics. When employed in qualifying beliefs, statements or propositions, it is usually considered in relation to fact or state of affairs. When such facts or state of affairs have to do with society and human interactions, truth is a social bond and performs an active role in the acts of sincerity and trust. It is for this reason that our commitment to truth is the soul of justice. In the world of positivist science, truth is empirical, while in everyday language truth is confessional. As a term 'truth' is honorific, it is something we always approve of, something we strive to attain or achieve (Lacey 1996: 358). This, it must be said, is so because truth is not only intricately linked with epistemic normativity but also possesses the character of moral prescriptivism. Some questions that represent the traditional concern constituting the focus of inquiry into the nature of truth are: What is it to call something true? Is truth necessarily a relation between what we say and the subject matter of reference? Is it a way of repeating or expressing a certain kind of approval or willingness to endorse it? Do we say a belief is true if, in a certain sense, it works or produces satisfaction? (Lacey 1996: 358). These questions run through the various dimensions and phases of human inquiries – be it science, philosophy or religion. While science seeks to determine 'that which is true', philosophy asks 'what is the nature of truth itself?' (Bunnin & Yu 2004: 703). In other words, while science inquires into the truth of nature, philosophy inquires into the nature of truth. This inquiry in philosophy has run almost exclusively through the confines of epistemology. In other words, inquiries in western traditions of science and philosophy are replete with epistemological dimensions in the analysis of the meaning and nature of truth. This is with little or no recourse to the ethical or moral dimension of the nature of truth. The present essay undertakes an analysis of the notion of truth in Esan philosophy paying significant attention to the moral dimension, the epistemological import notwithstanding. In the next section, the essay attempts a representation of truth as an epistemic ideal.

Truth as an Epistemic Ideal

In western history of ideas, attention to the analysis of the notion of truth is almost always characterized by epistemic considerations. The term *epistemic* is an adjective derived from *episteme*, a Greek word for knowledge. A proposition or statement, or claim is referred to as *epistemic* "if and only if it has some implication for what in some circumstances, is rationally worthy of belief" (Honderich 2005: 259). In the tradition of western epistemology, truth is contrasted with falsity (although whether truth and falsity are indeed polar opposites, as the principle of bivalence implies, is in itself a disputed issue; Honderich 2005: 926). Truth is viewed as a property that has a bearer, although there is no consensus as to what the bearer is. Some ascribe it to sentences (a group of words that make complete sense), others to statements (assertions) while some regard it to be propositions (what is asserted). Other candidates of truth are 'judgments' and 'utterances'. Therefore, some ask what renders a proposition true? While others ask what renders a sentence or an utterance of a sentence true? (Bunnin & Yu 2004: 703). The request here is to state the necessary and sufficient conditions for what truth is. And since truth involves a relation of features to reality, a natural answer is that, if a belief corresponds to reality, it is true. This is known in epistemology as the correspondence theory of truth. This theory, traditionally identified with Aristotle (384–322), states that "to say of what is that it is not, or of what is not that it is, is false, while to say of what is that it is, and of what is not that it is not, is true …." (Aristotle, *Metaphysics*, Trans. W.D. Ross. P7: 67–8).

The correspondence theory is perhaps the commonest of the theories of truth. This is so partly because 'correspondence' can be interpreted strictly or loosely. In its very strict sense, it involves a relation between two things, that which is true (a proposition, belief, judgment etc.) and that which makes it true (a fact or a state of affair). This interpretation is usually identified with G.E. Moore and Bertrand Russell in modern times, wherein a fact is taken to have a structure which the proposition copies or pictures (Lacey 1996: 358). This is echoed in Bertrand Russell's theory of meaning resting on the metaphysics of 'logical atomism'. The characteristic features usually identified with the correspondence theory of truth in western epistemology include the subject/object dichotomy between the knower and the known. This is enhanced by the element of detachedness by which the subject is distinguished and distinct from the object; human and the world, the scientist and nature, the philosopher and the ideas he relates with. This in western epistemology depicts the objectivity of knowledge. In western epistemology, we have presented as theories of truth not only the correspondence theory but also the deflationary theory of truth, redundancy theory of truth, the disquotational theory of truth, the performative theory of truth, the minimalist theory of truth, the semantic theory of truth, the pragmatic and the coherentist theories of truth.

In modern European philosophy, Heidegger takes his position from the etymological sense of the Greek word for truth, *aletheia*, that is 'unconcealment' or 'unhiddenness'. On this ground, Heidegger claims that truth in its most primordial sense is *Dasein's* disclosedness or uncoveredness, that is *Dasein's* openness to its possibilities. Being true therefore means being uncovered. At this primordial level, untruth is the fallingness of *Dasein's* being closed off. "The Being-true (truth) of the assertion must be understood as Being-uncovering" (Heidegger 1996: 220–221). In all, it can be said that "truth is the concern of all honest men; they try to espouse only true assertions, claims, theories, and so on" (Bunnin & Yu 2004: 703).

Truth as a Moral Ideal

As mentioned earlier, truth as an ideal is also manifest in the moral or ethical dimension. It is unarguably the fundamental essence of good, and our commitment to it is the soul of justice, the very ground for social reality. In other words, morality and its cognate ideals of good, trust, sincerity and justice rest on the reality of truth; they are what they are to the extent that they entail and/or imply the ideal of truth.

As a cognate ideal of truth, the 'good' for Plato is a perfect, eternal and changeless 'Form', while for Aristotle, truth as virtue is the main or sole good. Immanuel Kant also speaks of the 'good will' as the only unconditional good. In application, 'good' describes the dispositions, desires, intentions or actions of people and institutions. Trust, as a firm belief or reliability, stands out also as a cognate notion of truth; same goes for sincerity and friendship. Justice is yet another moral and social ideal founded on our commitment to the virtue of truth. It is the proper bonding and noninterference of classes in the society as well as harmony of the individual's elements (rational, spirited and appetitive). For Aristotle, it is equality and proportion in the enjoyment of values – treating equals equally and unequals unequally (Hamedi 2014: 1164–1165). These considerations present the reality of truth in its moral dimension, and this is a representation contained in the conception of truth in Esan philosophy. It is however necessary to state here that the understanding of truth in Esan philosophy is most appreciated when considered against a background of a certain metaphysics about the human person, and forms the platform for our study in the next subsection of this chapter.

The Human Person in Esan Metaphysics

In Esan metaphysics, the human person (oria/ohan) is a 'subject' rather than an 'object'. This 'subject' is a composite of body (egbe) and a *life force* (orion/ahun). The body or *egbe* is physical whereas *orion or ahun* is nonphysical. Put differently, the essential life force of *oria* is non-physical. Of course, the body (egbe) consists of, among other things, the physical head or brain referred to as *uhonmhon*. The exit of the *vital force* that is *orion* or *ahun* announces death. In Esan philosophy, the human person that is *oria* is the 'subject' of knowledge, morality, social values and spiritual reality. And so, constitute the 'subject' of ascriptions – in terms of knowing, loving, and judging – all expressed in relation to other 'subjects'. The human person therefore can be moral, ethical, spiritual and can possess cognitive capacities. As a rational and moral agent capable of natural and supernatural abilities, the subject's action, proposition, dispositions and thoughts can be evaluated as true, good, sincere, honest and perhaps modest. It is to the 'subject' of the human person or *oria* that these ascriptions can be applied. And here lies the ground for adjudging or evaluating the person's emotions, actions and dispositions as moral or otherwise. It is on the basis of this that the Esan people conceive of truth as one of the fundamental 'emissions' from the human person. Indeed, for them the consideration of a human being as *oria* or a person is sometimes tied to the possession of these ascriptions of truthfulness, honesty, goodness and sincerity to mention but a few.

There is of course some relationship between the metaphysics of the human person in Esan philosophy and epistemic ascription such as knowledge. The human person is not only the 'subject' of knowledge but also the 'subject' of moral values. It is to be taken seriously when one says "I do not know you". This is because knowledge in Esan discourse is more than information about reality. It is a 'living relationship' between the subject and reality or another 'subject'. And so, to say that 'I do not know you' is not just to deny cognitive acquaintance or access, but to reject a given intercourse that characterizes human knowledge. And so, it is usual to hear the dictum in Esan language *Ai yole abha len oria* (which literally translates as 'it is not said that I don't know someone'). This is usually taken to mean the person of reference is not regarded or is not worth it. It can also be said that Mr. 'A' is not a person (ona iyo ria). This is so because there is an observed moral deficit with regard to the subject of reference. In other words, the idea of *oria* or person is necessarily qualitative and intrinsically linked with integrity, truth and goodness. The foregoing situates the understanding of truth within the moral context of relationship.

Truth in Esan Philosophy

Truth as represented in Esan thought system is not only epistemic but also moral. This forms the point of divergence in this paper, emphasizing the moral standpoint of truth in Esan worldview. Of course, by its moral demands, some courageously pursue truth as an ideal, many cowardly avoid such ideal, and a few laments over its distortion (Lynch 2001: 1). To be specific, in Esan philosophy, truth is more of ascription to a subject over and above the proposition (object). The institution of truth-speaking or truth-telling in Esan thought system emphasizes the 'subject', underlying its integrity and ascribing virtue qualities to it. Such a human agent, a moral or epistemic subject is considered central in the worldview of any community. Consider the following: During a visit to an elderly family friend, the host declares a wish (prayer or supplication): "May someone known to be renowned for truth-telling or truth-speaking in a community not bear false witness against you". The import of this prayer is that members of the community would easily consider the trustworthiness of the 'witness' and accept such as true. In other words, if a supposedly habitual truth-speaking person makes a false claim concerning a matter or person, it is very likely that such claim would be accepted as worth it.

In Esan philosophy, truth is translated as *emhon-ata* or *ota-na-ta*. This literally means 'word', 'matter' or 'discourse' worthy of expression. Its component parts are *Emhon or ota* translated as 'word' or 'matter' or 'assertion' or 'statement' or 'discourse', and *ta* the verb 'to say', 'to assert' or 'to speak'. The question that looms large here is, what is it that makes a matter worth declaring or a proposition worth asserting? Closely related to the issue here is what has been put forward by Ludwig Wittgenstein in his work, *Tractatus Logico-Philosophicus* (1921). "The whole sense of the book" is, says Wittgenstein, "what can be said at all can be said clearly, and what we cannot talk about we must pass over in silence" (Wittgenstein 1921: 6.54). Here, the ideal of clarity constitutes a defining element of a worthwhile assertion. Of course, Wittgenstein is not alone in this belief. The father of modern philosophy, Rene Descartes. in one of his *Meditations* posits that we are not to accept any statement as true except if it is 'clear' and 'distinct' (Descartes 1988: 3:35). Even in his deferring position, Karl R. Popper did argue that error, confusion and obscurity are contradictions of truth (Popper 1962: 28). In the light of these, it is here asserted that for the Esan mindset, what is worth saying or worth asserting as a discourse or proposition is what is clear and distinct, devoid of confusion and obscurity. This, however, should be understood as an additional condition to the principle of correspondence or coherence represented in traditional epistemology, constituting the fundamental elements of truth, as '*emhon-ata*' or '*ota-na-ta*'. By this understanding, *emhon-ata*, while aligning to traditional epistemology goes further to demand additional conditions of clarity, which actually must aid correspondence and or coherence as principles. Yet closely linked with the elements of clarity and distinction and the elimination of confusion as well as obscurity are the moral ideals of sincerity, justice, trust, friendship and, above all, goodness. This would pass for the cluster of ideals that brings together the status of integrity in the thought, word and act of any moral agent. To be sure, thought brings forth discourse or word or assertion, discourse brings forth action and action brings forth habit and habit brings forth character. In all, character summarizes integrity or the lack of it. Indeed, in itself, character is hardly separable from the moral agent as it truly defines the 'being' of the person. In Esan philosophy, the man or woman of noble character, of virtue and integrity is identified as *Adaze*.

Conclusion

From the foregoing, although, '*emhon-ata*' or '*ota-na-ta*' has as its content a given discourse, it always has a person or a moral agent as its 'subject'. This as said earlier is in line with traditional epistemology that defines human knowledge in terms of subject relating to an object. Yet the relationship between the subject and object in traditional epistemology is either from rationalist or empiricist perspectives. And so, S's epistemic connection with 'P' is either rationalist or empiricist. The present essay is concerned with the relationship between subject and object as defined in terms of integrity and virtue. It is for this reason that this paper considers truth and truth-telling as moral or ethical dispositions of a person who can be described as *Adaze*. Usually identified with *Adaze* are the elements of sincerity and honesty, integrity and nobility – a person of 'grace' and admits of no 'disgrace'.

The chapter, therefore, does not restrict itself to the epistemology of truth, relying only on the ideation of discourse, but attempts a leap onto the realm of reality borne on the wings of existentiality. In other words, the idea of truth in Esan philosophy must be found expressed not only in *epistemic* ideas but also in the moral content of everyday life. We find this manifest in the dispositions of individuals and persons as well as institutions and relationships such as friendship, marriage, family life, politics, education and cultures. What gives acceptation at all times is the transcending presence of '*emhon-ata*' or '*ota-na-ta*'. It is in the light of this understanding that the Esan people of Southern Nigeria accept the claims of *Adaze* without investigating or inquiring into evidential grounds for acceptance. What is more? '*Emhon-ata*' easily identifies with not only epistemic justification but also moral prescription as well as ontological representation: Epistemological justification because it is characteristic of reliable knowledge, moral prescription because it is the ground for integrity and ontological representation because it is what really is.

It is at this point that one would reflect on the range of reference of *emhon-ata* in human discourse. It is easily found to relate with an aspect of human inquiry usually referred to in contemporary discourse as virtue epistemology, a discourse that "attempts to apply to epistemology the insight of virtue ethics" (Honderich 2005: 947). Its practitioners say that a justified belief is one that a virtuous cognizer, someone with the cognitive virtues would have such a person in Esan thought system is referred to as *Adaze* a virtuous cognizer (Honderich 2005: 947). Of particular consideration here is the condition of virtue responsibilism as it applies to belief, truth and knowledge. Virtue responsibilism emphasizes such intellectual virtues or *character traits*, such as "inquisitiveness, fair-mindedness, open-mindedness, intellectual carefulness, thoroughness, tenacity" (Baehr 2022), honesty and integrity. The above traits, they argue, derive from a responsible knower or inquirer.

Notes

1 The fundamental nature of this question to the human person is brought to the fore in the admonition that we must not leave this world as Pilate left the Praetorium with the unanswered question: What is truth? It is a question of knowing whether we live for something, or in vain. (See: Raniero Cantalamessa, "Cardinal Cantalamessa's Homily at the Vatican's Good Friday 2022 Liturgy". Online: www.catholicnewsagency.com/news/250993/full-text-cardinal-cantalamessa-s-homily-at-the-vatican-s-good-friday-2022-liturgy. Accessed May 10, 2022).
2 The Esan people are an ethnic group of Southern Nigeria who speak the Esan language. They are traditionally known to be agriculturalists, trado-medical practitioners, mercenary warriors and hunters. Esan language – Esan Edoid language is related to Edo, Urhobo, Owan, Isoko, Anioma and Etsako. This is a regionally important language in Nigeria, taught in primary schools in addition to being broadcast on radio and television. The Esan language is also recognized in the census of the United Kingdom. The people who reside in Esan land number about three million citizens in Nigeria. And there is a strong Esan-Diaspora.

References

Aristotle. *Metaphysics*. Trans. W.D. Ross. Sioux Falls, South Dakota: NuVision Publications, 2009.
Baehr, S. Jason. "Virtue Epistemology", Encyclopedia, 2004. Online: https://iep.utm.edu/virtueep/ Accessed: 13/01/2022.
Bunnin, Nicholas & Jiuan, Yu. *The Blackwell Dictionary of Western Philosophy*. Malden: Blackwell, 2004.
Coulet, Jean-Michel. (Ed.). *An Invitation to Faith: An A to Z Primer on the Thought of Pope Benedict XVI*. New York: K.S. Ginger Company Inc., 2007.
Descartes, Rene. *Discourse on Method and Meditations on First Philosophy*, Fourth Edition, Trans. Donald A. Cress. Indianapolis, IN: Hackett Publishing Company, 1988.
Hamedi, Afifeh. "The concept of justice in Greek philosophy, (Plato and Aristotle)." *Mediterranean Journal of Social Sciences*, Vol. 5, No. 27. (December 2014): 1164–5.
Heidegger, Martin. *Being and Time*. Trans. Joan Stambaugh. New York: State University of New York Press, 1996.
Honderich, Ted (Ed.). *The Oxford Companion to Philosophy*. Oxford: Oxford University Press, 2005.
Lacey, Robert A. *A Dictionary of Philosophy*, Third Edition. New York: Routledge, 1996.

Lynch, P. Michael. *The Nature of Truth: Classic and Contemporary Perspectives*. Cambridge, MA: Bradford Books, 2001.

Popper, K. Raimund. *Conjectures and Refutations: The Growth of Scientific Knowledge*. New York: Basic Books, 1962.

Wittgenstein, Ludwig. *Tractatus Logico-Philosophicus*. Trans. Pears and McGuinness. London: Kegan Paul, 1921.

8
FROM ONTOLOGY TO KNOWLEDGE ACQUISITION IN AFRICA AND THE CARIBBEAN

What Can Be Known for Certain?

Sandra McCalla

Introduction

Generally speaking, humans, regardless of oppression and their past or present struggles, philosophize as they seek to understand themselves and their place in the world. Philosophy and philosophizing are not solely reserved for a specific society, since all humans ask questions and seek solutions to everyday problems that often threaten their existence. Western scholars typically associate philosophy with rationality and reason and, on this, claim that Africans and Afro-Caribbeans do not have philosophy and cannot philosophize. On this view, Afro-Caribbean philosophy would be void of reason. As Masolo (1994) states:

> The birth of the debate on African philosophy is historically associated with two happenings: Western discourse on Africa and the African response to it …. At the centre of this debate is the concept of reason, a value which is believed to stand as the great divide between the civilized and the uncivilized, the logical and the mystical …. To a large extent, the debate about African Philosophy can be summarized as a significant contribution to the discussion and definition of reason or what Hegel called the spirit. Indeed, it is commonly referred to as the 'Rationality debate.'
>
> [1]

Sceptics on the rationality of philosophical discourses in other traditions rest their claims on the false premise that any act of philosophizing outside of mainstream academic Western philosophy is pseudo and irrational. According to Ochieng'-Odhiambo, such biased utterances were made by scholars such as David Hume, Karl Marx, L. Levy-Bruhl, E.E. Evans-Pritchard, Diederich Westermann, and John Carothers (Ochieng'-Odhiambo 2010: 8–9).[1] These scholars believed that, unlike, the non-western world, the Western world was the incarnation of reason. Contrary to the beliefs of the scholars mentioned above, all human beings are capable of rationality (Brown 1988: 2). It is therefore absurd to exclude some forms of philosophy and philosophizing from the category of reason. In an effort to hold meaningful discussions on Afro-Caribbean philosophy, I suggest that these sceptics dispel the myth that only Europeans philosophize and, thereby, take Afro-Caribbean philosophy from its ghostly existence to reality through an exorcism cure.

I seek to dispel scepticism associated with a false superior mainstream philosophy by arguing for an Afro-Caribbean epistemology situated within the ontology of the intellectual traditions of Afro-Caribbean people. I explore these traditions to show how Afro-Caribbean reality culminates in a unique epistemology (the study of how and what human beings know) in plantation and post-plantation existence.

The scepticism surrounding the existence of an Afro-Caribbean philosophy seems to be three-fold. Firstly, there is the notion that philosophy must be written, and since the written discourse on Afro-Caribbean philosophy is still developing, many sceptics of the existence of Afro-Caribbean philosophy question its authenticity. Secondly, persons of Afro-Caribbean descent are said to be backward and lack the intelligence needed to produce any meaningful philosophy (Ochieng'-Odhiambo 2010: 8). Thirdly, the compound nature of the concept Afro-Caribbean comes into question as some believe that the phrase Afro-Caribbean is a misnomer.

In a quest to explore these issues comprehensively, I divide the essay into three major sections. The first section explores the ontology of being within the Afro-Caribbean context. It proposes that Afro-Caribbean understanding of being (and/or reality) offers a tremendous footing on which Afro-Caribbean people understand the world and frame their epistemology. In the second section, I situate and explore knowledge as a socio-cultural construct and show that each culture construes knowledge differently, but that this does not mean that one way of knowing is superior to the other. Humans across cultures and societies are equipped with the capacity to know and understand as they seek to interact with the world, and Afro-Caribbeans are not exempt from this epistemological quest. The third section explores issues surrounding who can know and what can be known by examining the acquisition of knowledge from the Afro-Caribbean perspective. I show that knowledge is multidimensional. A perspectival form of knowledge is explored, using Nietzsche's perspectival views as a guide.

Afro-Caribbean Philosophy, History, and Ontology

Unlike Greek and Egyptian philosophy, Afro-Caribbean philosophy is a more modern development because of the newness of the Caribbean region (Gordon 2007: 145). It is with this in mind that Earl McKenzie traced the beginnings of Afro-Caribbean philosophy to the enslaved Africans who replaced the genocidally decimated Tainos in the sugarcane plantations in various Caribbean territories. According to McKenzie (2013):

Enslaved Africans arrived at a time when domestic slavery was widespread on their continent, and Trans-Sahara (Arabic) Slave Trade was also well-entrenched ... At the time of their arrival, these Africans had what later formally trained African Philosophers would call Ethnophilosophy: proverbs, myths, the thought of sages and so on.

13

McKenzie had no doubt that philosophical thinking existed in Africa. He proclaims that Africans, forcibly enslaved in the new world, were not void of philosophical thinking and ideologies, science and technologies, religions and the arts when they arrived in the Caribbean (McKenzie 2013: 13). They, however, had to adapt to a culture where their colonizers sought to enforce their own ideologies on them. These individuals were taken from various countries in West Africa in the Gulf of Guinea and sent to various locations in the Caribbean, including Jamaica and Barbados among others (Honeychurch 1995: 84). Due to cultural and other differences, all Africans did not enter the Caribbean holding the same philosophical beliefs on issues dealing with ethics, metaphysics, aesthetics, etc. These varied ideologies and views formed an interesting Afro-Caribbean philosophy.

Although McKenzie did not question the existence of philosophy in Africa, he continued his discussion by questioning if Africans had brought any philosophy with them to the Caribbean, and if they did, what aspects had survived (McKenzie 2013: 13). It is only logical that Africans would have brought their philosophy to the Caribbean, although some critics have labelled these as simply myths and proverbs. Some of these philosophical ideologies were mentally ingrained in their existence and remained with them despite circumstances of material exploitation and intellectual oppression. Aspects of philosophy and philosophical thinking therefore survived, manifesting new approaches to reality both in the minds and creative geniuses of Africans taken to the Caribbean. The outcome has been exhibited in the numerous thoughts and practices of phenomenal Caribbean thinkers such as Garvey, Rodney, Fanon, CLR James, Bob Marley, and many others.

Afro-Caribbean ontology and epistemology survived the Middle Passage and the centuries of Plantation dehumanization. It has also triumphed in formulating an authentic Afro-Caribbean philosophy in the post-colonial period. When McKenzie speaks of philosophical thinking, he seems to be referring to cognitive and theoretical knowledge to which he was introduced in the Western academy. However, these are not the only kinds of knowledge that are meaningful as he ambivalently speaks of retention. This only adds credence to the fact that Afro-Caribbeans had an epistemology to retain in the first place.

As Henry (1997) rightly states:

> Although grounded in the African experience, relocation in the Caribbean disrupted the discursively mediated equilibria that Africans had established between human agency and the imperatives of outer nature, inner nature, and

social life. Consequently, Afro-Caribbean people were forced to establish new balances in relations with these three planes.

11

This new social life and outer nature were independent and separate from what Afro-Caribbean people knew. They now found themselves in new existential positions which challenged them to recreate a philosophy that now suited this new condition. They, however, had their inner nature; they brought epistemes with them to the Caribbean which transmit easily into geographical and cultural borders' new formulations of coping and survival.

Thus, I agree with Henry (1997) that:

> Because of its independence on geography, inner nature was not experienced differently as a direct result of physical relocation. On the contrary, Africans brought their religious constructions of inner nature with them to the Caribbean. Consequently, there was little or no spiritual pressure to change the inner aspects of the new (Caribbean) mode of being-in-the-world or its African coding.

17

Afro-Caribbean people now found themselves in a unique position, but since they possessed the cognitive and practical capabilities needed to develop a philosophy based on this new position, they continued to triumph. Therefore, Afro-Caribbean philosophy is only distinguished from other kinds of philosophy based on cognitive exploration that considers socio-cultural relevance, geography, and the experiences of Afro-Caribbean people. This does not mean that some ideologies that exist in Afro-Caribbean philosophy are not found in any other kinds of philosophy existing in the world and vice versa.

I agree with Bewaji, Gordon, and others, who maintain that an autonomous Caribbean philosophy exists and is evident in various cultural elements. Thus, persons who profess that they know of Afro-Caribbean music, religions, politics, identity, etc. must also confess that an Afro-Caribbean philosophy exists; to do otherwise would equate to a categorical mistake as music, religion, politics, identity, and so on work separately and collectively to form the key manifestations of an Afro-Caribbean philosophy. Afro-Caribbean philosophy covers all areas including, but not limited to, metaphysics, ethics, applied ethics, logic, epistemology, and aesthetics. Afro-Caribbean philosophy is used here to mean an intellectual and practical discourse that reflects the views, beliefs, ideologies, and moral values of a people whose ancestry and realities combine aspects of African and Caribbean identities and ideals. "It involves philosophy about the region as well as the unique problems faced by people within the region" (Gordon 2007: 145–175).

There are some sceptics who maintain that an Afro-Caribbean philosophy does not exist, on the assumption that Afro-Caribbeans are not intelligent enough to produce a philosophy that is unique to themselves and their region

(Masolo 1994: 1). Some also hold the opinion that Afro-Caribbean philosophy and ontology are cognitively dependent upon European traditions and knowledge and are therefore not autonomous (Henry 2000: 2). This makes the task at hand a mammoth one, but I proceed from the premise that there is an Afro-Caribbean philosophy, as human beings across cultures and geographical locations have been producing philosophies from the beginnings of social engagements that often generate the need for critical reflections. In this regard, individuals across cultures have explored and asked questions such as: What is the nature of the physical world and the objects we find in it? Who am I? Why should I live a good (moral) life? What kinds of things exist? How can we respond to doubt about what we know? How one responds to these questions will depend on the ontologies of being and existence one espouses.

For emphasis, ontologies of being and existence are derivable from ideas, and propositions that are ingrained in proverbs, linguistic expressions, myths and folktales, religious beliefs and rituals, customs and traditions art symbols, and the socio-political institutions of people: to be sure, these are found in the theoretical and practical aspects of the cultures of peoples everywhere in the world (Gyekye 1987: ix). It is in this vein that it can be supposed that philosophical utterances and ideologies come in various forms.

In the context of the ontology of being of Afro-Caribbean philosophy, I argue that although it is ineffectual to have a dialogue about Afro-Caribbean ontology by dismissing African and Caribbean history and traditions, Afro-Caribbean philosophy is not solely dependent on these histories and traditions. This is because the understandings of ontology, being, and existence are not static, but dynamic. Indeed, there is no single narrative of the ontology component with regard to peoples' worldview about the nature and composition of reality. Notwithstanding, ontology may be defined as "the science of things existing, or things existing permanently" (Ramsay 1870: 1). In other words, ontology is the study of being or beings. It is concerned with the kinds of beings that exist and the nature of existence. Afro-Caribbean ontology, as used here, refers to what exists in terms of the Afro-Caribbean reality.

Since ontological discussions are dependent not only on the history of Afro-Caribbean people, given its linkages with the traditions of other struggles for existential space in Africa, the discussion here will also reflect the development of Afro-Caribbean ontology and epistemology within the wider African postcolonial era. This becomes relevant since Afro-Caribbean philosophy has aligned itself with the current situation in the region and beyond. That is, Afro-Caribbean people exist in an environment where their ontology of being is shaped by the freedom to think and explore the world, with a focus on issues that truly reflect who they are and not the ideologies of their colonizers. Post-colonial thinking and consciousness become more advanced and developed as Afro-Caribbean people seek to champion socio-economic, political, and cultural development leading to an ontology and epistemology that capture who they are as autonomous and intelligent beings. This autonomy is reflected in how Afro-Caribbean people created their own ontologies and epistemologies to include clear philosophical ideologies dealing with ethics, religion, aesthetics, metaphysics, logic, and epistemology.

As dominated human beings seek to find their places in the world, there will always be a struggle for ontological space. However, Afro-Caribbeans have held on to various ontologies of life that appraise their existence as they understand themselves, the world, and their place in the world. An ontology of life is formed by using social, psychological, and other elements and entities to shape one's sense of being, becoming, and belonging in the world. These ontologies are found in, but not limited to, economic, social and political affiliations, religion, and music.

There are various interesting ways to discuss the ontology of life within the Caribbean context. Headley's view of rum as an ontology of life within this context is an example. He states that "rum serves as a metaphorical basis for negotiating or transcending internal differences of political, social and cultural power" (Headley 2009: 241). I accept his view and explore the ontology of life that hinges on religion since an important part of the Afro-Caribbean culture is revealed in the variety of religious traditions that prevail.

Afro-Caribbean philosophy is unique, but this stems from the history of the Afro-Caribbean people, which was fraught with pain and much suffering as well as a struggle with identity. As Chamberlin (1993) writes:

> Blacks in the West Indies are not the only people with a history of oppression. But theirs is a special history, bringing with it a grim inheritance of someone else's images of difference and disdain, images that for five hundred years have conditioned their special and sometimes desperate need to determine for themselves who they are and where they belong.
>
> 28

Chamberlin's major contention rests with the African ontology and self-image, which slavery and its' many evils sought to destroy, through an epistemology of inferiority, insecurity, and ontological insufficiency. Does this grim image of self, this ontology of deficit, this imaginary inferiority hinder the development of wholesome Afro-Caribbean epistemology? The answer to this question is no. Even though Afro-Caribbean epistemology is a philosophy born of struggle, an ontology of resistance and an epistemology of otherness, the Afro-Caribbeans have managed to generate a powerful self-concept. As Afro-Caribbeans, they have learnt much from this twin evil of plantation slavery and colonial domination. They have learnt to use survival ethics at its best and have been using their rational faculties as well as their historical, social, and cultural legacies and experiences to shape an epistemology that depicts who they are, and what they know, individually and collectively. Afro-Caribbeans have built a philosophy that is unique and relevant to them.

So Afro-Caribbean philosophy depends on innate creativity for its instantiation. Enslaved Africans brought their religions with them to the Caribbean and many of these religions survived in pure forms, while others were creatively fashioned into various Christian beliefs. For example, Santeria is an Afro-Caribbean religion based on Yoruba beliefs and traditions with the addition of some Roman Catholic elements (Bascom 1951: 490–505). Revivalism and Spiritual Baptists are also forms of syncretism of the Christian faith and African spiritual beliefs. Others are stand-alone beliefs and continue to reflect the power of deities and ancestors. For example, Kumina, which can be traced back to ethnic groups in the Congo in Africa, managed to stand the test of time and survived any external influence (Bascom 1951: 491). Religious and spiritual existence is important to Afro-Caribbeans, as they hold a deep respect for the power of a Supreme Being, whether that being is referred to as God, Olodumare, Nyame, or Selassie. "This complex of Afro-Christian attitudes toward existence was radically historicised by the experiences of slavery and colonial domination" (Gordon 1997: 14). Enslaved Africans in the Caribbean relied on spiritual songs as they sought to navigate their new and strange reality. Some used religions as a coping mechanism. A belief in an afterlife, for example gave them hope of a new life free from oppression when their spirits would probably return to Africa where there would be no oppression and inhumanity. With this belief, Afro-Caribbean people have a sense of existence and belonging as well as a sense of freedom that can only be attained spiritually. This reassurance has made their belief in religion worthwhile and meaningful.

Today, this religious ontology of being, or ontology of life, continues to steer Afro-Caribbean philosophy and epistemology. Within Rastafarianism, for example one can find aspects of Afro-Caribbean ontology and epistemology that is akin to post-colonialism, since Rastafarianism is a relatively new movement (Price 2009: ix). As Price documented, "… adherents to this new worldview called themselves 'Rastafari'" (2009: x). Others would soon call them "Ras Tafarites," and later, "Rastafarians" (Price 2009: x). Scarred with the legacy of slavery and oppression, some persons within the Caribbean Island of Jamaica, where this religion started, readily welcomed "the Black King" in the form of Haile Selassie I, former Emperor of Ethiopia, whom they believed was sent to redeem the world. There are various branches of Rastafarianism. "Some believed Selassie was God. Some believed him a messiah, an incarnation of the Christ energy. Others saw him as a powerful leader whose words were divinely inspired" (Davis and Lee 2012: x). Rastafarians view Ethiopia as the promised land where blacks will be repatriated through an exodus from countries where they have been exiled or enslaved.

There are also some Afro-Caribbean people who seek to equate philosophy to Rastafarianism. On a recent visit to my dermatologist in Jamaica, she asked about my profession. I told her that I was studying philosophy, and her response was, "Oh, that Rasta thing." At first, I tried to fathom exactly what she meant, but her response adds credence to my point that for any philosophy to be worthwhile, it should incorporate the experiences and culture of the people. Rastafarian ontology of being should not be overlooked as Afro-Caribbean epistemology develops since aspects of this religion inform philosophy. Some of these philosophical underpinnings include aspects of freedom, consciousness, and morality. The concept of the "I and I" in Rastafarianism, for example reflects a sense of equality for all people; it depicts a group reality and oneness (Forsythe 1980: 62–81). Under this umbrella, what is known is that each person is equal. However, each person is independent but are mindful of their responsibility to each other.

So, from Rastafarianism, Afro-Caribbean people have garnered key ethical/character traits on how to treat self and others. From this altruistic framework, Afro-Caribbeans know the importance of valuing and respecting each other which amounts to living a good life. This is manifested in the communitarian approach, where the community is involved in the well-being of all others, and children are raised and cared for not only by family members but by community members as well. This approach has no place for the Cartesian ego since self is often sacrificed, the result of which is survival for all. It is from this ontology of existence, in the form of religion, music, the arts, and so on, that Afro-Caribbean epistemologies are formed.

Afro-Caribbean Epistemology as Socio-Cultural

As one seeks to grapple with the Afro-Caribbean reality, the words of Bob Marley and the Wailers (1973) song "Get up, stand up, stand up for your rights" holds significant relevance. This is so, since the discussions concerning the development of an Afro-Caribbean epistemology (and philosophy) continues to be fraught with scepticism from those who refuse to acknowledge that all races and ethnicities work together as well as separately to build nations. Also, as human beings stand for their rights, they concretize their autonomies. Despite this level of scepticism, it is evident that an Afro-Caribbean epistemology exists and continues to develop as societies evolve. In this section, I will show that the reality of slavery does not limit philosophical and epistemological production, but only seeks to enhance it. As Garvey (2019) rightly states, "A people without the knowledge of their past history, origin and culture, is like a tree without roots". As societies evolve, philosophy has seen a growth in knowledge development, and Afro-Caribbean philosophers are major contributors to this development. Here, I argue for Afro-Caribbean epistemology being a socio-cultural construct.

Epistemology is "a philosophical inquiry into the nature, condition, and extent of human knowledge" (Sosa and Kim 2000: ix). This knowledge involves different forms including memory, perception, other minds, induction, testimony among others. A human being evolves overtime, and although these changes account for the ontological components of an individual, they also have a significant connection to epistemology, since ontology is the start-point for knowledge creation. Individuals need to then know themselves before they can know the world; both kinds of knowledge help shape a collective epistemology.

It is often argued that sometimes in our attempt to acquire knowledge, we settle for a basic belief, which some argue is not synonymous to knowledge claims. Knowledge would then be classified as something that is justified, while a belief is just a hunch. Shope (2022) has argued that knowledge can only be found in the realm of science since in science, things are empirically tested and verified (25–70). This view is flawed, however, as there are several claims of scientific knowledge that were subjected to change or revision although they were at one point verified. In reducing everything that is worthy of acceptance to science, which the agenda of logical positivism, in its effort to discredit metaphysics, sets out to do, the other disciplines such as mathematics and logic would not be given the full respect that they deserve.

Bewaji is one Afro-Caribbean philosopher who has championed the development of Afro-Caribbean epistemology. In his writings, he shows that human beings across the world have always acquired and developed knowledge and that none of these forms or types of knowledge is more important than the other. As Bewaji (2007) states,

> ... in an increasingly competitive world, there can be no separation of knowledge from the wellspring of human realities ... namely life, death, pain, hunger, wealth, failure, and so on. Everything, including the process of becoming and extinction, depends on the presence or absence of knowledge.
>
> 14

It is a fact that human beings have existed for a number of years, having to fend for themselves in a world that they slowly come to understand and know. Philosophical thinking has then existed on all continents for as long as human beings have occupied them. Overtime, with the advancement of technology and globalization, knowledge of ourselves and the world has become more advanced, but this does not mean that the knowledge acquired now is more important and valuable than the knowledge acquired then. Knowledge can also be acquired without the knower being able to communicate that knowledge. By reasoning otherwise, one would be placing a limit on what one can know as there will be several times when individuals experience things that are 'real' knowledge claims, but that which they cannot communicate to someone else. Is knowledge something over and above experiences? Probably not, since knowledge is experience.

All human beings are suited to know as knowledge is internally as well as externally constructed. Given that epistemology is multifaceted, the archaic way of viewing epistemology/knowledge as only propositional and universal does not work, especially since we operate in open societies. It is for this reason that I view Afro-Caribbean epistemology as socio-cultural. Its socio-cultural nature is revealed where concepts such as truth, knowledge, and rationality can be interpreted using Afro-Caribbean social and cultural experiences. Even within this framework, some individuals will know differently from others based on subjective analysis and interpretations. In other words, an item of knowledge might not be true for all people and all societies as the issues, experiences, and problems that inform the knowledge will not be the same for everyone. These socio-cultural experiences exist in, but are not limited to, forms of religion, politics, ethics, consciousness, identity, and morality. Within this socio-cultural approach, issues surrounding spirituality, morality, consciousness, identity, and politics all play significant roles in epistemological development. In this socio-cultural milieu, there are forms of knowledge that are objectively and collectively agreed on, while there are others that are subjective and more akin to individual assessment and experience. These forms of knowledge will also not all be cognitive and theoretical as knowledge does not occur in a mental vacuum; it is also physical and practical.

Also, knowledge is more meaningful when placed in context, and this sociocultural approach allows for that. Since culture provides a blueprint which creates a model of self, the Afro-Caribbean has a cognitive and practical epistemological framework that, though born out of struggles, is not dependent on the oppressors' teachings. Henry alluded to the view that the distinguishing features of Afro-Caribbean philosophy do not lend themselves to this branch of philosophy being an autonomous discipline (Henry 2000: 1). This, however, is not the case, as evidence of an autonomous Afro-Caribbean philosophy is readily evident in the religious, social, cultural, ethical, and aesthetical realms, each of which can stand on its own. Philosophical reflections are therefore manifested in all these areas of Afro-Caribbean life. The question surrounding who can know and produce philosophy is then answered by saying that all human beings can know and philosophize irrespective of race, culture, and geographical location. However, as is indicated below, this response is often met with scepticism. According to Gordon (2008):

> The notion that philosophy was a peculiarly European affair logically led to the conclusion that there was (and continues to be) something about European cultures that makes them more conducive to philosophical reflection than others. But the problem that immediately emerges is one of accounting for and supporting such a claim when the people we call Europeans were (and continue to be) constantly changing, just as the global concept of the African emerged in the modern world, so too did the notion of the European.
>
> 6

Gordon's point is ontological as well as existential as it questions 'being' as well as being in the world. The illogical notion that European cultures are more conducive to philosophical thinking connotes an existential threat to all human beings outside the European culture since a culture that is not thought of as being able to philosophize is a non-existent one. All human beings can philosophize. The world is constantly changing and human beings, whether European, African, or Asian, change and evolve, as new knowledge is developed, acknowledged, and utilized.

Some academics hold the view that propositional knowledge (knowledge that) is the chief kind of knowledge, one that is subject to justification, verification, and proof, but, as Bewaji (2007) states, "to render something true or false does not affect claims to knowledge" (42). There is then no necessary connection between knowing and truth. For example, if through experience, I claim to know something that turns out to be true, the fact that it is true is not dependent on my knowledge of it. I can also know something to be true today and it changes tomorrow. This does not mean that I did not have knowledge of it yesterday. Similarly, when Afro-Caribbeans claim to know, this means that the knowledge is present to consciousness;

that is, they have an awareness, belief, or opinion that does not require justification. As Sartwell (1991) rightly states, if an agent has both a solid understanding of the belief and a genuine belief that it is true (which he claims entails "some degree of serious commitment to the claim"), then it should be counted as an instance of knowledge (157). If this commitment to the claim is evident, justification is not needed to declare knowledge. However, the agent has some degree of certainty (this occurs at various degrees) based on the nature of the claim.

To say that human beings can know only propositionally is to say that most forms of knowledge are not knowable since most cases of knowledge do not warrant a propositional analysis or justification. Propositional knowledge is too abstract and does not give credit to the knower. Since knowledge is socio-cultural, if one conforms to propositional knowledge, he/she stifles his/her autonomy. Knowledge is both theoretical and practical, and although there are different types of knowledge, none takes precedence over the other. That is, the different types are diminished neither in worth nor in hierarchy.

The socio-cultural epistemology that is advanced here accounts for both objective and subjective forms of knowledge, since it entails the knower or the agent, as well as what is known socially, culturally, and otherwise. As Bewaji (2007) states, "A careful assessment of knowledge is necessary based on the multi-dimensional nature of knowledge which is both objective and subjective" (42). Most traditional Western explanations of knowledge seem to primarily pay homage to objective rather than subjective knowledge. This strict emphasis on the objective component may be a weakness of the position of these traditional philosophers as both the objective and subjective components must work together to make valid knowledge claims, which will assist in underwriting patterns of behaviour and action. The major scepticism about the possibility of an Afro-Caribbean philosophy, for example stems from the lack of acknowledgement of both objective and subjective aspects of knowledge claims, especially, since some scholars believe that the Afro-Caribbean subject cannot function autonomously and is not suited to know.

Afro-Caribbean Epistemology as Perspectival

A perspectival form of Afro-Caribbean epistemology is offered in this section, and it is argued that since Afro-Caribbean people include a diverse group in terms of nationalities, cultural differences, and so on, only a perspectival form of epistemology can capture the totality of what encompasses such an Afro-Caribbean epistemology or gnosis. Perspectival knowledge is cognitively logical and is based on relevance of ideas and the epistemic needs of the people who occupy a specific time and space. This relevance is associated with the beliefs and value systems of these individuals. This perspectival analysis, although similar for some individuals and cultures, might differ in some respects if analysed through the lenses of someone from another cultural background or social setting, since socio-cultural beliefs and norms are value-laden.

Given that knowledge depends on a knower (the subject or individual), to overlook this component would not give an accurate representation of knowledge. Perspectivism is the view that ideas that are perceived are done from particular perspectives (Tuttle 2005: 97). This means that there are many possible conceptual schemes or perspectives from which judgements of truth or value can be made from a subjective or an objective perspective. This is often taken to mean that no way of seeing the world can be taken as definitively true or intrinsically superior a priori; this does not however mean that all perspectives are equally valid. But who determines the correctness and incorrectness of a perspective? Though this question remains a debate, it is defensible to say that a group or an individual cannot impose conditions of correctness and incorrectness on the rest of the world. Also, a perspective should not be considered wrong simply because some humans disagree on its tenets. Human beings experience the world selectively, based on traditions, values, and needs.

According to Nietzsche (1968), "insofar as the word 'knowledge' has any meaning, the world is knowable; but it is interpretable otherwise, it has no meaning behind it, but countless meanings – Perspectivism" (108). This means that what exists is perspectival knowledge that is derived from everyone's will; thus, it is countless. In other words, the world is knowable, but this knowledge is based on how each individual and culture interprets the world. Knowledge would then be subjective. In this interpretation, perspectivism is a will to power or a will to make known. I view perspectivism, first, as subjective knowledge that questions facts that are generated through personal experiences and, second, as objective knowledge which entails a responsibility that the knower bears to the self to attain the highest kind of knowledge possible.

Nietzsche (1968) connected perspectivism to desires by arguing that

> it is our needs that interpret the world; our drives and their For and Against (emphasis added). Every drive is a kind of lust to rule; each one has its perspective that it would like to compel all the other drives to accept as a norm.
> *481*

Nietzsche can be interpreted to mean that individuals rely on their needs and desires to guide them to a basic understanding of what exists. Individuals have different needs; so it follows that each will interpret the world from his/her perspective. This seems to indicate that it is not possible to hold beliefs about the world that are objective and devoid of value.

Nietzsche also asserts that our needs inform our interpretations of the world. My point of departure from Nietzsche's view is that knowledge should not be linked so much to desires, but rather to the quest to find what is true from a socio-cultural perspective irrespective of desires. An epistemology for any group would then be: first, an interrogation of already established socio-cultural facts in a quest to develop same and, second, using current situations to advance knowledge claims.

Whether the knowledge is objective or subjective, one cannot overlook the knower, as knowledge in any form requires a subject. The world and its contents are knowable from any perspective. Therefore, based on the nature of epistemology, it is unguided to impose one that is already established on a group. This is so as that imposed epistemology would be foreign to the knower. An imposed epistemology is 'unreal' as it embraces the ideologies of the imposers and not those of the knower. Since Afro-Caribbean epistemology is likened to the ontology of Afro-Caribbeans, epistemology within this framework can be said to be perspectival; it hinges on the history, tradition, culture, perspectives, and lived experiences of the people. This perspectival knowledge is however not always individual but includes a collective dimension. If various forms of knowledge are socio-cultural, as is espoused here, then such forms of knowledge are perspectival since they reflect a group reality or a collection of perspectives.

Gordon (2006) makes reference to a struggle for ontological space between blacks and whites, and he alludes to the fact that this struggle hinges on a normative enquiry between both groups (3–50). I agree with Gordon and argue for an Afro-Caribbean epistemology based on the premise that irrespective of the past, Afro-Caribbean people are free beings with the capacity to discern and think independently of others. They have been engaged in this for years with the aim of survival in a world to which they were imported. This survival mechanism indicates an epistemological framework developed through self-awareness as well as socio-cultural encounters; making it perspectival. This does not mean that there is no knowledge and understanding of the world in general, but an epistemology that reflects a culture and social experience truly reflects the people who create that epistemology. For example, Indian or Greek epistemologies are not the same as an Afro-Caribbean epistemology, as Indians and Greeks know from their unique socio-cultural perspectives. There will be similarities, but the differences can be remarkable.

Afro-Caribbeans are rational subjects whose consciousness qualifies as an authority of knowledge, both individually and collectively. Since Afro-Caribbeans have contributed significantly to knowledge development in all professions and disciplines, scepticisms surrounding the existence of an Afro-Caribbean epistemology are not warranted. For example, the contribution of Afro-Caribbeans to the field of medicine is phenomenal, starting with the African folk doctors who took knowledge of the use of herbal medicine with them to the Caribbean. It has been documented that some plantation owners relied on the medical knowledge of Africans who were able to administer medical care to them during times of illness.

According to Bailey (2002), for example "enslaved African folk doctors were often sought after for their medical knowledge, which in most cases was based on traditional forms of healing and preventing sickness" (52). Among the Africans, there was also the "black conjure doctor" who provided alternative medicine. In his view, "… the black conjure doctors were African healers who used 'magic' plants, spells and suggestions to heal. These doctors were far ahead of Europeans in their appreciation of the power of the mind over the body" (Bailey 2002: 52). These African healers were powerful within the enslaved communities because of the knowledge they possessed. Some critics referred to this kind of healing as 'obeah' and 'witchcraft' since they did not understand the healing power of herbs.

Furthermore, Afro-Caribbeans have expanded knowledge of the use of herbs, such as nutmeg, dandelion, rice weed, marijuana, wild cherry, fever grass, etc., to cure illnesses such as cold and fever, diabetes, joint pain, measles, and headache. This kind of knowledge is perspectival as it is generated by Africans and Afro-Caribbeans and its use has been passed down from one generation to the next. The value of this knowledge is understood from the perspective of those who generate and create that knowledge. Scepticism regarding the use of herbs as a cure for illnesses is now on the decline as alternative medicine has spiralled into a major industry and serves as a source of medical treatment for millions of people across the world.

Conclusion

The views presented here should not be interpreted to mean that Afro-Caribbean ontology and epistemology are radically different in all respects from other kinds of epistemology. The key point is that ontologies and epistemologies will differ in nature and kind, but all are the same in terms of purpose and relevance to the people who use and engage and encounter themselves in these ontologies and epistemologies. No human existence has an epistemology or ontology that is conclusive; each develops as knowledge evolves, so each group and society must always be in a state of readiness to revaluate their ontology of life and existence as well as their capacity to know. This is such that each racial and ethnic group, society, and culture should take the initiative and re-examine its place in the world. Denying Afro-Caribbean epistemology would be synonymous to denying Afro-Caribbean ontology, phenomenology, and existence, especially since epistemology is perspectival in nature.

Since Afro-Caribbean people exist, there is an Afro-Caribbean epistemology as all conscious beings have the capacity to know and develop an epistemology. Therefore, since there is an Afro- Caribbean ontology, there is an Afro-Caribbean epistemology. The Afro-Caribbean struggles are real, factual, and true as is Afro-Caribbean epistemology. So although degrees of certainty will vary, what Afro-Caribbeans can know for certain is embedded in the physical and spiritual world as well as in areas that transcend the disciplines of philosophy, science, mathematics, religion, and economics. Knowers employ both an individualistic and collectivist framework to attain their epistemological aims. Degree of certainty will depend on the knower or the agent as well as the source of the claim. However, the level of certainty does not diminish a knowledge claim.

Note

1 Friedrich Ochieng'-Odhiambo (2010), *Trends and Issues in African Philosophy* (New York: Peter Lang Publishing), pp. 8–9. See also, the writings of L. Levy-Bruhl (1923), *Primitive Mentality*, E.E. Evans-Pritchard (1980), *Theories of Religion*, Diederich Westermann (1969), *The African To-day and To-morrow*.

Bibliography

Bailey, E. J. 2002. *African American Alternative Medicine: Using Alternative Medicine to Prevent and Control Chronic Diseases*. Connecticut: Greenwood Publishing Group.
Bascom, W. R. 1951. "The Yoruba in Cuba." *American Anthropologist*, vol. 53, no. 4: 490–505.
Bewaji, J. A. I. (2007). *An Introduction to the Theory of Knowledge: A Pluralistic Approach*. Ibadan: Hope Publications.
Brown, H. I. (1988). *Rationalism*. New York: Routledge.
Brown, L. (2004). *African Philosophy: New and Traditional Perspectives*. New York: Oxford University Press.
Chamberlin, E. (1993). *Come Back to Me My Language: Poetry and the West Indies*. Chicago: University of Illinois Press.
Davis, S. and Lee, H. (2012). *The First Rasta: Leonard Howell and the Rise of Rastafarianism*. Chicago: Chicago Review Press.
Forsythe, D. (1980). "West Indian Culture through the Prism of Rastafarianism." *Caribbean Quarterly*, vol. 26, no. 4: 62–81.
Garvey, M. (2019). "Marcus Garvey quotes." www.buyblackmovement.com/MarcusGarvey/Quotes/Index.cfm> Accessed 4/8/2019.
Gordon, L. R. (1997). *Existence in Black: An Anthology of Black Existential Philosophy*. New York: Routledge.
———. (2006). "African-American Philosophy, Race, and the Geography of Reason." In *Not only the Master's Tools: African-American Studies in Theory and Practice*, Lewis Gordon and Jane Anna Gordon (ed.). Boulder: Paradigm, pp. 3–50.
———. (2007). "What is Afro-Caribbean Philosophy?" In *Philosophy in Multiple Voices*, George Yancy (ed.). Maryland: Rowman & Littlefield, pp. 145–175.
———. (2008). *An Introduction to Africana Philosophy*. Cambridge: Cambridge University Press.
Gyekye, K. (1987). *An Essay on African Philosophical Thought: The Akan conceptual scheme*. New York: Cambridge University Press.
Hales, S. D. and Rex, W. (2000). *Nietzsche's Perspectivism*. Champaign: University of Illinois Press.
Headley, C. (2009). "A Study in Comparative Ontologies: Root Metaphors and Existence." In *Conversations in Philosophy: Crossing the Boundaries*, F. Ochieng'-Odhiambo, R. Burton and Ed Brandon (eds.). Newcastle: Cambridge Scholars Publishing, pp. 241–250.
Henry, P. (1997). "African and Afro-Caribbean Existential Philosophies." In *Existence in Black: An Anthology of Black Existential Philosophy*, L. Gordon (ed.). New York: Psychology Press, pp. 11–36.
———. (2000). *Caliban's Reason Introducing Afro-Caribbean Philosophy*. New York: Routledge.
Honeychurch, L. (1995). *The Caribbean People- Book 1*. Surrey: Nelson Caribbean.
Marley B. and The Wailers. (1973). "Get up Stand up." CD ROM, Album: Burnin.
Masolo, D. A. (1994). *African Philosophy in Search of Identity*. Bloomington: Indiana University Press.
McKenzie, St. Hope E. (2013). *The Loneliness of a Caribbean Philosopher and Other Essays*. Kingston: Arawak Publications.
Nietzsche, F. (1968). *The Will to Power*. Walter Kaufmann and R. J. (eds. and trans.). Hollingdale. New York: Vintage Books.
Ochieng'-Odhiambo, F. (2010). *Trends and Issues in African philosophy*. New York: Peter Lang.
Price, C. (2009). *Becoming Rasta: Origins of Rastafari Identity in Jamaica*. New York: New York University Press.
Ramsay, G. (1870). *Ontology, Or, Things Existing*. London: Walton.
Sartwell, C. (1991). "Knowledge is merely true belief". American Philosophical Quarterly, vol. 28, no. 2: 157–165.

Shope, R. K. (2002). "Conditions and Analysis of Knowing." In *The Oxford Handbook of Epistemology*, Paul K. Moser (ed.). New York: Oxford University Press, pp. 25–70.

Sosa E. and Jaegwon Kim. (2000). *Epistemology an Anthology*. Malden: Blackwell.

Tuttle, H. N. (2005). *Human Life is Radical Reality: An Idea Developed from the Conceptions of Dilthey, Heidegger, and Ortega y Gasset*. New York: Peter Lang.

9

ELẸ̀ẸRÍ AS OMỌLÚÀBÍ

The Interface of Epistemic Justification and Virtue Ethics in an African Culture

Abosede Priscilla Ipadeola

Introduction

Ever since justification became popular as a proviso for defining knowledge, there have been series of attacks on it as an epistemic condition. An aspect of the onslaught is Gettier's attack on the three conditions – justification, belief, and truth (the JTB account of knowledge) as sufficient conditions for a knowledge claim. The other aspect has revolved around how to define justification. On the note of defining or determining justification, there have been analyses of the different theories of justification and different types of justification. Therefore, volumes have been written in Western epistemology on the nature of justification, especially on the question of defining justification. For example, a view of justification known as foundationalism, which dates to Descartes, holds that to justify a claim about knowledge, the justifier must either be a basic belief or grounded on a basic belief. This conception of justification is riddled with many contradictions, chief among is that the theory itself cannot pass for a knowledge claim because it is neither a fundamental belief nor founded on a foundational belief.

To remedy the flaw of foundationalism, coherence theory of justification defines justification in terms of consistency between beliefs. According to this view, a belief is justified, or a subject possesses a justified belief only if the belief is consistent with other beliefs within the system. Like the foundationalist theory that coherentism criticizes, it has also been variously criticized. A significant objection to the coherentist theory of justification is that it is circular. In other words, if we are to establish justification of belief A by ascertaining coherence between A and the other beliefs within the system, say B, C, D, E, and F, which all, in turn, depend on each other and A for validation, then it follows that belief A ultimately 'relies' on itself for justification. There is no justification evident or implied within the coherentist theory for this circularity of the justification process. This is the most debilitating

DOI: 10.4324/9781003182320-13

flaw of the coherentist theory of justification. Apart from foundationalism and coherentism, which seems to examine the nature of justification in terms of its structure, there are various other conceptions of justification, which may be understood to bother on the requirement of justification. These include internalism, externalism, reliabilism, and evidentism. Internalism contends that justification of a belief relies on the internal knowledge of the knower, externalism argues that external sources of knowledge justify a belief, reliabilism stresses the importance of justifying beliefs through reliable means, while evidentism emphasizes the importance of evidence to justification.

Justification came into prominence as a condition for knowledge claims when Theaetetus defined knowledge as true account and logos, which has come to be popularly known as 'justified true belief'. This definition also called the traditional definition of knowledge has been widely discussed over decades by generations of epistemologists in different parts of the globe. This definition was somewhat taken as infallible until Gettier wrote his famous essay, "Is Justified True Belief Knowledge?" Since Gettier published his seminal essay in 1963, the enterprise of epistemology has not remained the same. To Gettier, belief, truth, and justification are not sufficient conditions for a knowledge claim. The implication of this is that Gettier's diatribe eroded the substratum of traditional epistemology, leaving different epistemologists to argue in different directions about the consequences of his critique of the JTB account of knowledge. However, despite the various solutions suggested to salvage epistemology, contemporary epistemologists find themselves going back to analyze and review the three traditional conditions of knowledge. In a sense, epistemologists are fixated on the three conditions because it has been difficult to completely jettison them or to generate more viable alternatives.

This chapter, though written decades after Gettier's onslaught, goes back to examine one of the conditions of knowledge – justification – with reference to an African culture. The chapter argues that testimony is fundamental to the justification of a knowledge claim, and that character underlies a knower's qualification to bear testimony.

The Nature of *Ìmọ̀* (Knowledge) in Yorùbá *Weltanschauung* (*Ìwòye*/Worldview)

African philosophy emerged from the milieu of a mélange of controversy, skepticism, resistance, and defense, among others. The birth of African philosophy was surrounded by the aura of an intellectual battle between Afrocentrism and Afro-skepticism. While Afro-skeptics doubted the capability of Africans to engage in independent, critical, and rigorous conceptualization that could pass as philosophy, Afrocentric scholars challenged the skeptics of African philosophy and described their position as a token of racism, oppression, and Eurocentric hegemony. However, in the attempt to affirm the existence and relevance of African philosophy, certain dominant questions came to the fore. Hence, the acceptability or otherwise of the discourse of African philosophy grossly depends on how well the questions are addressed. Prominent among the questions are two main ones, which are: (a) what is African philosophy? (b) If African philosophy exists, what is its nature and/or content? These two questions have largely shaped the practice of African philosophy and African epistemology, which is a subdiscipline of African philosophy, cannot afford to disregard the questions. In order for African epistemology to be considered relevant and extant, it must equally answer questions about the existence, nature, and content of African philosophy. This is because,

> The question whether or not there is an African epistemology cannot be addressed without taking due cognisance of the answer to the question whether or not an African philosophy exists. A negative answer to the latter would imply a negative answer to the former. Similarly, to assert the existence of an African philosophy is also to imply the existence of an African epistemology, to the extent that an African epistemology is a subset of African philosophy.
>
> *Kaphagawani and Malherbe 1998, 25*

Afrocentrists and other African scholars who contend in defense of African epistemology are aware of the importance of clearly articulating the basic epistemological concepts from the African perspective if it would be tenable that there is indeed a variant of epistemology that is African. Hence, there have been different analyses and interpretations of important epistemological constructs like knowledge, truth, justification, and belief within the purview of different African cultures over the years.

Hallen and Sodipo did a beautiful analysis of ìmọ̀ (knowledge) among the Yorùbá in their renowned work *Knowledge, Belief and Witchcraft: Analytic Experiment in African Philosophy*. They explained, for instance, that ìmọ̀ is acquired directly from firsthand experience, while ìgbàgbọ́ is gotten from a report or secondhand information. In other words, knowledge among the Yorùbá, according to Hallen and Sodipo, presupposes that the subject knows the object of knowledge 'by acquaintance.' Any belief that one does not experience directly cannot be called knowledge, but merely remains a belief (ìgbàgbọ́). It is, therefore, imperative to note that what justifies a knowledge claim, for Hallen and Sodipo, is experience or acquaintance. Any other means is only capable of giving a belief rather than a form of knowledge.

However, the dichotomy between ìmọ̀ (knowledge) and ìgbàgbọ́ (belief) is not as sacrosanct as Hallen and Sodipo made it seem. This is because the distinction between ìmọ̀ (knowledge) and ìgbàgbọ́ (belief), according to them, is experience or acquaintance. Nevertheless, the Yorùbá do not always insist on experiencing a phenomenon before they claim to know it. Hence, the popular saying *afọgbọ́n ọlọ́gbọ́n sọgbọ́n ló gbọ́n* (They are wise who take wisdom from other people's experience). The Yorùbá also say *ọgbọ́n ọlọ́gbọ́n ni kìí jẹ́ ká pe àgbà ní wèrè* (learning from other people or acquiring wisdom (or knowledge) from them makes us acknowledge the wisdom of the elders). Therefore, a vital source of knowledge among the Yorùbá from pristine era is oral communication. The Yorùbá used the oral culture, symbols, and pictorial carvings to preserve their indigenous knowledge for centuries before the advent of documentation. As such, if only experience validates knowledge, then the idea of indigenous knowledge is a mirage.

The Yorùbá hold that the ancestors are very important members of the community. The living elders refer to their ancestors as the elderly ones who oversee the affairs of the community. There is a sense of continuity held by each community between the living and the dead. Hamminga gives an apt illustration of the conception of continuity of knowledge among an African people. In his words,

> [o]ur community is a tree. (Dead) ancestors are roots giving energy to the adults. Adults form the trunk. They in turn supply the branches, leaves and flowers, our children. The tree *knows*. 'We know.' The tree is the knowing subject.
>
> *Hamminga 2005, 58*

The Yorùbá hold the idea that society is a continuum from generation to generation. Hence, the knowledge inherited from the forebears is never categorized as mere beliefs or denied the epistemic status of *ìmọ̀* (knowledge). In other words, whether *ìmọ̀* (knowledge) is acquired from direct experience, inherited from the ancestors, or gotten from the experience of a contemporary, the important validation for each to qualify as *ìmọ̀* (knowledge) is the justification (*ìfìdímùlẹ̀*) conferred by *ẹ̀rí* (testimony). It is important to note, however, that *ẹ̀rí* (testimony) does not stand alone. The kind of person that the *ẹlẹ́ẹ̀rí* (testifier) is determines the acceptability of the *ẹ̀rí* (testimony). This takes propositional knowledge from the level of the individual knower, which is all that matters in traditional epistemology, to the level of the community, which is important in a traditional African society. Among the African, knowledge is not knowledge until the knower shares it. For shared knowledge to be justified, however, *ẹ̀rí* (testimony) is key.

Many polemical essays have been published by different scholars on the question of the peculiarity of African communality. Some scholars have argued, for example, that communality is merely an attribute or index of every primitive society. For such scholars, it is erroneous or misleading to claim that communality is exclusively African. I am not oblivious of the arguments for and against the idea of communality in studies about Africa. However, this objection does not invalidate the claim that pre-colonial Yorùbá people advocated communal living as evident in some of their sayings. The Yorùbá say, for example, *igi kan kìí dá igbó ṣe* (a tree does not make a forest), *ẹnikan kìí jẹ àwá dé, ọ̀pọ̀ ènìyàn ló ń jẹ jọ́ńmọ̀n* (one person cannot say 'we have arrived', many people form a community), *èrò ẹnikan kò jọ bọ̀rọ̀* (only one person's counsel is never adequate), *àìkọ́ọ̀wọ̀ rìn ejò ló ń fìyà jẹ wọ́n* (individualism is the bane of snakes [snake here is figurative. It refers to anyone who likes to go or act solo]). From these, it is evident that knowledge cannot remain at the level of the individual. It must pass from the individual to the community through the justification process of *ẹ̀rí* (testimony).

It is not everyone who qualifies to be ẹlẹ́ẹ̀rí (testifier). Age, social status, and other prestigious qualities do not suffice to qualify one as an ẹlẹ́ẹ̀rí (a testifier). Rather, an ẹlẹ́ẹ̀rí (a testifier) must be a person of proven integrity. How is a person of integrity identified? A person of integrity must be known as ọmọlúàbí (a virtuous person) before they qualify to be a reputable ẹlẹ́ẹ̀rí (testifier) that can provide ìmọ̀ (knowledge). This is because the Yorùbá recognize that a person who is not ọmọlúàbí (a virtuous person) would be ẹlẹ́ẹ̀rí-èké (false witness). Therefore, the important distinction between a good witness and a bad witness is the concept of ọmọlúàbí (a virtuous person). Who then is ọmọlúàbí (a virtuous person)?

Ọmọlúàbí (Virtuous Person) as Axiom for Ẹ̀rì (Testimony)

The concept of ọmọlúàbí (virtuous person) applies to and underlies so many other concerns among the Yorùbá. Although, ọmọlúàbí is both a descriptive and normative moral construct, it also illuminates the idea of the human person as a being (ontology) and a knower (epistemology). Considering the nexus between ọmọlúàbí and epistemology underscores the significance of certain questions. For instance, it is imperative to ask: Who or what is ọmọlúàbí? What is the nature of the nexus between the ethical idea of ọmọlúàbí (virtuous person) and the epistemic notion of justification? And last, but not least, how can the ethos of ọmọlúàbí (virtuous person) help address epistemic quandaries in contemporary Africa?

> The omoluabi is an epitome of moral rectitude. Such an individual is dignified and guided by culturally approved standards of behaviour. To become an omoluabi, emphasis is laid on the cultivation of virtues such as patience, respect for others, teachability, self-control, hardwork, diligence. The moral import of being a person imbued with character is evident in the fact that personhood, within the Yorùbá moral universe, is earned.
>
> *Adeboye 2020, 123*

Ọmọlúàbí (virtuous person) signifies the rounded description or quintessence of good character among the Yorùbá people of West Africa. It is both normative and descriptive as a moral concept, and it is both internalist and externalist as an epistemic construct. It is normative because people bring children up to value and exhibit the qualities of ọmọlúàbí (virtuous person), and children are also nurtured and encouraged to grow up into an ọmọlúàbí (virtuous person). However, when a person displays the good character, they are described as an ọmọlúàbí (virtuous person). Corroborating the idea that ọmọlúàbí (virtuous person) is both prescriptive and descriptive among the Yorùbá, Wright (2021) notes that ọmọlúàbí (virtuous person) refers to:

> An indigenous concept that *prescribes* the right mannerism and conduct of an individual in a specific social milieu. The concept of *omoluabi* stems from

the belief that a person has to exhibit certain behavioral traits to qualify as responsible and reputable in society. *Omoluabi* is the philosophical and cultural concept used by the Yorùbá to *describe* someone of good and virtuous nature.

42, emphasis mine

The Yorùbá stress *ìwà rere* (good character), *ìwà pèlé* (gentle character), *ìwà ìrèlè* (humility), *sùúrù* (patience), *ogbón* (practical wisdom), and *òdodo* or *òtító* (honesty or truthfulness) as the essential qualities of *omolúàbí*. *Ìwà rere* (good character) is one of the important qualities of *omolúàbí*.

> *Ìwà rere* (good or appropriate character) occupies the center of the social existence of the Yorùbá. The Yorùbá show their children the path of good character from childhood. They have various sayings, proverbs, adages, folklore, tales, and fables by which they teach children the importance of good character. For the Yorùbá, good character is superior to opulence and beauty.
>
> Ipadeola 2021, 111

A person of good character considers other people in terms of how their behavior is going to affect the natural order of the community before they act. The Yorùbá hold that the community is an interconnected system or structure that only one act of wickedness, impunity, or rashness could unbalance, and everyone's existence could thereby be jeopardized. Meanwhile, whether a person imbibes the traits of *omolúàbí* (virtuous person) imparted by the family and community or the person fails to imbibe the traits goes on to determine the kind of person the fellow is. Someone who exhibits the character-traits of *omolúàbí* (virtuous person) is called *omo rere* (a good child) or *ènìyàn rere* (a good person [if the fellow is an adult]), while a person who lacks the character-traits of *omolúàbí* (virtuous person) is referred to as *omo burúkú* or *ènìyàn burúkú* (a bad child or a bad person).

Ìwà pèlé (gentle character) is one of the identifying qualities of *omolúàbí* (virtuous person). *Omolúàbí* (virtuous person) must not be rash or given to hot temper. The Yorùbá acknowledge the destructive nature of hot temper. Therefore, they consider *ìwà pèlé* (gentle character) and its cognate *suuru* (patience) as signs of moral maturity that identify *omolúàbí* (virtuous person). The Yorùbá hold that "anger does not do anything for anyone; patience is the father of good character; those who develop patience will enjoy a long life" (Karade 2020, 22). *Ìwà ìrèlè* (humility) and *ogbón* (practical wisdom) are also very important in the making and for the purpose of identifying *omolúàbí* (virtuous person). *oolúàbí* (virtuous person) must balance *ogbón* (practical wisdom), *ogbón àgbà* (wisdom from maturity), and *ogbón inú* (adroitness) with *ìwà ìrèlè* or *ìteríba* (humility).

However, a very important quality of *omolúàbí* (virtuous person), which although is a moral element, yet serves as the basis of the relevance of the concept of *omolúàbí* (virtuous person) to epistemology is *òtító* (truth). *Òtító* (truth) is a moral cum epistemological concept among the Yorùbá. This is because it describes a situation or proposition and also describes, prescribes, and proscribes a person's or group's character or disposition. Imperatively, òtítọ́ (truth) is a cardinal but not the only quality of an ọmọlúàbí (virtuous person). Being olóòtítọ́ (truthful person) demands that one speaks the truth even when it is not or is not likely going to be in the person's interest. The Yorùbá believe that òtítọ́ (truth) is a very powerful cosmic force that should be promoted and must not be acted against. An Ifa verse, which is one of the important guides for the appropriate behavior among the Yorùbá states, for instance, that "[N]o matter how powerful wickedness is, righteousness overcomes it at the end. The power of falsehood is transient and ephemeral; truth although seemingly slow and weak overcomes falsehood in the end" (Karade 2020, 25). Òtítọ́ (truth) does not function alone. It functions in conjunction with other virtues of ọmọlúàbí (virtuous person). The virtuous status of ọmọlúàbí is not attained overnight. This is like what Wiredu avers about the nature of truth among the Akan people of Ghana. According to him, truth in Akan is both cognitive and moral.

The family plays a significant role in the upbringing of a person to be ọmọlúàbí (virtuous person). This is because in traditional Yorùbá societies, "The family was the most sacred and important institution among the Yorùbá, as it is the most effective agent of socialization where children are taught lessons in honor and shame to become an ọmọlúàbí" (Phillips 2011, 138). However, the entire community brings every child up in a typical traditional African society. Hence, the Yorùbá say ẹnìkan ní í bímọ, igba ojú ní í wò ó (one person gives birth to a child, but 200 persons nurture the child). At the age of innocence, the entire community guide and nurture every child and inculcate in them the ethos of ọmọlúàbí (virtuous person).

Ìmọ̀ (knowledge) requires ẹ̀rí (testimony) to be justified. However, it is only ènìyàn rere (good person) who can validate a knowledge claim. Ènìyàn rere (good person) is ọmọlúàbí (virtuous person) who possesses the requisite pedigree of good character traits and veracity to bear testimony that validates a knowledge claim. In other words, although the Yorùbá accord enormous respect to age, it is character rather than age that qualifies an individual to be an ẹlẹ́ẹ̀rí (testifier). Hence, [i]t is important to note that old age does not automatically confer prestige, respect, and honor. Old age only complements the values associated with good character for social unity and progress. The lack of normative character and its associated elements renders old age or the place and essentiality of an aged person rather irrelevant and incongruent (Omobowale 2014, 218).

Is Epistemic Tyranny a Threat to Yorùbá Epistemology?

Having looked at the position of the Yorùbá on the importance attached to the ethical idea of ọmọlúàbí (virtuous person) as a justifier of a knowledge claim, certain questions are germane. A critical question which anyone who holds the notion that the testimony given by ọmọlúàbí (virtuous person) is sufficient for a knowledge claim cannot gloss over is that of guarding against epistemic tyranny. What this means, for instance, is how can the entire weight of epistemic justification be placed on a single individual without such an individual using their position of privilege as a means of oppression or tyranny against the structure or gamut of knowledge production? Going by the onslaught of the critics of virtue ethics, one could raise similar criticism against the Yorùbá idea of ọmọlúàbí (virtuous person). Swanton (2021) argues, for example, that:

> ... the measure of what is right, good, and advantageous is a virtuous agent, then if you are virtuous, you are the arbiter of right action. If you are not, then you should ask a virtuous agent. Call this basic view qualified agent virtue ethical epistemology. However, this view has been subject to considerable criticism and its unpalatability for many has been a potent reason for rejecting virtue ethics altogether. Objections which have been leveled against qualified agent virtue ethical epistemology come in three types, which I label thus:
>
> (a) The lack of transparency objection
> (b) The monological objection
> (c) The virtuous agent is not an expert objection.
>
> *300*

Looking critically at Swanton's objection to virtue ethics, none of the three objections debilitates ọmọlúàbí (virtuous person) as a virtuous person because the idea of ọmọlúàbí (virtuous person), especially about the concept of justification (ìfidímùlẹ̀), is undergirded by a more fundamental concept, which is examined in detail in the subsequent section. Another popular objection to virtue ethics is that of reconciling the interests of the moral agent with the interests of the collective. To put it pithily,

> The major objection concerns the compatibility of universal love and self-love, both of which are central components of the profiles of virtues. The objection has two main facets. The first concerns the apparent downplaying of personal merits in an ideal of universal love, and a consequent apparent downplaying of individual worth. Even if this problem can be resolved, there remains a fundamental complaint that ideals of universal love valorize various forms of weakness and resentment, demanding problematic forms of egalitarianism and excessive self-sacrifice.
>
> *Swanton 2003, 146*

The concern of reconciling self-love with universal love, which is believed to place the burden of 'excessive sacrifice' on the individual fails to enervate the virtue ethical theory of ọmọlúàbí (virtuous person) because the Yorùbá do not hold a binary or oppositional view of the collective versus the individual. The two cannot exist without each other. Individuals form the whole and they, in turn, need the collective to function as individuals. This understanding is popular among the Yorùbá as it is one of the ethos inculcated into the individual from childhood. Hence, John

Mbiti says in most parts of Africa, the dictum 'I am because we are' (and not 'me versus them') underlies and influences most of their considerations and actions. In other words, although sacrifices are to be made, it is not one-sided and, therefore, not a burden on the virtuous person, like the objection implies.

Another objection to virtue ethics is that there is no guide to turn to in specific situations and this could make a virtuous person settle for a bad option when confronted with making a moral decision. It is argued, for instance, that

> virtue ethics is unlikely to be able to provide anything like manual or an instruction book – of the kind that comes along when, for instance, buying a new TV – containing a few easy steps that any normally developed adult could always turn to in order to determine what to do in the circumstances.
> Johansson and Svensson 2018, 503

Again, this criticism does not hold against the virtue ethical idea of *ọmọlúàbí* (virtuous person) because *ọmọlúàbí* (virtuous person) does not act in isolation. Apart from the check provided by *ilẹ* (earth), as explicated in the following section, members of the community (living and dead – ancestors) also hold *ọmọlúàbí* (virtuous person) accountable for their actions. In other words, that a person is *ọmọlúàbí* (virtuous person) does not exonerate them from being sanctioned if they err. Consequently, the following section examines a formidable check on *ọmọlúàbí* (virtuous person) as a justified testifier in the process of knowledge production.

The Phenomenon of *Ìfidímùlẹ̀* (Justification) in Yorùbá Epistemology

From times past, the Yorùbá have relied on oral communication or testimony (*ìjẹ́ẹ̀rí*) as an important tool of 'grounding' knowledge. Justification in Yorùbá is called *ìfidímùlẹ̀* (literally, to establish or ground an argument or proposition). *Ilẹ* in *ìfidímùlẹ̀* (justification) is what the Yorùbá call earth or the ground. Therefore, the Yorùbá concept of justification is foundational, although completely different from the notion of foundationalism in Cartesian epistemology. Therefore, the idea of foundationalism in Yorùbá epistemology is not affected by the objections that made Cartesian foundationalism odious and necessitated the emergence of coherentism and other theories of justification. This is because "[t]he orderly whole in which classical African knowledge operates is contextual and *bound* to the elements, workings, processes and cycles of the sacred universe, not to an abstract law" (Martin, July 2008, 957).

Yorùbá creation stories and myths preponderantly hold that Earth is the material cause of humans (in the sense of Plato's types of causes). According to those stories, *Olódùmarè*, the Supreme Being, saddles two deities with the task of creating human beings, and both rely on earth as the basic material. It is held that *Ajàlá* sculpts the head of every human being that is sent to the earth (*ilé ayé*) from heaven (*ikọ̀lé ọ̀run*), after which he brings the head to *Ọbàtálá/Òrìsànlá*, the artist deity, who molds humans out of clay (Kaplan 2008, 152). The Yorùbá, therefore, do not believe that only one deity is solely responsible for the creation of humans. Perhaps, this lends credence to the saying among the Yorùbá that *Ìsí wò ó, Ìkòrò wòó. Ohun a bá dìjọ wò, gẹ́gẹ́ ní í gún* (both *Ìsí* and *Ìkòrò* should look carefully at the matter, for a matter examined by more than one person is mostly error free). According to Adegbindin (2017):

> *Olódùmarè*, or the Supreme Deity, always charges *Àjàlá*, the divine, heavenly potter, with the responsibility of molding or casting the individual's head before she departs from heaven to begin her sojourn on earth. After molding different sizes of anatomical heads, *Àjàlá* follows the protocol of bringing the molded heads before *Òrìshà-ńlá*, a Yorùbá divinity, who is expected to fill these empty heads with some divine lots.
>
> 325

In other words, *Ilẹ̀* (earth) plays a vital role in the understanding of justification (*ìfidìmúlẹ̀*) among the Yorùbá because it is the origin of every human being. *Ilẹ̀* (earth) as the basic substance is also known as the grand witness to every knowledge claim. *Ilẹ̀* (earth) is, therefore, believed to be able to punish anyone who gives false or misleading testimony. In a situation where someone's testimony is doubted, even if the person is known as an *ọmọlúàbí* (virtuous person), the person could be asked to prove the veracity of their claim by swearing or taking an oath by *Ilẹ̀* (earth). If the person is being mischievous, *Ilẹ̀* (earth) as the overall witness knows and such a person would be sanctioned. The belief that *Ilẹ̀* (earth) does not compromise and justly issues a penalty if someone errs by giving a piece of false or misleading information or testimony is widely held among the Yorùbá. The Yorùbá understand that everything that is done is done upon earth, hence the capacity of *Ilẹ̀* (earth) to ensure justice. "A betrayer (of a friend, family, etc.) in Yorùbá is called *Òdàlẹ̀*, literally meaning one who betrays the land [or earth]" (Na'Allah 2010, 170). Therefore, the Yorùbá say *ọdàlẹ̀ bá 'lẹ̀ kú, ẹni bá da'lẹ̀ á bá'lẹ̀ lọ* (a betrayer dies with the land/earth, anyone who betrays goes with the earth). This does not mean that the Yorùbá hold that earth dies. The Yorùbá believe that *Ilẹ̀* (earth) is eternal, hence they say *kàkà kí ilẹ̀ kú, ilẹ̀ á ṣá ni* (rather than dying, the earth would only become sterile). Hence, it is important to note that the caveat is simple: if one betrays the Earth by giving false testimony (*ẹ̀rí*), then one would be penalized by the immortal element that witnesses all that one experiences or does.

The analysis on the significance of *Ilẹ̀* (earth) accentuates the double-check that underlies *ẹ̀rí* among the Yorùbá. In other words, although the Yorùbá consider the ethical basis of *ọmọlúàbí* (virtuous person) essential in validating a testimony, the privilege vested in *ọmọlúàbí* (virtuous person) is not absolute. After a person has cultivated the virtue of *ọmọlúàbí* (virtuous person), they are still put in check by *Ilẹ̀* (earth) – the amaranthine habitat of all humans and the grand witness to all events. This serves to forfend epistemic tyranny. Ergo, *ẹ̀rí* (testimony) can produce *ìmọ̀* (knowledge) or justify a knowledge claim contrary to the popular view of knowledge production among the Yorùbá, championed by Hallen, Sodipo, and some other contemporary African epistemologists. Knowledge acquisition is, therefore, not based on glib concepts or phenomena, but founded on the virtue ethical notion of *ọmọlúàbí* (virtuous person), who is in turn cognizant of the implication of unbalancing the ontological and cosmological order by giving false testimony.

Conclusion

This chapter has critically examined the African (Yoruba) conception of justification (*ìfidímúlẹ̀*). This essay has argued, for example, that knowledge (*ìmọ̀*) among the Yoruba is not acquired from firsthand experience alone. Rather, if secondhand information is justified by testimony from a virtuous person (*ọmọlúàbí*), then it qualifies to be referred to as knowledge. The essay underscored a cardinal attribute of *ọmọlúàbí* (virtuous person) as a moral cum epistemological concept that makes the virtue ethical notion of *ọmọlúàbí* (virtuous person) relevant in the purview of African epistemology. The essay pointed out that *òótọ́* (truth) in conjunction with other values of good character makes it possible for *ọmọlúàbí* (virtuous person) to give testimony that justifies secondhand information to be a knowledge claim.

In Western (traditional) epistemology, truth is an epistemic condition that stands with belief and justification to form knowledge. Among the Yorùbá, however, truth and other character traits jointly make a person an *ọmọlúàbí* (virtuous person). Similarly, being an *ọmọlúàbí* (virtuous person) is the condition required by a knower to justify a knowledge claim. To guard against epistemic tyranny, however, the Yoruba hold that *Ilẹ̀* (earth) is the impartial judge and witness which sanctions every act of giving false or misleading testimony. In all, this chapter has critiqued the intersection between epistemology, ontology, and ethics among the Yoruba people of West Africa.

References

Adeboye, O. 2020. "A Starving Man Cannot Shout Halleluyah": African Pentecostal Churches and the Challenge of Promoting Sustainable Development. In Philipp Ohlmann, Wilhelm Grabb, and Marie-Luise Frost (Eds.), *African Initiated Christianity, and the Decolonisation of Development: Sustainable Development in Pentecostal and Independent Churches*. Oxon: Routledge, pp. 115–135.

Adegbindin, O. 2017. Sophia, Phronesis and the Universality of Ifa in African Philosophy. In Adeshina Afolayan and Toyin Falola (Eds.), *The Palgrave Handbook of African Philosophy*. New York: Palgrave Macmillan, pp. 315–332.

Hamminga, B. 2005. Epistemology from the African Point of View, Bert Hamminga. In *Knowledge Cultures: Comparative Western and African Epistemology*. Amsterdam: Rodopi, pp. 57–84.

Ipadeola, A. P. 2021. *Ìdàgbàsókè*: An African Notion of Organic Development Ethics. *Journal of Development Societies*, Vol. 37, No. 1, pp. 98–115.

Johansson, J. and Svensson, F. 2018. Objections to Virtue Ethics. In Nancy E. Snow (Ed.), *The Oxford Handbook of Virtue*. Oxford: Oxford University Press, pp. 491–507.

Kaphagawani, D. N. and Malherbe, J. G. 1998. African Epistemology. In P. H. Coetzee and A. P. J. Roux (Eds.), *The African Philosophy Reader*. London: Routledge, pp. 259–319.

Kaplan, F. E. S. 2008. Twice-Told Tales: Yorùbá Religious and Cultural Hegemony. In Benin, Nigeria, Jacob K. Olupona and Terry Rey (Eds.), *Òrìṣà Devotion as World Religion: The Globalization of Yorùbá Culture*. Wisconsin: University of Wisconsin Press, pp. 128–165.

Karade, B. I. 2020. *The Yorùbá Handbook of Religious Concepts*. Boston, MA: Weiser Books.

Martin, D. 2008. Maat, and Order in African Cosmology: A Conceptual Tool for Understanding Indigenous Knowledge. *Journal of Black Studies*, Vol. 38, No. 6, pp. 951–967.

Na'Allah, A.-R. 2010. *African Discourse in Islam, Oral Traditions and Performance*. New York: Routledge.

Omobowale, A. O. 2014. An Ethnographic Textual Analysis of Aging and the Elders in South Western Nigeria. *Canadian Journal of Sociology*, Vol. 39, No. 2, pp. 211–230.

Phillips, O. F. 2011. Peacemaking and Proverbs in Urhobo and Yorùbá Marital Conflicts: Part 2. *African Conflict and Peacebuilding Review*, Vol. 1, No. 2, pp. 136–152.

Swanton, C. 2003. *Virtue Ethics: A Pluralistic View*. Oxford: Oxford University Press.

Swanton, C. 2021. *Target-Centred Virtue Ethics*. Oxford: Oxford University Press.

Wright, Bankole Oluwaseun. 2021. Navigating Morality in the Plays of Stella Oyedepo. In Bosede Funke Afolayan (Ed.), *Nigerian Female Dramatists: Expression, Resistance, Agency*. New York: Routledge, pp. 39–51.

PART IV

African Epistemology in Applied Context

10
ONTO-NORMATIVE MONISM IN THE ሐተታ (ḤĀTETA) OF ZERA YAQOB
Insights into Ethiopian Epistemology and Lessons for the Problem of Superiorism

Björn Freter

Introduction

In this contribution,[1] we will analyse the *ḥāteta* (Ge'ez, ሐተታ, English, "inquiry"),[2] written by Ethiopian scholar, Zera Yaqob, ዘርአ:ያዕቆብ, *Seed of Jacob* (Sumner, 1976: 4, I).[3] His philosophy resists a division into the basic disciplines customary in Western philosophy; his arguments, as we wish to propose with caution, combine metaphysics, ethics, and epistemology, in a way that is almost impossible to separate. We will thus not identify purely epistemological principles in his philosophy. However, since Zera Yaqob is deeply concerned about truth, we still find profound philosophical insights about knowledge and being and their relationship to one another. We will finish our reconstruction of some of the main ideas of the *ḥāteta* (ሐተታ, inquiry), with some rather critical notes on some of the hidden premises of the *ḥāteta* and their seemingly superioristic implications.

'All Things Are Good if We Ourselves Are Good'

Zera Yaqob was, according to his testament, born in Aksum in 1592 in the Ethiopian calendar which equals 1599 in the Gregorian calendar (Sumner 1976: 3). Despite poverty, his father ensured that Zera Yaqob received an excellent education. During his educational years, Zera Yaqob learned to keep his opinions on the interpretation of the Holy Scriptures to himself, as his opinion often differed from those of the Franğ[4] and his Ethiopian colleagues: "I withheld my opinion and hid in my heart all the thoughts of my mind" (Sumner 1976: 4, I). Despite his caution during his years as a teacher, as Zera Yaqob writes, "many of my friends came to dislike me" (Sumner 1976: 3, II). He states that he surpasses his friends "in knowledge and love of one's neighbour" (Sumner 1976: 3, II). While he was teaching, Zera Yaqob refused to declare what the Franğ or the Coptic scholars taught as good or bad;

rather, he claims that "all things are good if we ourselves are good" (Sumner 1976: 5, II). This was not well received. Charges were brought against Zera Yaqob many times, but, according to his narration, God protected him, until "a certain enemy of mine" (Sumner 1976: 5, II) went to the king and accused Zera Yaqob of misleading the people and attempting to incite them to "rise for the sake of our faith, kill the king and expel the *Franğ*" (Sumner 1976: 5, II). Afraid for his life, Zera Yaqob "took three measures of gold" and "the Psalms of David", with which he prays and fled at night (Sumner 1976: 5, II). He found shelter in a cave where he "lived for two years until [King] *Susənyos* died" (Sumner 1976: 5, II). In this cave, Zera Yaqob writes, "I have learnt more [...] than when I was living with scholars" (Sumner 1976: 17, IX). Some of the thoughts he developed in this cave he would later present to the reader in his *ḥāteta* (ሐተታ, inquiry), which he wrote down around 1667, about 30 years later. In his cave, Zera Yaqob meditated, at times for "whole days on conflicts between men and their depravity and on the wisdom of their creator who is silent while men do evil in His name and persecute their fellow men and kill their brothers" (Sumner 1976: 53, III).

Zera Yaqob, as we learn from his autobiography, was existentially exhausted by the troubling ways of his contemporaries. This might be one of the reasons why he was drawn so much to the *Psalms* (see Dawit Worku 2012: 107–108). We will begin this investigation of Zera Yaqob's thought with a look into these *Psalms*.

Existential Exhaustion

In *Psalm* 116[5] (MT = 114-115 LLX), we hear the psalmist cry out

> The snares of death encompassed me;
> The pangs of Sheol laid hold on me;
> I suffered distress and anguish. (Ps. 116:3 MT = 114:3 LXX)

In this peril, God has heard his cry. The psalmist is overjoyed:

> [1] I love the LORD, because he has heard
> my voice and supplications.
> [2]Because he inclined his ear to me,
> therefore I will call on him as long as I live. (Ps. 116:1-2 MT = 114:1-2 LXX)

A full life "of close harmony and careful obedience" (Ross 2016: 428) will be possible again,

> [8] For you have delivered my soul from death,
> my eyes from tears,
> my feet from stumbling.

Onto-normative Monism in the ሐተታ (ḥāteta) of Zera Yaqob   **147**

> ⁹ I walk before the LORD
> in the land of the living. (Ps. 116: 8-9 MT = 114:8-9 LXX)

Even in his darkest hour (see Isaiah 58:10), the psalmist could stay true to his faith:

> ¹⁰I kept my faith, even when I said,
> 'I am greatly afflicted'; (Ps. 116:10 MT = 115:1 LXX)

The greatest affliction did not cause the psalmist to lose his faith in YHWH. However, he had one confession to make:

> ¹¹I said in my consternation,
> 'Everyone is a liar.' (Ps. 116:11 MT = 115:2 LXX, see Romans 3:4)
> [אֲנִי אָמַרְתִּי בְחָפְזִי כָּל־הָאָדָם כֹּזֵב׃]
> [ἐγὼ εἶπα ἐν τῇ ἐκστάσει μου
> Πᾶς ἄνθρωπος ψεύστης.]

In his haste – בְחָפְזִי (*châphaz*), ἔκστασις (*ekstasis*) – the psalmist lost faith in his fellow humans: he became carried away and called everyone a liar (כֹּזֵב, *kâzab*). At this moment, when the psalmist was abandoned by all human companions, he realised that YHWH did not abandon him. God, as Paul would later express it, is perceived as ἀψευδής, *apseudes, without lie* (Titus 1:2.), as one who is incapable of lying.

Let us now turn back to our Ethiopian philosopher. Zera Yaqob would experience a similar existential abandonment. He asks: "Is everything that is written in the Holy Scriptures true?" Since he cannot find an answer, he decides: "I shall go and consult scholars and thinkers; they will tell me the truth" (Sumner 1976: 7, IV). Zera Yaqob thus investigates their teachings, but he cannot be satisfied. He was searching for the *truth*, but he could only find what is in the *heart* of his contemporaries. After all, "[w]hat will men tell me other than what is in their heart?" (Sumner 1976: 7, IV). What can be found in the heart (ልብ, *lebb*, see Dawid 2012: 186–188) of his fellow human beings is apparently not the same as the sought-after truth (ጽድቅ, *ṣedq*; see Leslau 1987: 548). Everyone, Zera Yaqob continues to bemoan, saying: "My faith is right, and those who believe in another faith believe in falsehood and are the enemies of God" (Sumner 1976: 7, IV).

During Zera Yaqob's investigation, Frang, Jewish, Islamic, and Ethiopian scholars claim that their faith is right and that, consequently, any other faith must be wrong, and moreover, by living according to any faith other than their very own, the other becomes an enemy of God. Everyone seems to claim that the friends of God are only those who are like oneself. Zera Yaqob cannot agree to reconcile himself to this. He posits that no human can be a judge in this matter. How should humans be able to determine the truth, "for all men are plaintiffs and defendants between themselves" (Sumner 1976: 7, IV). For Zera Yaqob, the investigation into faith in search of truth could not yield a result of any metaphysical significance. Zera Yaqob could only find, as James says, *amici seculi, friends of the world* (James 4:4), and they were only invested in worldly matters. Therefore, Zera Yaqob decides to turn inward to find out about the truth, and he prays[6]: "O my creator, wise among the wise and just among the just, who created me with an intelligence, help me to understand, for men lack wisdom and truthfulness" (Sumner 1976: 7, IV). And this is the moment when Zera Yaqob cites from his beloved *Psalms*. He continues: "as David said, no man can be relied upon" (Sumner 1976: 7, IV).

The psalmist and Zera Yaqob are existentially exhausted, and in their exhaustion, they both arrive at the same sad finding of the untrustworthiness of their fellow human beings. However, there is an important difference. The psalmist, as we have seen, spoke in a haste, he had "to admit to blurting out a hasty charge that every human being is false. Clearly, this accusation is something for the speaker to own up to and make up for. [...] The unstated implication is: Not everyone is false" (Charney 2010: 257). Zera Yaqob, on the other hand, cannot agree with that. His comprehension of the human being, ሰብእ (*säbə'ə*, see Sumner 1978: 277 and Leslau 1987: 534), is different from that of the psalmist. After consulting his fellow scholars, Zera Yaqob is profoundly disturbed. He exclaimed that "no man can be relied upon" not when he found himself abandoned in his moment of life-threatening danger, but rather when he, without being in any imminent danger, examined his questions with his fellow scholars. These scholars were open to the conversation and shared what they had to share; they did not abandon Zera Yaqob. The existential exhaustion of Zera Yaqob does not culminate in the horror of being abandoned by the human other, but in the horror of finding the human other to be untrustworthy. And to make matters even worse, Zera Yaqob cannot even trust himself: "As my faith appears true to me, so does another one find his own faith true" (Sumner 1976: 7, IV). This is the moment in which Zera Yaqob adds – *en passant* – a most important *epistemological* and at the same time *metaphysical idea* of his *ḥāteta* (ሐተታ, inquiry). He says: "but truth is one [አሐቲ ('*äḥätti*)]" (Sumner 1976: 7, IV).

Äḥättism

We frame this onto-normative monism as perceived by Zera Yaqob as *äḥättism* – derived from አሐቲ, '*äḥätti*, meaning 'one' (see Leslau 1987: 13). Äḥättism, the theological onto-normative monism, seems to be understood as the *reality how it ought to be*.[7] Everything *ought to be* in accordance with äḥättism – what is in accordance with it ought to be like this and what is not in accordance with it ought not to be like this but instead to be in accordance with äḥättism. The äḥättism is hence of foundational metaphysical and epistemological importance. God determines what ought to be. The original meaning of the Ge'ez word for God እግዚአብሔር (*'əgzi'abəḥer*) is "Sovereign of all things" (Sumner 1978: 128). What is, what ought to be, and thus what can truly can be known depend on the äḥättism. Onto-normative monism or äḥättism refers to the idea that all of reality ought to be in accordance with the one will of the one God.

Onto-normative Monism in the ሐተታ (ḥāteta) of Zera Yaqob **149**

The ähättism immediately produces up another question: why is there a diversity of faith expressions? Zera Yaqob has a rather disturbing explanation, which will introduce a most important *anthropological idea* of the ḥāteta (ሐተታ, inquiry). He says:"Why do men lie over problems of such great importance, even to the point of destroying themselves?" (Sumner 1976: 7, IV). This is quite a surprising turn. Zera Yaqob assumes that when his coevals instruct him about their faith, they in fact lie. They do not err, they are not making a mistake, and they do not, in all honesty, believe something that turns out to be untrue: no, human beings simply lie, ሐሰወ (ḥasäwä). The human being (ሰብእ, säbə'ə) is neither ἀψευδής (apseudes, without lie) nor merely fallible. It is much worse: the ሰብእ (säbə'ə) is a pseudophile. Indeed, the

> gə'əz word for 'lie' is one of the most frequent keywords of the Ḥatätas [of Zär'a Ya'əqob and Wäldä Ḥəywât]: a sign of a deep and constant concern for the universal abuse that has been made of the truth that shines in the human heart, but is veiled and obscured by human bigotry
>
> Sumner 1978: 97

Ḥasäwäism

This anthropological finding of pseudophilia can be framed as *ḥasäwäism* – derived from ሐሰወ, ḥasäwä, "to lie", originally "to veil", "to cover all-round" (Sumner 1978: 97; see Leslau 1987: 267). The ḥasäwäism, too, seems to be understood as *present factual reality as it is*. The present factual reality is impacted by the antecedent onto-normative ähättism. Ḥasäwäism ought not to be a factual reality, since it is *not* in accordance with reality as it ought to be, it is not in accordance with the ähättism. There ought not to be a diversity of faith that arose from the human beings' notorious lying, but, in accordance with the oneness of truth, there ought to be a oneness of faith.

The onto-normative monism of truth is, if we interpret Zera Yaqob correctly, equivalent to the onto-normative monism of God himself – if not identical to it. The oneness of truth means, in its deepest ontological consequence, nothing less than the oneness of God (see Deuteronomy 6:4 and the usage of אחד, *echad*, *one* in this verse). The singularity of truth, i.e. the *singularity* of God, normatively necessitates, according to Zera Yaqob, a *singular* expression of faith. This is, even though it is not the factual reality that ought to be, it is the immediate practical consequence of the epistemo-metaphysical principle. God, if it is truly God who is experienced, is experienced as the *same* one by everyone. The divine singularity nullifies – or rather depletes – whatever diversity we might find amongst the human beings' understandings of faith to produce the one true faith expression.

Zera Yaqob continues his investigation. He wants to understand what is at the root of the notorious tendency to lie of the human being. He finds either a misguided entitlement:"Convinced that they know all, they do not attempt to investigate the truth" (Sumner 1976: 7, IV) or a misguided trust in the ancestors: "Their hearts are curdled because they assume what they have heard from their predecessors and they do not inquire whether it is true or false" (Sumner 1976: 7, IV).

Human Nature

Zera Yaqob inquires even further: there must be an underlying reason "[w]hy [...] all men do not adhere to truth, instead of [believing] falsehood?" (Sumner 1976: 7, IV). Zera Yaqob finds an answer, and again, his thought is fairly unsettling: it lies in the "nature of man [ፍጥረተሰብ, *fəṭrätä säb*] which is weak and sluggish. Man aspires to know the truth and the hidden things of nature, but this endeavour is difficult and can only be attained with great labour and patience" (Sumner 1976: 7, IV). The weak and sluggish human nature is the problem (see Dawit Worku 2012: 177–181), a well-known presumption in Jewish and early Christian thought from *Genesis* to the *Epistle to the Romans*. The human being has all that is necessary to do what ought to be done. Zera Yaqob is as confident as the psalmist: God "will listen to us" (Sumner 1976: 7, IV); however, it is up to us to call him. There is, according to Zera Yaqob, a natural yearning for God: "God did not create me intelligent without a purpose, that is to look for him and to grasp him and his wisdom in the path he has opened for me and to worship him as long as I live" (Sumner 1976: 7, IV). We are directed toward God, we have a God-given ability, and we are obliged (see Kiros 2006: 185) to become close to him. However, this is hard work, as Zera Yaqob points out – this time using the authority of Qohelet or, in the understanding of Zera Yaqob, Solomon (see Lauha 1978: 29 and Schwienhorst-Schönberger 2004: 41–43, 54–56):

> [13]With the help of wisdom I have been at pains to study all that is done under heaven; oh, what a weary task God has given mankind to labour at!
>
> *Qohelet 1:13*

That which constitutes a rather pessimistic theological lamentation of the early Qohelet (see Schwienhorst-Schönberger 2004: 191) is, scil, that God made it a "weary task" (עִנְיַן רָע, περισπασμὸν πονηρὸν) for us to understand "all that is done under heaven", is perceived by Zera Yaqob as a rather dry fact of the *conditio humana*. While (early) Qohelet bemoans the hardship that God placed upon us, Zera Yaqob bemoans the unwillingness of humans to simply accept this *conditio humana* and to critically investigate what ought to be done. We are not making reality out of the God-given possibilities. We are reluctant to actually do the necessary work. "[P]eople", as Zera Yaqob points out, "hastily accept what they have heard from their fathers" (Sumner 1976: 8, IV). People refuse to critically examine, they shy away from, as Zera Yaqob calls it, the ሐተታ (*ḥāteta*, inquiry; see Dawit Worku 2012: 149–151 and Sumner 1978: 101–111, see also Leslau 1987: 248). The ሐተታ (*ḥāteta*, inquiry) is the foundational investigative procedure, the "one and supreme criterion for his entire philosophy" (Dawit Worku

2012: 150), that has to be applied to find the truth about faith. God gave us all we need:

> Our soul has the power of having the concept of God and seeing him mentally; likewise it can conceive of immortality. God did not give this power purposelessly; as he gave the power, so did he give the reality.
> *Sumner 1976: 14, VII*

In fact, we do not even need other humans for this. Let us remember, Zera Yaqob told us: "I have learnt more while living alone in a cave than when I was living with scholars" (Sumner 1976: 17, IX).

The ሐተታ (ḥāteta, inquiry)

Zera Yaqob does not explicate a method of the ሐተታ (ḥāteta, inquiry). He instead provides us with examples of his investigations. What is most impressive here is the breathtaking autonomy – "[e]xcept for the Psalms and a few Biblical passages the [ḥāteta] does not quote any other texts" (Wion 2015: 234) – and originality of thought (see Krause 2003: 332 and Sumner 2006: 174). Zera Yaqob does not even shy away from fundamentally criticising the biblical scriptures (see Gutema 2001). He inquires about the idea that:

> all men are created equal in the presence of God [see Herbjornsrud 2017 and see the further the critical commentary on Herbjornsrud by Burke 2020]. and all are intelligent, since they are his creatures; he did not assign one people for life, another for death, one for mercy, another for judgment.
> *Sumner 1976: 12, VI*

It is the reason (ልቡና, ləbbuna), asserts Zera Yaqob confidently, that "this sort of discrimination cannot exist in the sight of God" (Sumner 1976: 12, VI) even though Moses was sent to teach only the Jews, and David himself said: "He never does this for other nations, he never reveals his rulings to them" (Sumner 1976: 12, VI; see Psalms 147:20 MT = 147:9 LXX). Zera Yaqob even argues against the psalmist (Sumner 2006: 181–182, n. 5) for the equality in *coram deo*, i.e. equality in the *presence of God*. Zera Yaqob asks us to "think why all men agree that there is a God, creator of all things?" (Sumner 1976: 12,VI). He answers:

> Because reason in all men knows that all we see was created; that no creature can be found without a creator and that the existence of a creator is pure truth. Hence all men agree on this.
> *Sumner 1976: 12, VI*

When looking at the beliefs taught by humans and not by *pure reason*, we do not find agreement. The *Coram-deo*-equality is the truth because, as we understand Zera

Yaqob, in *pure reason* reflecting on *what every human necessarily has to agree upon*, we find a *necessarily consensual insight*, i.e. "all men are created equal in the presence of God". The ሐተታ (*ḥāteta*, inquiry) seems to be a meditative procedure of emptying all empirical elements in order to be able to use a purified reason, which is now open for the evidence of divine truth.

"To a person", says Zera Yaqob,

> who seeks it, truth is immediately revealed. Indeed he who investigates with the pure intelligence set by the creator in the heart of each man and scrutinizes the order and laws of creation, will discover the truth.
>
> *Sumner 1976: 9, V*

> Our reason which our creator has put in the heart of man teaches all these things to us.
>
> *Sumner 1976: 16, VIII*

Conducting ሐተታ (*ḥāteta*, inquiry) means to *reduce* – this is the reason why Zera Yaqob is sometimes compared with his contemporary, Rene Descartes (see, for instance, Sumner 1978 and Sumner 1999: 175–177) – our thought, so that we are able to investigate with pure intelligence. This pure intelligence is our thought as "set by the creator", allowing us, quasi-deindividualised and even all alone, to discover the universal creational truths. And if we do so, we will necessarily leave all ḥasäwäism behind and, because we are thinking äḥättismically, we will find exactly the same truth as anyone else conducting the ሐተታ (*ḥāteta*, inquiry).

The Will

We have learned that Zera Yaqob assumes that God gave us all we need to become close to him. However, he does not move our will towards him for us, he does not will our will;[8] we need to move our will ourselves: "God created man to be the master of his own actions so that he will be what he wills, good or bad" (Sumner 1976: 8, IV). God "[did] not create us perfect", in fact, he made us "with such a reason as to know we are to strive for perfection as long as we live in this world" (Sumner 1976: 15, VIII). Perhaps, Zera Yaqob imagined this perfection to be of transcended reality similar to that described by Augustine, who explains in *De civitate dei*, that in the City of God, humans will:

> no longer be able to take delight in sin. This does not mean, however, that they will have no free will. On the contrary, it will be all the more free, because set free from delight in sinning to take a constant delight in not sinning. For when man was created righteous, the first freedom of will that he was given consisted in an ability not to sin, but also in an ability to sin [potuit non peccare, sed potuit et peccare]. But this last freedom of will be

greater, in that it will consist in not being able to sin [hoc autem nouissimum eo potentius erit, quo peccare non poterit].
Augustine 2013: 1179 = XXII, 30/Augustinus 1993: II, 632 = XXII, 30

Of course, Augustine adds, this is "not [...] a natural possibility, but a gift of God [munere dei]" (Augustine 2013:1179 = XXII, 30/Augustinus 1993: II, 632 = XXII, 30). Zera Yaqob might have agreed with this, too. In stark contrast to Augustine, however, Zera Yaqob presumes that we can work towards this gift.

We are striving towards God seemingly naturally, but to direct that desire towards God, to will the good, has to be willed by us. To make this good will (or its opposite) and its corresponding practical action, a factual reality is quasi the human contribution to the divine creation: "God did not create man to be evil, but to choose what he would like to be, so that he may receive his reward if he is good or his condemnation if he is bad" (Sumner 1976: 8, IV). Should a liar "who desires to achieve wealth or honours among men" need to use foul means to achieve these goals, that liar will do so and claim "he is convinced this falsehood was for him a just thing" (Sumner 1976: 8, IV). This liar will be followed by those who are too lazy to conduct a proper ሐተታ (ḥāteta, inquiry), those who will "believe in the liar's strong faith" (Sumner 1976: 8, IV). This happens all the time as people "believe wholeheartedly in astrology [...], and in all kinds of magical art and in the utterances of soothsayers" (Sumner 1976: 8, IV).

The "predecessors" brought these lies into the world to obtain "wealth and honours" or "to rule the people" (Sumner 1976: 8, IV). Those who followed "accepted their fathers' faith without question", even added "stories of signs and omens" and thus "made God a witness to falsehood and a party to liars" (Sumner 1976: 9, IV). Zera Yaqob finds only radically self-involved humans (see Abera 2016: 436), as we can say, in loose accordance with an expression Luther developed in his doctrine on original sin, *homines curvati*, humans curved in on themselves (see Luther 1961: 159).

We find here the motivational root of the ḥasäwäism. There is something humans want, they want "to achieve wealth or honours among men" (Sumner 1976: 8, IV) or they want to worship, but they are reluctant to do the work of the ḥāteta (ሐተታ, inquiry), they are reluctant to develop their personal relationship with God by using the "reason which our creator has put in the heart of man" (Sumner 1976: 16, VIII). Humans are thus either yearning for goods that are irrelevant *sub specie aeternitatis (under the heading of eternity)*, or they are seemingly turning in the right direction but are actually only walking along a path that others have built, with the help of lies, for them.

Cognitive Dissonance

If we understand Zera Yaqob correctly, all this happens perhaps not in all, but certainly in many cases, quite intentionally. Humans lie and thus create a pseudo-reality – a reality, as we have seen before, that ought not to be, because it is not in accordance with äḫättism – in order to obtain something that they *do not have* but want or that they *ought not to have* but want. And most humans do in fact know that they do what they are not supposed to do, they know that they are fighting against their very own "reason which our creator has put in the heart of man" (Sumner 1976: 16, VIII). "The law of nature", insists Zera Yaqob, "is obvious, because our reason clearly propounds it, if we examine it. But men do not like such inquiries, they choose to believe the words of men rather than to investigate the will of their creator" (Sumner 1976: 14, VII).

Zera Yaqob seems to explain that we actively try to denaturalise ourselves; that we actively want to unknow the natural yearning to will what God wills. And, most importantly, we do this to pseudo-achieve what we know we ought to achieve. The humans of whom Zera Yaqob speaks do not deny God, they pseudo-follow him, and their lies are told not only to the hearts of their fellow humans but also to themselves. Zera Yaqob makes the stunning observation of a cognitive dissonance (see on this concept Festinger 1962) *avant a lettre*.

Ambivalence, Love and Superiorism: A Personal Note

I have attempted to understand the astounding work of Zera Yaqob, and so far, I have mostly endeavoured to reconstruct what I have found in the ḥāteta (ሕተታ, inquiry). However, there is an important word of caution that I need to express. The reader will have already noticed during the reconstruction that a tension exists between the truths of pure reason, such as: "Worship God your creator and love all men as yourself. […] Do not do unto others that which you do not like to be done unto you, but do unto others as you would like others to do unto you" (Sumner 1976: 14, VIII), and the anthropological finding of ḥasäwäism as it is expressed here: "We cannot, however, reach truth through the doctrine of men, for all men are liars" (Sumner 1976: 13, VII).

We are led to believe that humans are either selfishly inventing lies or keeping lies alive because they are too lazy to find out the truth. This is the origin of the diversity of faith according to Zera Yaqob: lies and laziness. He, thus, radically *invalidates all diverse human religious experience*; he denies *all existential seriousness of these diverse experiences*. And, at the same time, he invents, with the technique of the ḥāteta (ሕተታ, inquiry), a philosophical *modus operandi* that exempts him from his own relentless critique.

The seriousness of Zera Yaqob cannot be doubted. His work, in my understanding, gives no cause whatsoever to doubt that he calls for the equality of human beings (explicitly including female human beings – see Sumner 1976: 20–22, XII). The call to love one another, and the insistence that all we do can be good "if we ourselves are good" (Sumner 1976: 5, II) are written with the deepest sincerity; his beliefs, as Teodros Kiros has pointed out, are of *"existential seriousness"* (Kiros 2017: 195).

However, it seems that there are more hidden premises to these ideas than Zera Yaqob admits. A human moving towards God by pure reason via ሕተታ (*inquiry*, ḥāteta) will be, according to the teachings of Zera Yaqob, in more superior harmony with God than another human being caught in ḥasäwäism. This is certainly what Zera Yaqob ascribes to himself; this is the position from which he feels entitled to call all human beings liars. Zera Yaqob, who considers his theology to be undeniably true, is the *one* human being entitled to call all *other* human beings liars and to call upon all these other human beings to change.

This is undoubtedly a *superiorist* self-understanding, since according to his own theory, Zera Yaqob knows better than others what *is* and *what ought to be*. Zera Yaqob would have to admit that, with regards to his insights and his self-proclaimed ability to critically inquire, he is superior to his fellow human beings. We are moving into extremely dangerous terrain here. Zera Yaqob does not explicitly say it – but, it seems, we, the *other* human beings, have to ask him: *What now, Zera Yaqob? What do we do with all these insights authorised by you, the superior authority, Zera Yaqob, who is himself authorised by the most superior authority God? What do we do if our inquiry simply does not lead us where you have gone?*

As a white Western scholar, unfortunately I feel I can imagine the answer given what *my* ancestors have done with this kind of epistemic foundation – and I have to admit that I am not sure whether it is my euro-western self-consciousness that is causing me to bring this bias into the discussion of the most honourable Zera Yaqob. Zera Yaqob developed a sophisticated theory connected with a deep practice of personal spiritual exercise.[9] If this theory were to be true however, if there is in fact an *ought-to-be-reality*, the next step would be to convert the *ought-to-be* into an *is*. This would be the dreaded next step. A comprehensive realisation of Zera Yaqob's philosophy would require, in the name of love, in the name of equality, in the name of God, *forcing* his fellow human beings to do what ought to be done for the sake of their own happiness. This is horribly close to something that my euro-western people have done so many times and what they continue to do. We declared equality and we then hid – usually within the concept of the 'human being' – so many implications that made it possible to extol this virtue of equality while simultaneously acting against it (see Freter 2018, Freter 2020, and Freter 2021). The *Declaration of Independence* might be one of the most famous texts documenting this. It declares freedom for all, but actually, as David Cooper already stated in 1783, its "blessings were only meant to be the *rights* of *white men*, not of *all men*" (Cooper 1783: 14).

Zera Yaqob was even aware of the problem, with his amazing finding of cognitive dissonance *avant a lettre* having been rightly celebrated above. And yet he still slipped into the dissonant trap, still he committed the superiorist fallacy of centring his self-understanding as superior. Zera Yaqob assumed he achieved knowledge about reality as it is in itself and from that allegedly superior knowledge, he inferred what ought to be. He assumes to have found the superior guideline to correct reality where is fails to be what he knew it ought to be, he assumes to have superior knowledge that lets him understand how other human beings ought to be. Indeed, Zera Yaqob does not tell us how this superior knowledge about how beings ought to be would be practically enforced. However, from what we know about his thought, it seems rather inevitable that the practical realisation of Zera Yaqob's onto-normative monism as it is in its core a superiorism would be suppressive reality, a reality incapable of accepting difference.

I am aware that these are rather dark conclusions. If my thoughts are indeed somewhat accurate, they seem to show that superiorism can emerge in any geographic location. However, and this is most intriguing and crucial, this superiorism of the *ḥāteta* (ሐተታ, inquiry) factually never became a violent reality as was the case with the philosophical *inquiries* of the euro-western Enlightenment. The Humean, Kantian, Jeffersonian, Hegelian, and so many more superiorisms became violent political realities. These euro-western inquires became aggressive and violent realities in the form of colonial genocide, capitalistic exploitation, and sexual oppression, to name just a few manifestations. There are unfortunately so many more examples. Superiorism is a danger that seems to go together with the human undertaking of searching for truth, i.e. the knowledge of what actually is and what actually ought to be. However, this danger as unavoidable it seems to be as a possibility does not necessarily become reality. In the so-called Western philosophy it was prominent from its earliest days, but it came to reality in its most aggressive from since the 18th century. The central task of contemporary Western philosophy, in my understanding, has to be the radical, the relentless, and the unadorned fight against all forms of superiorism, that is its radical desuperiorisation (see Freter 2020, Freter 2021, and Freter and Freter 2021).

Conclusion

In conclusion, as a white scholar seeking to be inclusive of the philosophical contributions of all peoples, the philosophy of Zera Yaqob has revealed to me astute insights from the 17th century confirming the need for critical inquiry and the dangers of cognitive dissonance that pose so many challenges to us in the 21st century. At the same time, this investigation has also revealed a cautionary tale for postcolonial scholars as they seek to avoid the destructive superioristic hierarchies that the Enlightenment left in its wake.

Notes

1 My heartfelt thanks go to Yvette Freter and Kerry Jago for their ongoing support and to the editors Peter Ikhane and Isaac Ukpokolo for their endless patience. My special thanks go to Jonathan Egid for his detailed comments on an earlier draft of this chapter.
2 We will cite Zera Yaqob from the translation by Claude Sumner as provided in Sumner (1976: 1–25). We will refer to the page number followed by the chapter number in roman numerals.
3 On the question of authorship of the *ḥāteta*, (ሐተታ, inquiry), see Getatchew 2017 and the review by Merawi and Kenaw (2019).
4 "A foreigner. Here: the 'Europeans,' the 'Portuguese,' 'the Catholics'" (Sumner 1976: 4).

5 Biblical texts are quoted – unless indicated otherwise – using the standard editions: Masoretic Text is taken from *Biblica Hebraica Stuttgartensia*, 4th ed., Greek text is taken from *Septuaginta*, ed. Rahlfs, 2 vols., 8th ed., further Greek text and Latin text are taken from *Novum Testamentum*, ed. Nestle-Aland, 26th ed., the English text follows the *New Revised Standard Version, Anglicised*.
6 "For Zara Yacob, prayer is a modality of philosophizing with the aid of *hatata* and *hasassa*" (Kiros 2017: 200).
7 This seems to be a truly 'African' thought. See Nkulu-N'Sengha (2005: 43): "African epistemology is grounded on the fundamental belief that reality is one, that is, everything is interconnected in a web of relationships. […] African epistemology rejects all forms of dualism […]".
8 For comments on the western thoughts in this regard, see Freter (2016: 209–278).
9 See Sumner (1999: 183): "Hence rationalism in Zera Yacob goes hand in hand with a deeply religious sense and even with piety towards an all-merciful and all-wise creator".

References

Abera. T. 2016. "Rationality and ethics in Zara Yacob's 'Hatata.'" *Imperial Journal of Interdisciplinary Research*, vol. 2, no. 2: 431–439.
Augustine. 1993. *De civitate dei libri XXII. Vol. II.* Stuttgart, Leipzig: Teubner, Alfons Kalb (ed.).
Augustine. 2013. *The city of God against the pagans.* Cambridge.: Cambridge University Press, Robert W. Dyson (ed.).
Burke, J. 2020. "Assessing Zera Yacob's Relationship to the Enlightenment." www.academia.edu/43292077/Assessing_Zera_Yacobs_Relationship_to_the_Enlightenment. Accessed 31/5/2021.
Charney, D. H. 2010. "Performativity and persuasion in the Hebrew Book of Psalms: A rhetorical analysis of Psalms 116 and 22, 257." *Rhetoric Society Quarterly*, vol. 40, no. 3: 247–268.
Cooper, David. 1783. *A serious address to the rulers of America, on the inconsistency of their conduct respecting slavery: Forming a contrast between the encroachments of England on American liberty, and American injustice in tolerating slavery.* London: Trenton.
Dawit Worku, K. 2012. *The Ethics of Zärʿa Yaʿəqob. A reply to the historical and religious violence in the seventeenth century Ethiopia.* Roma: Edictrice Pontifica Università Gregoriana.
Festinger, L. 1962. *A theory of cognitive dissonance.* Stanford: Stanford University Press.
Freter, B. 2016. *Wirklichkeit und existentiale Praxis. Vorarbeiten zu einer Phänomenologie der Normativität entwickelt an narrativen Texten der altgriechischen, neutestamentlichen, mittelhochdeutschen und klassischen deutschen Literatur.* Berlin: Lit.
Freter, B. 2018. "White supremacy in euro-western epistemologies. On the West's responsibility for its philosophical heritage." *Synthesis Philosophica. Journal of the Croatian Philosophical Society*, vol. 15: 237–249.
Freter, B. 2020. "Decolonization of the west, desuperiorisation of thought, and elative ethics." In *Handbook of African philosophy of difference*, Elvis Imafidon (ed.). Cham: Springer, 105–127.
Freter, B. 2021. "Desuperhumanizing whiteness." In *Implications of race and racism in student evaluations of teaching: The hate u give students*, LaVada Taylor (ed.). Lanham, Boulder, New York, London: Lexington, pp. 159–178.
Freter, B. and Freter, Y. 2021. "Embracing a decolonial epistemological approach in African higher education." In *Decolonisation as democratisation. Global insights into the South African experience*, Siseko H. Kumalo (ed.). Cape Town, South Africa: HSRC Press, s.l., 127–150.

Getatchew Haile. 2017. "The discourse of Wärqe: Commonly known as Ḥatäta zä-Zär'a Ya'ǝqob." In *Ethiopian studies in honour of Amha Asfaw*, Getatchew Haile (ed.). New York: Getatchew Haile Publishers, 57–72.

Gutema, Bekele. 2001. "Zarayaqob: Ein äthiopischer Philosoph." *Polylog. Zeitschrift für interkulturelles Philosophieren*, vol. 7: 68–74.

Herbjørnsrud, D. 2017. "The African Enlightenment." https://aeon.co/essays/yacob-and-amo-africas-precursors-to-locke-hume-and-kant. Accessed 31/5/2021.

Kiros, T. 2006. "Zera Yacob and traditional Ethiopian philosophy." In *A companion to African philosophy*, Kwasi Wiredu (ed.). Malden, Oxford, Carlton: Blackwell, pp. 183–190.

Kiros, T. 2017. "An interpretative introduction to classical Ethiopian philosophy." In *The Palgrave handbook of African philosophy*, Adeshina Afolayan and Toyin Falola (eds.). New York: Palgrave Macmillan, pp. 181–207.

Krause, A. 2003. "Spezielle Metaphysik in der Untersuchung des Zar'a Jacob (1599-1692)." *Archiv für Geschichte der Philosophie*, vol. 85, no. 3: 331–345.

Lauha, A. 1978. *Kohelet*. Neukirchen-Vluyn: Neukirchener Verlag.

Leslau, Wolf. 1987. *Comparative Dictionary of* Geʻez (Classical Ethiopic). Geʻez-English / English- *Geʻez* (Classical Ethiopic).

Luther, M. 1961. *Lectures on Romans*. Wilhelm Pauck (ed.). Louisville: John Knox Press.

Merawi, F. and Kenaw, S. 2019. "Is there an Ethiopian philosophy? Rereading the Hatetas of Zara Yaecob and Walda Hewat in the context of knowledge production." *Ethiopian Journal of the Social Sciences and Humanities*, vol. 15, no. 1 (Special Issue): 59–75.

Nkulu-N'Sengha, M. 2005. "African epistemology." In *Encyclopedia of black studies*, Molefi Kete Asante and Ama Mazama (eds.). Thousand Oaks, London, New Delhi: Sage Publications, pp. 39–44.

Ross, A. P. 2016. *A Commentary on the psalms: Volume 3 (90-150)*. Grand Rapids: Kregel Publications.

Schwienhorst-Schönberger, L. 2004. *Kohelet*. Freiburg, Basel, Wien: Herder.

Sumner, C. 1976. *Ethiopian philosophy. Volume II. The treatise of Zär'a Ya'ǝqob and of Wäldä Ḥǝywât. Text and authorship*. Addis Ababa: Commercial Printing Press.

Sumner, C. 1978. *Ethiopian philosophy. Volume III. The treatise of Zär'a Ya'ǝqob and of Wäldä Ḥǝywât. An analysis*. Addis Ababa: Commercial Printing Press.

Sumner, C. 1999. "The significance of Zera Yacob's philosophy." *Ultimate Reading and Meaning*, vol. 22, no. 3: 175–177.

Sumner, C. 2006. "The light and the shadow: Zera Yacob and Walda Heywat: Two Ethiopian philosophers of the seventeenth century." In *A companion to African philosophy*, Kwasi Wiredu (ed.). Malden, Oxford, Carlton: Blackwell, pp. 172–182.

Wion, A. 2015. Review of "Dawit Worku Kidane, The ethics of Zär'a Ya'ǝqob. A reply to the historical and religious violence in the seventeenth century Ethiopia." *Oriens Christianus*, vol. 98: 232–235.

11
PERSONALISM AND AN AFRICAN EPISTEMOLOGY OF PERSONHOOD

Philip Edema

Introduction

The work seeks to achieve an epistemological interpretation in the discourse of the ontological nature and understanding of the human person from an African perspective. The discourse of the human person especially from an African perspective is not a recent phenomenon. As a matter fact, different philosophers and scholars of different disciplinary approach have interrogated this reality of 'who the person is'. The outcome of such research has generated further interrogations and one of such is what this chapter focuses on.

This chapter is an attempt to examine the epistemic status of the human person from an African standpoint. The argument on what constitutes the nature of the human person is popular within the realm of applied ethics and its subsets, bioethics. The debate has also been extended to the comparative study of the person between Western and African ontological frameworks. However, this chapter attempts to take this discourse beyond the realm of applied ethics, to the realm of the epistemic status from an African perspective. In doing this, the author raises some fundamental questions: to what extent can we determine when a person becomes a person? What are the criteria for knowing the person? What are the conditions for knowledge of the truth about the human person in regard to his personal beginnings? The debate in Western philosophy is polarised between when a person truly is a person and the point at which a person can be considered a person. Is it at conception, that is, at the embryonic stage, or is personhood acquired at a later stage of human development?

To achieve this, the author examines the general nature of personalism. This is vital to the entire discourse, given that the above questions can be answered by looking at personalism as conceived in the West and its implications for an

African epistemology of the person. Other sections of the chapter include African Personhood and African Epistemology, African Epistemology of the Person and Conclusion.

The Idea of Personalism

Essentially, the concept 'personalism' focuses on the human person within the realm and perspective of philosophical discourses. It is a philosophical school of thought that promotes the value and dignity of man as a unique being. It emphasises the ontological and existential character of man and provides a solid foundation for the ethical framework for the understanding of human life. Importantly, the different narratives about the human person have taken a lot of perspectives and forms since the ancient epoch to the postmodern age. These discourses have raised a lot of arguments and counterarguments about the proper place of man in the recent times. This is why Battista Mondin rightly argued that:

> Man is the supreme question for man. That this is the principal and fundamental question for us as men is an obvious thing, because every other interrogative, every other question (about the earth, the sky, the moon, the stars, the air, the water, atoms, cells, etc., even about God) acquires relevance only with reference to our being... Who is man? This is the interrogative of all interrogatives, the most pressing and piercing of all. It is an old interrogative, yet it is always new; it is concrete, not abstract; personal, not generic.
>
> *Battista Mondin 1985: 7*

The above citation lays a solid credence to our understanding of personalism as a fundamental aspect of philosophy and anthropology and that the discourse concerning man is very important and fundamental.

Historically, personalistic ideas and thoughts were said to have developed around the 19th century as a response to a crisis of Western society society. It was a crisis of values, dehumanised tendencies and a response to depersonalisation in the rationalism, the positivism, the Enlightenment, the pantheism, Hegel's absolute idealistic panlogism, individualism, the political collectivism, materialism, the psychological and evolutional determinism (Dancak 2017: 51). Simply, it was conceived that these theories mentioned above were developed with the intention of side-lining the dignity and values attached to the human person and as such, personalists took it upon themselves to rescue man from total annihilation and false anthropology. Again, personalism encapsulates various philosophical schools and systems, which share the common feature of emphasising the fact that the person presents a source as well as an aim for philosophical and theological researches or the researches of humanities and science. Further still, it focuses on the person and his relations towards the society and world to the extent that the person is becoming a unifying ontological and epistemological principle in various approaches of different sciences (Dancak 2017: 51).

Thomas Williams and Jan O. Bengston citing K. S. Grzegorz affirmed that for personalists, the human person should be the ontological and epistemological starting point of philosophical reflection. Besides, the concerns of personalists include the investigation of the experience, the status, and the dignity of the human being as person, and regard this as the starting point for all subsequent philosophical analysis (Holub 2018: 254). Elsewhere, Thomas D. Williams stated that personalism,

> focuses on the reality of the person (human, angelic, divine) and on his unique dignity, insisting on the radical distinction between persons and all other beings (non-persons) …and as a philosophical school, personalism draws its foundation from human reason and experience.
>
> *Williams 2004: 164*

Carlo Petrini and Sabina Gainotti submitted that personalism focuses on our common shared human nature and that all human beings deserve respect. In addition, they aver that personalism strongly emphasises the protection of the weakest and the sickest persons in society (Petrini and Gainotti 2008: 626).

Furthermore, to reiterate the essence of the principles of personalism as person centred, Elio Sgreccia stated that:

> [P]ersonalistic tradition has its roots in man's reason itself and in the heart of his freedom: the human being is a person, because he is the only being, whose life is able to reflect upon himself, to self-determination. He is the only being that is able to understand and find the sense of life and to give sense to his expressions and conscious language. Reason, liberty and conscience represent as Popper says, an "emerging creation" that cannot be reduced to the flux of the cosmic and evolutionistic laws. This happens, thanks to a spiritual soul that forms and gives life to his physical reality and that contains and forms the body. The sense of universe and the value of humanity are contained in every human being: the human being is a unit, a whole and not a part of a whole. Society itself refers to the human being: the person as an aim and a source for society.
>
> *Sgreccia 1999: 21–22*

In essence, Sgreccia and Popper were able to show that the human person determines his or her life by decision h/she makes. Besides, the person though part of the cosmic order is not subjected to the changes of the cosmic and evolution laws for the simple reason that the person is a spiritual being, a creation of a divine being and s/he place in the society is very paramount. As such, the person is perceived as an ultimate fact, s/he is the centre and the foundation of the entire reality, either from the ethical or political point of view.

Personalism attempts to unravel the mystery and the character of the existence of man by placing s/he at the centre of all reality such that every discourse revolves around h/she for the benefit of the common good. In man's expression and choices, we come to know who h/she is, the kind of values s/he upholds and how such values impact either negatively or positively on humanity. This is the truth about the human person. This is what makes the person a truly dignified entity. This truth, for the personalists, is irreplaceable and it is unique in itself. Beyond this, this work also recognises the position of philosophers or scholars who holds a different opinion about human persons as non-spiritual beings. These are materialists, and who believe in the dignity and uniqueness of human persons as well.

Regarding the major themes in personalism, Pavol Dancak revealed that among personalists, the top position in the hierarchy of beings belongs to the person for the simple reason that the person is a spiritual being, possesses autonomy, possesses ability to make free decisions and express himself through acts as well as creativity (moral behaviour, art, religion, philosophy, science and technology). Furthermore, personalists emphasise that:

> man as the person should never be regarded as an instrument, because in his very nature he is goal of activity...development of the person should be superior to all particular values realised in the life of an individual as well as society.
> *Dancak 2017: 52*

Rigobello, as cited by Thomas D. Williams, bifurcates the strains of personalism into two categories: personalism in a strict sense and personalism in a broader sense. Personalism in the strict sense puts the person at the centre of a philosophical system that originates from an "intuition" of the person himself, and analyses the personal experience that is the object of this intuition. The method it adopts draws extensively from phenomenology and existentialism, departing from traditional metaphysics. In this sense, the original intuition is really that of self-awareness by which one grasps values and essential meanings through unmediated experience. The knowledge produced by reflecting on this experience is nothing more than an explication of the original intuition, which in turn generates an awareness of a framework for moral action (Williams 2004: 165). G. P. Bowne and Emmanuel Mounier belong to this strand of personalism.

In the broader sense, personalism integrates a particular anthropological and ethical vision into global philosophical perspectives. As such, the person is not considered as the object of an original intuition, nor does philosophical research begin with analysis of the personal context. Rather, in the scope of a general metaphysics, the person occupies the central place in philosophical discourse, but this is not reduced to an explication or development of an original intuition of the person (Williams 2004: 165–166). Thus, this does not constitute an autonomous metaphysics, but it offers an anthropological–ontological shift within existing metaphysics and draws out ethical consequences of the shift (Dancak 2017: 124).

African Personhood and African Epistemology

In constructing an African epistemic understanding of the human person, it is vital to begin by briefly examining the nature of African epistemology. Didier Kaphagawani and Jeanette Malherbe stated that all humans have the capacity to know; and that epistemology is available to all cultures, tribes or races. The implication of this is that presuppositions and bases of knowledge claims vary from culture to culture. The way an African lay claim to knowing something is different from the way in which a Chinese or European, for instance, would arrive at and assert his or her knowledge. Following from this, Kaphagawani and Malherbe concluded that since there are sociocultural and different ways of acquiring knowledge, its stands to reason that an African articulation and formulation of knowledge is an African epistemology (Kaphagawani and Malherbe 2003: 260). For Anselm Jimoh, African epistemology focuses on what African mean and understands when he makes knowledge claim. This involves how the African sees or talks about reality (Jimoh 2017: 124). Jimoh's view clearly aligns with Kaphagawani and Malherbe argument as stated above.

Furthermore, Jimoh assert that African epistemology is essentially and necessarily rooted in African ontology. Simply put, the epistemological view of the traditional African is in consonance with his/her metaphysics. Jimoh supported his submission by quoting Placide Tempels that "true wisdom which is knowledge for an African person, is to be found in ontological knowledge…ontological knowledge is the intelligence of forces in their hierarchy, their cohesion and interaction" (Jimoh 2017: 125). Thus, for Jimoh, epistemology essentially is about the claims we make regarding the facts of our experiences and these facts are always interpreted with certain assumptions, concepts, theories and worldviews. This shows that there is an important and necessary relationship between ontology and epistemology (Jimoh 2017: 125). In a similar vein, Peter Ikhane adds that "African epistemology makes reference to the perception of reality, which was common to the cultures of Africans" (Ikhane 2017: 141). Ikhane cited Mbiti thus, "African cultures contain complex knowledge systems based on an understanding of a sacred universe sustained by a synergy of individual, ancestral, communal, spiritual, natural, and cosmic forces that animate all of the physical reality" (Ikhane 2017: 141). On the basis of this, Jimoh may be read to have submitted that a good grasp of African culture and ontological conceptions of reality will enable us to understand the African approach to knowledge.

Within Africa, the human person is given a higher epistemic recognition in comparison with the Western ontology. This shall be examined within the scope of African – Igbo ontology. According to Chikezie Onuoha, in Igbo worldview, and indeed, among most African worldviews, the human person occupies an important place in the society. For instance, the concept of personhood is all encompassing within an African context. It has some significant implications on virtually all events of life. Specifically,

> the realities of sickness and healthcare are examples where the concept of personhood plays a significant role. The Igbo thought on the place of human being strikes a balance between his or her personal identity as a unique individual person and his or her collective identity as a member of a community.
>
> *Onuoha, 2007: 235*

The discourse of personhood in the Igbo society occupies a fundamental place in their quest to know and understand the cosmos. The Igbo notion of person is basically metaphysical. Etymologically, "human being" means *mmadu* or *madu*, depending on the dialect (Chielonoza 1998: 31). It is a combination of two words: *mma* and *du* or *di* meaning beauty or goodness. The *mma* as aforementioned denotes 'good', 'a good' or 'the good'. Then, *'di'* is from an Igbo verb *'idi'* meaning 'to be' (Chielonoza 1998: 32). Thus, *mmadu* and *mma di* actually mean the same thing, which could be 'beauty' or 'goodness'. Chielonoza Eze emphasises that "there is no doubt that there is beauty in creation and no doubt that creation is good. Thus, *mmadu*, as the Igbos hold, is the hallmark and ultimate proof of the existence of beauty and goodness" (Chielonoza 1998: 32). It is also important to point out that *mma* which is derived from another dialect as *madu* means *muo* (spirit). This implies that spirit is seen in the person too. From this, we could understand that the Igbos also refers to person as, *ndi mmadu na ndi mmuo* – human person and spiritual person (Metuh 1991: 109). Justin Ekennia alluded to the fact that the strict biological and scientific distinction is almost absent in their reflections on human being and human person. The human person is essentially an integral being, constituted of physical, spiritual and metaphysical elements (Ekennia 2003: 26).

Following from this, the Igbo hold a dualistic conception of the person. A person in Igbo traditional thought has a composition of *ahu* (body) and *mkpuruobi/mmuo* (soul) not just body or a soul alone, but the conglomeration of these two realities defines the person (Uzoma 2019: 139.) The *ahu* (body) is a very important part of the human person that houses the soul and gives it form in a physical world. The *mmuo* (spirit) serves as the principle of performance; the *ahu* serves as the ground for changes and makes the whole enquiry into the concept of person possible (Okoye 2011: 59). The *ahu* is also seen to be in charge of the spirit during consciousness; therefore, once the soul is detached from the body, the individual is said to be dead (Onwuategwu 2020: 7). The *mmuo*, which is also used interchangeably with *mkpuruobi* (soul), on its part, accounts for the immaterial aspect of the human person. The *mkpuruobi*:

> forms and completes the innermost being and so it is the main essence of a being that makes it what it is. It is also a unit of life and *that* which enables the *mmadu* (man) comprehend, connect and commune with *Chukwuokike* and other metaphysical realities.
>
> Onwuategwu 2020: 7

Simply, the *mmuo/mkpuruobi* is incorporeal, indestructible and remains the immortal element in the human person. It is the vital force and the source of life of any human person. At death, it is *mmuo* that survives, while the *ahu* (body) disintegrates.

African Epistemology of the Person

Having established earlier that personalism focuses on the dignity and value of man as a unique being, this section draws some personalistic implications from the

African epistemology of the human person as against Western perspectives. There is no denying the obvious that there is sufficient evidence that traditionally, many, if not all; Africans uphold a dualistic notion of reality. In other words, that existence is partly physical and partly spiritual is a belief held by Africans, though, expressed in diverse forms. They also accept the reality and the intrinsic interrelationship of both the sensible (perceptible and physical) and non-sensible (non-perceptible and spiritual) aspects of reality (Edema 2018: 187). This view was buttressed by Elvis Imafidon thus:

> In a typical African ontology, there exists a universe of two realms of existence in African ontology; the visible and invisible; independently real but intrinsically linked to form a whole. The beings or entities existing in these two realms of existence are lively and active in varying degrees because they are vitalized, animated, or energized by an ontological principle or essence or force, given them by the Supreme Being.
>
> *Imafidon 2014: 38*

The Igbo perception of the person reveals that the person is a composite of different entities. Again, it is observed that, though there are differences with reference to the constituting parts of a person according to the different scholars cited, there is an agreement that the person consists basically of a material aspect and spiritual aspect. This presupposes dualism. The Igbo (as an instance of the African) conception of the human person therefore embraces and transcends the Western. That is, the African idea of the person transcends the physical. It is a conglomeration of the physical and metaphysical. Therefore, this is diametrically opposed to the Western notion of the human person that revolves around materialism, functionalism and physicalism.

In giving justification for the above, Justin Ekennia asserted that in analysing the nature of the human person in Igbo ontology, the strict biological and scientific analysis found in the modern Western narratives is almost absent in their (Igbo) reflections on human being and human person. The human person is essentially an integral being, constituted of physical, spiritual and metaphysical elements (Ekennia 2003: 26). Justin Ekennia further notes that *chi* is a unique life force, which each person possesses. No two individuals have the same *chi*; it is considered as the Igbo principle of individualisation. Thus, each person is unique and irreplaceable. *Chi* is present at birth. In this regard, Ekennia argues that *chi* is present in the human embryo/foetus. The Igbo believe that a child is a gift from God (*nwa sin a chi*) – the reason *chi* is called 'a personal god'. *Chi* is described as the supreme God as shared by each individual but more especially in his capacity as giver and author of destiny. By this same fact, *chi* is an emanation or participation of the supreme God. According to Ekennia, the Igbo construe the foetus as a human person and it automatically shares the life force of the Supreme Being right from the moment of conception (Ekennia 2003: 27). The position of Ekennia we may argue falls in line with some western moral philosophers who are of the view that personhood begins at the moment of conception. This, of course, is a departure from those (functionalists) who reduced personhood to entities who possess capacities for consciousness and rationality. To this, Chikezie Onuoha stated that:

> ... the functionalists' position may be said to be radical and perhaps not representative of western positions or only a form of reductionistic positions within the West. Nevertheless, it may not be denied that western liberal cultures have individualistic tenets, which serve as basis for the various notions of personhood held by different individual writers.
>
> *Onuoha 2007: 234*

Contrasting this Western view of the human person and the African view, Onuoha maintained that thinkers like Tangwa claim that the African notion of the person is not and cannot be different from Western notion for the fact that both understand the person to be fully self-conscious, rational, free and self-determining being. In response, Onuoha argued that it could be said that for him, what defines the human species is the universals of culture not their particularities. Onuoha further quizzed about where Tangwa locates the apparent difference between the two cultures since each recognises the various developmental stages of human being and the qualitative differences rooted on the degree of attainment of positive human attributes or capacities. Tangwa made it clear that the difference lies in the fact that the African concept does not draw the same conclusions as are drawn from the Western theory. He writes that the difference between a mentally retarded individual or an infant and a fully self-conscious, mature, rational and free individual do not entail, in the African perception, that such an individual is outside the inner sanctum of secular morality. Moreover, such a condition does not imply that they can or should be treated with less moral consideration. Unfortunately, Western notion of personhood is preoccupied with drawing out such a consequence (Onuoha 2007: 234). Based on this, Onuoha submitted that the African concept of personhood is totally different from what obtains in the West. He further premised his reasons on the following:

> The African notion does not make a distinction. It applies to the human being in all its developmental stages and to all its possible conditions. This is the case because Igbo thought rejects the purely materialistic conception of the person that characterizes Western conception. In order words, it rejects scientific materialism especially the aspect that denies objectivity to anything that cannot be proved in a laboratory experiment. One should note that the concept of personhood in this sense is not solely determined by its descriptive content, but also by its normative value as understood in African philosophy.
>
> *Onuoha 2007: 256*

In addition, and taking the discourse to the realm of bioethics which involves ethical issues, human and scientific experimentations, Onuoha argued that the Western approach to bioethics is characterised and dominated by a 'right approach'. Simply, "most of the ethical problems are couched in the language of rights, such as human rights, individual rights, woman rights, patient rights, embryo rights, children's rights and animal rights" (Onuoha 2007: 256). The implications of this, Onuoha stated, is that in the first place, little or no attention is paid to the meaning of life and the common good. Secondly, an ethic that is severed from a sense of ultimate orientation, that is, an ethic without telos, is encouraged. As such, human life, in this sense, is no longer seen from a holistic perspective for the reason that the 'right' language seems to be congruent with an individualistic orientation. This, for Onuoha, is not good enough, because the Igbo culture and most African cultures emphasise the interdependence of individuals, family and community (Onuoha, 2007: 257).

In a similar vein, Ebunoluwa Oduwole, arguing from the Yoruba conception of personhood, noted that there is a sense in which the embryo/foetus could be described as a person. She premised her reasons on the fact that

> the embryo/fetus possesses the *ara*, *emi* and *ori* which are necessary to be able to achieve the normative as one goes on interacting with the society. She says, *ori* (human destiny) suggests that there is life and individuality before birth that needs to be actualized; hence, the embryo has a right to live to actualize this destiny.
>
> *Oduwole 2010: 74*

Furthermore, Oduwole, arguing from the 'potentiality argument', noted that the Yoruba:

> ... often say *eyin ni di akuko* (meaning, it is the egg that becomes the hen). They believe strongly that there are many developmental stages in life. For instance, there is the early, middle and late. Life has to begin somewhere and we do not go from nothing to something. Life begins at the moment of conception and it is at this moment that a human being is biologically under construction from early to middle to late terms and then birth.
>
> *Oduwole 2010: 74*

Thus, the Yoruba, from available indications, submits that life begins at conception and the embryo/foetus is at least a potential human being. If we consider the idea of *ori*, the embryo/foetus is an individual that has a right to life from the moment of creation. As such, rather than the Yoruba claim that the embryo/foetus is not a person because it cannot perform certain functions, the Yoruba is likely to suppose that the embryo/foetus will grow/develop to have ability to perform such higher functions (Oduwole 2010: 74).

Following the same line of argument, George Ehusani has asked; do we have the absolute right or authority to produce or dispose our kind or to introduce radical mutations into the nature of the human species? The question raised about the right and authority to produce or dispose in the above concern such techniques as in vitro fertilisation and artificial insemination, surrogate motherhood, extracorporeal gestation, foetal experimentation and sex pre-selection and lately, sex change, embryonic stem cell research, male pregnancy, cloning and so on. Ehusani considers these techniques and procedures immoral and inhumane. For example, they involve:

> ... the super-ovulation of the woman by artificial means for the procurement of a large number of her ova; the procurement of the male semen in the laboratory by way of masturbation; the freezing of live human embryos for indefinite periods of time; and the discarding or wilful destruction of embryos produced in excess, and the commercialization of the womb, by which a woman gets pregnant only to surrender the fruit of the womb at any stage of its development for a fee. Experimentation with the foetuses has at times involved such a bizarre act as the slicing open of the rib cage of a still living human foetus (in order to observe the heart action); and the removal of vital organs of live foetuses for study.
>
> *Ehusani 1991: 215–216*

These procedures are inimical to the traditional African who not only treats the foetus as human life, but also sees 'life' in the umbilical cord of a new born baby. This simply explains why the umbilical cord is buried in ritualistic manner, away from the public view. The traditional African attaches serious importance and dignity to the life of the new born child. The average African believes strongly in the spiritual reality and connection of the umbilical cord of the child; this is the sole reason it is disposed carefully for the protection of the child. In addition, Ehusani asserted that the first thing we must take note of is the fact that, among the traditional African persons, the bifurcation of metaphysical and anthropological dualism that seem to divide reality as seen in western philosophy, science and theology does not exist. In other words, the African person does not have a problem in understanding the intersecting coexistence of both the physical and the visible, spiritual and invisible forces of the universe. In other words, there is no contradiction in them. There is a kind of symbiotic relationship between them; a harmonious interrelationship. The two worlds intersect in a dynamic communion such that the dichotomy between the sacred and the profane, matter and spirit, the supernatural and the natural, that define the Western worldview, is strikingly absent in Africa (Ehusani 1991: 291–220).

In all of these, one is tempted to ask, where is the epistemological thesis of the human person situated? The answers are not far-fetched. One of the issues I have sort to clarify at some point, in this work, is to articulate that, to some degree of certainty, African mode of knowing is different from others, say, Western or Asia. Specifically, if there are sociocultural and different ways of acquiring knowledge in Africa, then its stands to reason that an African articulation and formulation of knowledge is an African epistemology. On this, and from Jimoh's argument that authentic African epistemology is rooted in African ontology which includes our worldviews, experiences, facts, assumptions and theories, one would immediately understand that essentially, the notion or idea of the human person in African thought, as depicted in Igbo ontology, reveals the epistemic perspective of the human person. In this vein, the African notion of personhood takes the notion of personhood to describe the human person throughout its developmental stages from conception onwards. For instance, the Igbo believe that the embryo is a person and subsequently shares the life force of the Supreme Being right from the moment of conception. This, taken to be the African understanding of personhood, an African epistemology of the person, against the Western notion of person, does not subscribe to materialistic conception or scientific materialism regarding the human person, particularly when such denies objectivity to anything that cannot be proved in the laboratory.

Livio Melina has provided an insight into the epistemic status of the human personhood. She essentially argued that the act of knowing the human person must begin from the moral status of the human embryo; this is premised on the fact that the human being is to be respected and treated as a person from the moment of conception. Supporting her submission, she said, "The act of knowledge of the personal dignity of the embryo is also immediately an act of ethical self-questioning on the part of the subject, called to recognize him as such" (Melina 2007: 97). Clearly, what Melina's argument is about is that to justify our knowledge of the human person, it is important we look at the beginning of life. Thus she added:

> To know is not a neutral, purely speculative act; it is also 'recognition' of the dignity of a subject in a situation which inevitably has a practical nature… Must we not then admit that the ethical questioning begins precisely from the very act of knowing…The point…is to bring to light the subjective conditions for knowledge of that specific truth about the human being in regard to his personal beginnings.
>
> *Livio 2007: 98*

No doubt, Melina's submissions, above, was not in reference to African perspective on the notion of the person. However, one can safely conclude that her arguments has further substantiated the position that to understand the true nature of the epistemic nature and character of man, especially from the African perspective, it is important to begin from the beginning of life; that is, from conception. In this vein, an African epistemology of the person can be taken to consist in respecting human persons at all stages of human development. It finds the reasonableness of this by reference to the fact that African ontology does bifurcate between the spiritual and the physical; that is, African ontology is non-reductionistic and functionalistic as seen in Western philosophy and science.

Conclusion

In essence, what this chapter attempts to achieve is that while most scholars of African origin analyse or do a comparative study of the nature and character of the idea of the human person in Africa, attention is usually given to the ontological or ethical perspectives thereby neglecting the epistemic aspect. In other words, the conditions for the epistemic status of the truth of the human person are silent in such literature. Thus, this work has brought to limelight the basis on which to determine the epistemic status of the human person from an African perspective when the criteria established above are seen in the relation between African ontology, ethics and epistemology. To emphasise one of these to neglect the other two is inadequate simply because they are all related. This is not to dismiss the Western perspectives and orientations; rather, what this work has been able to show is that the understanding of the human person across cultures provides the avenue and space for further interrogation. Indeed, knowledge of persons and of oneself across cultures is vital in answering or proffering solutions to myriads of existential issues bedevilling humanity.

Works Cited

Chielozona, E. 1998. "Man as mma-du: Human Being and Being Human in Igbo Context." *The West African Journal of Philosophical Studies*. Vol. 1, No. 1: 27–48.

Copleston, F. 2003. *A History of Philosophy Hobbes to Hume*: Vol. 5. London: Continuum.

Dancak, P. 2017. "Personalism-The Philosophical Movement for Development." *Advance in Social Science, Education and Humanities Research*. Vol. 124: 51–55.

Edema, P. 2018. "Beyond Fractured Epistemology: A Discourse on the Idea of Personhood and Personalism in Igbo and Yoruba Thought Systems". *Synthesis Philosophica*. Vol. 65: 179–196.

Ehusani, G. O. 1991. *An Afro-Christian Vision (OZOVEHE): Toward a More Humanized World*. Lanham: University Press of America, Inc.

Ekennia, J. 2003. *Bio – Medical Ethics: Issues, Trends and Problems*. Owerri: Barloz Publishers.

Eze, C. 2018. "Man as mma–du: Human Being and Being Human in Igbo context." *The West African Journal of Philosophical Studies* 1(1): 27–48.

Ezedike, E. U. April 2019. "The Concept of Human Person in African Ontology: A Critical Reflection on the Igbo Notion of Man." *African Research Review*, Vol. 13 (2), No. 54: 131–137.

Fletcher, J. 1972. "Indicators of Humanhood: A Tentative Profile of Man." *The Hastings Center Report*. Vol. 2, No. 5: 1–4.

Grzegorz Holub, K. S. 2018. "Is a Post-Human Personalism Possible"? *FILOZOFIA*. Vol. 25: 253–262.

Ikhane, P. 2017. "Epistemic Insight from an African Way of Knowing" in Isaac Ukpokolo (ed.). *Themes, Issues and Problems in African Philosophy*. London: Palgrave Macmillan, pp. 137–144.

Imafidon, E. 2014. "Life's Origin in Bioethics: Implications of Three Ontological Perspectives: Judeo-Christianity, Western Secularism, and the African Worldview" in E. Imafidon and J. Bewaji (eds.). *Ontologized Ethics: New Essays in Africa Meta-Ethics*. Lanham: Lexington Books, pp. 133–150.

Iroegbu, P. 2000. *Kpim of Personality: Treatise on the Human Person*. Nekede Owerri: Eustel Publications.

Jimoh, A. K. 2017. "An African Theory of Knowledge" in Isaac Ukpokolo (ed.). *Themes, Issues and Problems in African Philosophy*. London: Palgrave Macmillan, pp. 121–136.

Kaphagawani, D. N., and Malherbe, J. G. 2003. "The Question of African Epistemology" in Pieter. H. Coetzee and Abraham. P. J. Roux (eds.) 2nd. *The African Philosophy Reader*. London: Routledge, pp. 259–319.

Lowe, E. J. 1995. *Locke on Human Understanding*. Tim Crane and Jonathan Wolff (eds.). New York, USA: Routledge.

Melina, L.1997. "Epistemological Questions with Regard to the Status of the Human Embryo" in Juan De Dios Vial Correa and Elio Sgreccia (eds.). *Identity and Statute of Human Embryo: Proceedings of the Third Assembly of the Pontifical Academy for Life*. Vatican City: Liberia Editrice Vaticana, pp. 123–127.

Metuh, I. 1991. *African in Western Conceptual Schemes: The Problem of Interpretation* (Studies in Igbo Religions). Jos: Imico Press.

Mondin, B. 1985. *Philosophical Anthropology*. Bangalore: Theological Publications.

Oduwole, E. 2010. "Personhood and Abortion: An African Perspective." *LUMINA*. Vol. 21, No. 2: 1–10.

Okoye, C. 2011. "'Onwe': An Inquiry into the Igbo Concept of the Self." *Ogiris: A Journal of African Studies*. Vol. 8. No. 1: 51–66.

Onuoha, C. 2007. *Bioethics across Borders: An African Perspective*. Dissertation for the Degree of Theology in Ethics. Uppsala: Acta Universitatis Upsaliensis.

Onwuategwu, I. N. 2020. "The Concept of Hylomorphism in Igbo Ontology: An Analytic Approach." *The Journal of Philosophy, Culture and Religion*. Vol. 3, No.1: 1–9.

Petrini, C., and Gainotti, S. 2008. "A Personalist Approach to Public – Health Ethics." *Bulletin of the World Health Organization*. Vol. 86, No. 8: 624–629.

Rudman, S. 1997. *Concepts of Person and Christian Ethics*. Cambridge: Cambridge University Press.

Sgreccia, E. 1999. *Bio-Ethics: Origins, Epistemological Justification and Orientations in The Family and Bio-Ethics: Trends, Implications and Challenges. Seminar Papers on the Family, Marriage and Bio-Ethics*. Ghana: AECAWA Publications.

Sutton, A. 2008. *Christian Bioethics*. London and New York: T&T Clark.

Thomas, D., and Williams, L. C. 2004. "What Is Thomistic Personalism." *Alpha Omega*. Vol. VII. No. 2: 163–197.

Uzoma, E. E. 2019. "The Concept of Human Person in African Ontology: A Critical Reflection on the Igbo Notion of Man." *African Research Review*. Vol. 13(2), No. 54: 131–137.

Wildman, J. 2007. "Substance, Nature, and Human Personhood". CedarEthics Online. Paper 29. http://digitalcommons.cedarville.edu/cedar_ethics_online/29

12

KNOWLEDGE, BEING, AND THE CASE FOR AN AFRICAN EPISTEMOLOGY

Dennis Masaka

Introduction

Uneven power relations of cultures from the global North and global South have over the years tended to decide the fate of some knowledges of the latter and propped up that of the former as legitimate one (Ramose, 2016: 546; Masaka, 2021: 260). While the knowledge tradition of cultures of the global North continues to flourish unencumbered by negative influences from other cultures, the same has not been the case with knowledges from the global South and Africa, in particular. These knowledges have lately been measured against the epistemological order of the dominant cultures as if it embodies credentials for a transcultural knowledge. Under the banner of standardisation, self-ascribed and defended by some cultures in the global North, deviations from that knowledge tradition have often led to overt and covert doubts about the standing of such knowledges as knowledges *qua* knowledges (Graness, 2015: 79; Masaka, 2018: 287–288). But then, such a position if successfully held as the criterion of knowledge production would neatly disqualify knowledges, whose production disregards contentious and provincial standards of knowledge formation emanating from the global North. There lies the problem of trying to base knowledge production across the world to a particular epistemological order (Mudimbe, 1988: 85–86). As Anke Graness (2015: 84) has aptly noted, such canonisation of knowledge "is part of a meaning-producing process that does not escape an inherent capacity to become a discourse of domination".

My intervention in this chapter is to argue that a human being's particular location and conditions of existence, gives birth to certain knowledges and knowledge claims. That these knowledges and knowledge claims deviate to some degree from the dominant epistemology from elsewhere is no cause for intellectual disillusionment if one's preeminent concern is that of creating fresh and unmediated paths for authentic self-understanding among African cultures. Any claims militating against this organic nature of human life will only lead to creation of knowledges that are essentially unhelpful to self-understanding. I take self-understanding as the foundational prerequisite for creating knowledge in any culture whether from the global South or North. Regrettably, the temptation to fashion knowledge creation along the lines of the dominant epistemology that dominated cultures seek to sidestep has often been too tempting for some (Mudimbe, 2003: 212). However, this mode of thinking will not lead to knowledges borne out of authentic locations and existential conditions of knowers from the dominated cultures, such as Africa. A new and transformational way of thinking to address the present power relations becomes necessary, one 'that would not take the history of ideas that any one culture claims is universal as a starting point' (Vest, 2005: 14). Rather, one that takes a particular culture's point of location and conditions of existence as the fundamental starting point becomes inevitable.

The chapter is organised as follows: in the first section, I discuss what the dislocation from thinking and creating knowledges on terms and conditions of one's existence means to the quest for the African self-understanding unmediated by alien epistemological orders. With this in mind, in the second section, I defend the position that the African could be better disposed to talk of and about herself or himself than what others from elsewhere may think they can or consider as the correct way to do so. Such a feat can only be successfully attained by respecting and remaining true to the idea that cultures across the world may not have the same epistemological questions that underpin knowledge formation so are their conditions of existence. This will then justify the need for diverse epistemologies underpinned by diverse terms and frameworks. The substance of this reasoning is that the African ought to be a preferred producer of knowledge about herself or himself. In the third section, I articulate the clarion call for disputed knowers in Africa and elsewhere to produce knowledge along lines of their terms and conditions of existence. This is not an invitation to seek or solicit acceptance in the 'family of knowledges' because no culture is there to offer this acceptance as history has shown. The temptation will be to dominate or attempt to destroy subaltern knowledges. In this light, dominated cultures ought to produce their own knowledges from their different and diverse vantage points. In this liberatory trajectory, the African ought to be the first point of reference concerning knowledge production about and of herself or himself; that is, she or he should be one that takes her or his conditions of existence as a veritable point of departure. This is necessary in nurturing conditions that would allow the flourishing of authentic African epistemologies.

Epistemic Dislocation

Doubts about an African's mettle to produce knowledge that measures to the assumed ideal have been broadly debated. The general argument from sceptics has been to throw into doubt what an African claims to know not on her or his terms but on assumed ideal 'universal' standards of what qualifies as knowledge. But this contention is wrong-headed because the African constructs knowledge by answering to questions that arise from her or his conditions of existence or being. Moreover, the 'universal' has been aptly shown to be essentially a particular narrative that deceptively claims transcultural appeal and application (Taiwo, 1998: 5–6; Dussel and Ibarra-Colado, 2006: 505; Ramose, 2016: 551; Dunford, 2017: 389–390). The same might be true of cultures from other geopolitical centres. So, the said standards to which an African has to measure to may simply be a lure to pander to the epistemological order of dominant cultures (Matolino, 2015: 433; Masaka, 2017: 444–445) leading to epistemic dislocation. With this in mind, the ideal or the standard is just but a source of dislocation and not sign of excellence.

In this section, the struggle of the African with dislocation is the main focus. I first discuss briefly the problem of dislocation of the African from thinking and creating knowledges on terms and conditions of her or his existence. Thereafter, I ponder what this would mean to the quest for self-understanding unmediated by hegemonic terms and frameworks. I argue that the lure of making it to the assumed 'knowledge grade' through bowing to the argument of standardisation is a lost cause that is unhelpful to African cultures and other dominated ones elsewhere in their quest for self-assertion. The idea underpinning this position is that knowledges and knowledge claims are generated in reference to conditions of being and not from some detached and abstract or Ivory Tower–like vantage points as some advocates of standardisation may want to claim.

The African has faced a number of challenges on a number of fronts most notably in efforts to assert an inalienable right to be a knower. Her or his humanity has often been questioned by those who think that they represent ideal human beings (Taiwo, 1993: 898). Failure to fit into the latter's model of humanity is reason for disqualification from their own contentious categories. This has been extended to her or his capacity to produce knowledge (see Nyamnjoh, 2012: 129). Though such claims may appear to be simply self-serving strategies to disorient those that are marked for conquest and subjugation, they have serious implications on knowledge projects of dominated cultures. Essentially, a question that can be posed is: to whose design and purpose should knowledge production in Africa be? This is a significant question that calls attention to politics of knowledge where dominated cultures are proscribed from epistemic freedom to create knowledge on their own terms and conditions of existence because it is not considered as knowledge proper (Ndlovu-Gatsheni, 2018: 20). As a result, they are forced, or at best encouraged to produce knowledge along the lines of the dominant cultures' epistemological paradigm if they are to be certified as legitimate producers of assumed knowledge *qua* knowledge. Nevertheless, this is a negation of the idea that 'conceptions of knowledge, of what it means to know, of what counts as knowledge, and how that knowledge is produced are as diverse as the cosmologies and frameworks' (Santos, Nunes and Meneses, 2007: xxi) that underpin them. While this sounds quite compelling, it might be purposely and strategically downplayed. However, the claim of standardised knowledge is a useful tool for those inspired to conquer and maintain their dominance over dominated cultures but essentially a source of trepidation for the conquered cultures.

Producing knowledge on alien terms is an overarching point of entry for epistemological dislocation. By epistemological dislocation, I mean being displaced from one's epistemological locus through being made to underpin knowledge construction on terms and frameworks that do not emerge from one's conditions of existence (Graness, 2015: 81). In this scenario, the knowledge one produces has marginal significance to oneself and one's circumstances. While on the face of it, it might be identified as useful knowledge, it has serious deficiencies because it is not geared towards the circumstances that it is meant to respond to. In fact, it is essentially dislocated from people and purposes for which it is intended to serve. But then, an interlocutor might argue that such knowledges produced on terms and frameworks of alien cultures have proved to be useful to countries in Africa over the years. For that reason, one might say we cannot change what has worked for dominated cultured then and perhaps now. While, to some extent, this might be a plausible claim, it largely loses the salient reason behind such a liberatory move, which is to ensure that knowledges produced in cultural traditions in Africa arise from terms and conditions of existence of their peoples. The reason is that knowledges and knowledge claims answer to conditions that give rise to them. It is possible that with time they may be adopted by other cultures but it would appear more plausible to ensure that the knowledge used in a specific locus emerges and is shaped by authentic terms of its producers.

Epistemic dislocation has serious implications for the quest for self-understanding that ought to be the veritable response to this problem. The focus of the knower is diverted from issues that are fundamental to one's conditions of existence. Yet, producing knowledge that answers to one's conditions of existence ought to be the preeminent focus of a knower. Attempting to satisfy some standards set elsewhere of what qualifies as knowledge will only help to alienate knowledge produced to the circumstances it is supposed to be applied. In light of this major problem, which is an outcome of epistemic dislocation, there is need to focus on ensuring that knowledges that dominated cultures produce are underpinned by the terms and conditions of their existence. With this in mind, Vest (2005: 14) is right in calling for the end of:

> *perverse preoccupations* with proving to mainstream (read Western) philosophers that the wisdom traditions of [these] non-European cultures could also qualify as philosophy. We need to begin to be more critical of this need which Southern philosophers feel to prove ourselves.

And in being critical of it, it is necessary to highlight that focus must be on creating knowledges steeped in respective circumstances of the dominated cultures and not the unhelpful quest to 'match' some 'standards' of what qualifies as knowledge which are prescribed from other geoepistemic centres. This liberatory step does not require mediation from terms and frameworks of dominant cultures but must be driven by terms and frameworks emerging from the circumstances of an African knower.

The African Knower

Following from the position defended above, in this section, I defend the position that the African could be better disposed to talk of and about herself or himself than what others from elsewhere may think they can or consider as the correct path to do so. While this dimension has been widely shared by some African scholars (Dladla, 2017; Ndlovu-Gatsheni, 2018: 20–21), I explicitly defend it by noting that such an endeavour could be successfully done by respecting and remaining true to the idea that cultures across the world may not have the same questions that underpin knowledge formation. If this is so, I suppose that it will then allow for the existence of diverse epistemologies underpinned by diverse terms and frameworks. The substance of this reasoning is that the African ought to be a preferred producer of knowledge about herself or himself especially if it is acceptable that knowledges and knowledge claims are borne out of conditions of existence of human beings.

That circumstances and conditions of existence of diverse cultures in Africa and more generally in the global South and global North may share significant differences may be hardly contested. The terms and frameworks of knowledge production in the global North may not be expected to be the same as those of some cultures from the global South. The colonial experiences that cultures from the global South have suffered significantly mark them as having different existential conditions that require a more suited transformational turn. This then offers support to the contention that those better disposed to produce knowledge that is more suited to a particular culture's conditions of existence are people from within it. This is supported by Okere, Njoku and Devisch (2005: 3) who argue that all knowledge starts off from local roots where, by 'local roots of knowledge', they refer to:

> any given culture's unique genius, and distinctive creativity which put a most characteristic stamp on what its members in their singular context and history meaningfully develop as knowledge, epistemology, metaphysics, worldview. This particularity in the nodes and mode of knowledge is often a result of that mutual push and pull between the people and the potential in their history and life-world, their task-related networks and living communities.

What can be discerned from these averments is that particular communities or cultures produce their own local knowledges that answer to their existential circumstances and terms. The fact that knowledge is first of all local is an indication of the fact that particular conditions of existence are the first sources of knowledges before such knowledges are possibly adapted to different social-cultural contexts. But, essentially, the point is that every culture has its own internal systems of producing knowledge that help to answer and understand their circumstances. In so doing, they may be interested in understanding other cultures more generally.

However, the testimony of a particular culture about its own attributes ought to be given overarching recognition and respect as representative of its life story and how it masters its conditions of existence and the world more generally. This then helps to support the view that the quest for self-understanding ought to be the focus of knowledge creation and not the contentious clamour for standardisation of what knowledge is and how it ought to be created (see Curry, 2011a, 2011b).

With this in mind, there may not be a 'correct way of producing knowledge' that ought to be adopted by all cultures. Accenting to this position is to fall into the trap of the hegemonic narrative of standards that may, on the face of it, appear well-intentioned purportedly supporting the production of knowledge on 'universal' terms and frameworks, yet it conceals the salient epistemicide against alternative ways of knowing (Santos, Nunes and Meneses, 2007: xxi). This forfeits responsibilities of cultures to produce knowledges that by definition and practice emerge from their respective existential circumstances. This is the tragedy of epistemic dislocation. It renders dominated cultures largely confined to non-local systems of knowledge production whose end product may not be so much useful to their diverse and evolving conditions of existence. It is for this reason that I consider that the African knower ought to come to the fore and assert her or his right to produce knowledge that speaks to her or his existential circumstances. The reasons for supporting this call are further articulated. I take it to be the case that what a particular culture considers as knowledge emerges from, and provides answers to nagging questions that it faces at it tries to understand itself and the world more broadly. What needs to be emphasised here is that there are salient questions that underpin production of certain kinds of knowledges from vantage points of particular cultures. In addition, since existential circumstances significantly differ from one culture to another, some nagging questions that these cultures ponder are different, so are the answers to them.

With the above view in mind, the knowledge produced in response to these questions would not be expected to constitute transcultural but essentially local claims. If this is taken as the point of departure for knowledge production in Africa and elsewhere, then cultures will produce knowledges that respond to questions emerging from their respective existential circumstances. This might not be the kind of scenario that friends of standardisation of knowledge production might favour as they are largely driven by the desire to find something like a 'common denominator' that ought to underpin knowledge production across the world. However, as I have shown, this is an untenable position as it suppresses diversity of epistemological questions and conditions of existence of different cultures for purposes of foregrounding a contentious standardisation narrative. African cultures cannot entrust this important task to cultures from other geopolitical centres nor will their terms and frameworks be used to underpin veritable knowledge production for the former. The onus is on Africans to work towards self-understanding than for other cultures to pretend to be better positioned to speak authoritatively about them. Their testimony must define what is known about them and how they conceive the world more generally.

Motivations of an African Knower

In the previous section, I have shown that an African knower ought to produce knowledge underpinned by local terms and conditions. In this section, I seek to argue that this is not a task meant to seek accommodation or acceptance in the 'family of knowledges'. The reason is that such a purpose is ill-conceived and deviates significantly from the liberatory stance that ought as its preeminent focus to steer clear of temptations to negotiate compromises with the dominant epistemology, and focus on developing distinctive knowledges that directly answer to respective cultures' evolving challenges and aspirations. In so arguing, I appeal to the works of Tommy J. Curry (2011a: 140, 2011b: 316) that have highlighted the dangers of seeking accommodation and coexistence with dominant cultures. Although Curry's averments are meant to highlight the predicaments of preoccupations of African-American philosophers, I intend to use them to articulate how an African knower could explicitly focus on producing knowledge that answers to her or his conditions of existence. The reason is that African-Americans and others from the global South, with Africa as a point of reference, face similar colonial experiences. After briefly outlining Curry's (2011a, 2011b) central averments relevant for my purposes here, I show what they might mean to an African knower's quest to take a transformational turn and focus on producing knowledge steeped in her or his culture and conditions of existence.

Curry (2011a: 139) notes that African-American philosophy has been famous for noting the inadequacies of European philosophical thought. However, "this practice has the effect of not only distracting Black philosophers from understanding the thought of their ancestors, but formulates the practice of Africana philosophy as 'racial therapy' for whites" (Curry, 2011a: 139). The reason is that such a preoccupation means that African-American philosophers are saddled with questions that are unhelpful in understanding their self-history as they seek to transform the colonial logics of Western philosophical thought so that it would appear non-dominant in their quest to forge integration with a philosophy that has entrenched hostilities to other cultures. This appears to be a lost cause as it ignores what ought to be the overarching guiding principle of charting black thought on its terms and frameworks. With this in mind, Curry (2011a: 140) laments African-American philosophy's marginal focus on issues of fundamental significance to blacks; that is, the articulation of "the actual historical positions that many Black authors held outside Africana philosophers' criticisms of European thinking". Though seeking racial harmony, equality and audience with oppressors may be praised in some quarters, it is pursued at the expense of focusing on understanding of black self-history and their conditions of existence (Curry, 2011a: 140). Because of the preoccupation with finding space within the hegemonic European philosophical tradition, "African-American philosophy has failed to inquire seriously into the culturally particular epistemologies of African-descended people, preferring instead to read into Black thought decidedly European philosophical continuities" (Curry, 2011a: 144–145). This leads to the temptation to underpin black thought on terms and frameworks of the dominant European philosophical thought which is a serious normative and methodological flaw.

Curry's (2011a, 2011b) averments are very important to my understanding of what African knowers need to do in order to seriously invest in articulating knowledges that are underpinned by terms and questions that emerge from their respective cultures and conditions of existence. This might on the face of it prove to be a daunting task especially given that such a liberatory move ought to be accomplished within the context of an environment in which one philosophy has, over some centuries, been projected as the dominant one if not the only one worth the title. More so, the majority of Africans some of whom are entrusted to produce liberatory knowledges that depart from entanglements in the dominant European philosophical thought have been educated in this latter philosophical tradition. Perhaps, for the sake of seeking comfort in what they have 'grown' to know as philosophy, namely European philosophical thought, Africans may be tempted to ensure that knowledges they produce purportedly from their respective conditions of existence find resonance with European philosophical thought. Doing so may be thought to be a strategic move to make knowledges purportedly emerging from African cultures to be part of what has been considered as knowledge from the perspective of the dominant cultures. As a result, there have been efforts to find equivalences between knowledges 'emerging' from African cultures with philosophical traditions from the Euro-North American world. However, these equivalences are false and problematic as has been articulated by Curry (2011a, 2011b) with reference to African-American philosophy and as I proceed to show concerning knowledge production in Africa.

There is need to depart from the comfort but false zones of seeking a place in the dominant philosophy and focus on self-understanding as the overarching mission of an African knower. I call efforts to find equivalences with the dominant epistemology 'false' basically for two reasons. First, these efforts presuppose that there are abstract terms and frameworks of producing knowledge that are detached from any specific cultural context. This appears not to be the case especially when one realises that existential circumstances between cultures from the global North and global South may be significantly different. Differences also exist among cultures within these respective geopolitical centres. With this in mind, efforts to find equivalences among knowledges emerging from these diverse backgrounds are simply misdirected. Second, it presupposes that the dominant epistemology offers the standards for which the dominated epistemologies must always strive to match. However, this is a contentious expectation given that the so-called standards of knowledge production are essentially subjective to particular cultures. As a result, to pretend that a particular and provincial knowledge paradigm is the reference point for knowledge production for all other cultures is implausible (Chimakonam, 2017: 12). It is a wrong strategy for the African knower as she or he ponders ways of trying to produce knowledge that identifies with her or his conditions of existence. Seeking to be allowed space into the knowledge canon of the dominant culture only helps to aid epistemic dislocation than to authenticate a knowledge paradigm of a dominated culture as one may envisage. These two reasons help to show that the African knower ought to avoid these false zones of standardisation and become true to her or his terms and existential situations as she or he seeks to produce knowledge that is useful to her or his existential situations.

However, one might argue that there is nothing wrong at all with aspiring to be part of the 'family of knowledges'. According to this reasoning, knowledges produced from subaltern regions of this world have a right to assert a stake in the global knowledge economy. This is often done in order to show that indeed knowledge does not emerge from a uni-source and producer but from pluri-sources and producers (Masaka, 2019: 304). Granted, this is quite convincing especially in the light of the predicaments of subaltern knowledges when placed in comparison to the dominant epistemologies. But, one ought to be wary of seeking the help of the dominant cultures to allow subaltern ones to be part of the 'family of knowledges'. The dominant epistemology may not 'allow' parity with subaltern epistemologies as the latter may think but may actually seek to suppress them so that it retains its dominance. In this light, subaltern epistemologies, such as those from African cultures, must seek to develop themselves unencumbered by wishful thinking that the dominant epistemologies may seriously enter into dialogue with them that will possibly result in parity of existence and influence. The reason is that the uneven power relations currently existing between the dominant epistemologies and subaltern ones are not 'natural' but have been artificially created by the former so as to assume dominance over the latter. Going into the future, this may not change even though optimism for a positive change may be worth envisioning. The uneven worth ascribed to the two knowledges are not a result of an objective process. Even though such a process existed, it would ideally be untenable as knowledge may not be reasonably compared on the basis of an abstract standard. If such a standard ever existed, especially when one accepts as I do that knowledges emerge from diverse cultures and conditions of existence. As a result, there are strong reasons to renounce insinuations of the existence of 'general' knowledge (Santos, 2007: 67) that is unattached to any specific culture. In light of this, such concerns ought not to be a source of worry for an African knower. She or he ought to be guided and motivated by a quest for self-understanding if she or he is to produce knowledge inspired by terms and existential situations of her or his culture.

Concluding Remarks

The African knower faces a daunting task as she or he seeks to construct knowledge that answers to her or his terms and conditions of existence. In this chapter, I have confined myself to imagining how an African knower might contribute to knowledge production about her or his existential situations and the world at large from her or his veritable vantage point. I consider this as the best possible course of action if we are to have authentic knowledges emerging from diverse cultures. The assumption underpinning this contention is that an African knower will be able to overcome alien terms and conceptual frameworks that she or he has over the years grown to be accustomed to and relied upon as she or he seeks a fresh start to knowledge production, one that is liberatory. Nevertheless, doubts have been expressed about chances of a successful escape of an African knower from entanglement in the dominant epistemology and methods that underpin it. If this is accepted, it would essentially forestall meaningful chances of overcoming epistemic conquest and attain epistemic liberation that countries and more specifically cultures in Africa envision. Despite possible doubts about the emergence of a typical African knower unencumbered by terms and frameworks of the dominant epistemology, there might be a way out of epistemic conquest. It is quite promising that a number of African thinkers have begun to highlight problems with the basis of knowledge production in Africa. Such a legitimate concern is essential in grounding a transformational step that would lead an African knower on a path of veritable knowledge production that takes as foundational, terms and frameworks of one's culture and conditions of existence.

References

Chimakonam, J. O. (2017). Conversationalism as an Emerging Method of Thinking in and beyond African Philosophy. *Acta Academica*, 2, pp. 11–33.

Curry, T. J. (2011a). On Derelict and Method: The Methodological Crisis of African-American Philosophy's Study of African-Descended Peoples under an Integrationist Milieu. *Radical Philosophy Review*, 14 (2), pp. 139–164.

Curry, T. J. (2011b). The Derelictical Crisis of African American Philosophy: How African American Philosophy Fails to Contribute to the Study of African-Descended People. *Journal of Black Studies*, 42 (3), pp. 314–333.

Dladla, N. (2017). Izwe Elethu: A reply to Rafael Winkler's 'Who has the authority to speak about identity?' *Huffington Post*, www.huffingtonpost.co.uk/entry/izwe-elethi-a-reply-to-rafael-winklers-who-has-the-authority_uk_5c7e991ae4b078abc6c13cb8. Accessed 03/01/2023.

Dunford, R. (2017). Toward a Decolonial Global Ethics. *Journal of Global Ethics*, 13 (3), pp. 380–397.

Dussel, E. and Ibarra-Colado, E. (2006). Globalization, Organization and the Ethics of Liberation. *Organization*, 13 (4), pp. 489–508.

Graness, A. (2015). Questions of Canon Formation in Philosophy: The History of Philosophy in Africa. *Phronimon*, 16 (2), pp. 78–96.

Masaka, D. (2017). Challenging Epistemicide through Transformation and Africanisation of the Philosophy Curriculum in Africa. *South African Journal of Philosophy*, 36 (4), pp. 441–455.

Masaka, D. (2018). The Prospects of Ending Epistemicide in Africa: Some Thoughts. *Journal of Black Studies*, 49(3), pp. 284–301.

Masaka, D. (2019). Attaining Epistemic Justice through Transformation and Decolonisation of Education Curriculum in Africa. *African Identities*, 17 (3–4), pp. 98–309.

Masaka, D. (2021). Knowledge, Power, and the Search for Epistemic Liberation in Africa. *Social Epistemology*, 35 (3), pp. 258–269.

Matolino, B. (2015). Universalism and African Philosophy. *South African Journal of Philosophy*, 34(4), pp. 433–440.

Mudimbe, V. Y. (1988). *The Invention of Africa: Gnosis, Philosophy, and the Order of Knowledge.* Bloomington: Indiana University Press.

Mudimbe, V. Y. (2003). Globalization and African Identity. *CR: The New Centennial Review*, 3 (2), pp. 205–218.

Ndlovu-Gatsheni, S. J. (2018). *Epistemic Freedom in Africa: Deprovincialization and Decolonization.* London: Routledge.

Nyamnjoh, F. B. (2012). 'Potted Plants in Greenhouses': A Critical Reflection on the Resilience of Colonial Education in Africa. *Journal of Asian and African Studies* 47(2): 129–154.

Okere, T., Njoku, C. A. and Devisch, R. (2005). All Knowledge Is First of all Local Knowledge: An Introduction. *Africa Development*, XXX (3), pp. 1–19.

Ramose, M. B. (2016). Teacher and Student with a Critical Pan-Epistemic Orientation: An Ethical Necessity for Africanising the Educational Curriculum in Africa. *South African Journal of Philosophy*, 35 (4), pp. 546–555.

Santos, B. D. S. (2007). Beyond Abyssal Thinking: From Global Lines to Ecologies of Knowledges. *Review*, 30 (1), pp. 45–89.

Santos, B. D. S., Nunes, J. A. and Meneses, M. P. (2007). "Opening Up the Canon of Knowledge and Recognition of Difference." In *Another Knowledge Is Possible: Beyond Northern Epistemologies (Reinventing Social Emancipation: Towards New Manifestos)*, edited by B. D. S. Santos, xix–ixii. London: Verso.

Taiwo, O. (1993). Colonialism and Its Aftermath: The Crisis of Knowledge Production. *Callaloo*, 16 (4), pp. 891–908.

Taiwo, O. (1998). Exorcising Hegel's Ghost: Africa's Challenge to Philosophy. *African Studies Quarterly*, 1 (4), pp. 3–16.

Vest, J. L. (2005). The Promise of Caribbean Philosophy: How It Can Contribute to a 'New Dialogic' in Philosophy. *Caribbean Studies*, 33 (2), pp. 3–34.

INDEX

Note: Endnotes are indicated by the page number followed by "n" and the note number e.g., 3n4 refers to note 3 on page 4.

active empiricism, theory of 80, 83
Adegbindin, O. 8
African belief system 20, 24, 168
African communitarian community 97, 99
African communitarian epistemology (ACE) 35, 39, 40, 50; African theory of knowledge 41; characterisation of 41; knower's rational activity 35; knowledge/truth 42–5; social, cultural and communitarian process 38; theorising knowledge 36
African communitarian knowledge: critical discourse 91–3; self-unconscious 91
African communitarian ontology 92, 97, 100–3; conception of personhood in 101; discourse of 103; individual and 100–2; individuality and criticality in 101; and knowledge 97–100; nature of 92; radical 101
African communitarian tradition 98
African communo-cognition 55
African cultural traditions 82
African cultures 3, 163, 172; challenges 174; colonial experiences 176; epistemic dislocation 175; self-understanding 172, 173, 177; sub-Sahara 44
African-descended people 178
African epistemology 1, 2, 3n4, 8, 20, 28, 92, 93; African knower 176–7; delineation of 19; epistemic dislocation 173–5;
externalist and internalist notions 4; meaning/discourse of 1–12; motivations, of African knower 176–7; overview of 172–3; personhood 162–4; pre-colonial life-forms of 21
African knower: African epistemology 176–7; motivations of 178–80
African knowledge system 12, 39, 92, 139
African metaphysical ideas, about ontology 93
African metaphysicians 67
African metaphysics 67
African notion, of continuum implies 29
African ontology 41, 92–4, 163, 165; ontological frameworks 159; ontological notion 94
African-oriented epistemology 11
African philosophy 55, 64, 66
African Philosophy Reader, The 68
African political emancipatory ideology 5
African traditional belief systems 1
African traditional court systems 100
African traditional idea 98
Afro-Caribbean culture 120
Afro-Caribbean epistemology 116, 120, 122; philosophical reflections 124; socio-cultural 123
Afro-Caribbean ontology 117, 121
Afro-Caribbean people 118, 119, 121, 128

Index

Afro-Caribbean philosophy 116
Afro-Caribbean reality 116
Afro-communitarianism 57
Afro-communitarian philosophy 56
Afro-relational approach 63; defending from objections 74–6
Afro-relational vs. Western-individualist ontologies: definitions of 64–7; hypothesis of 67–9; natural object, essence of 67–9; objections defending 74–6; overview of 63–4; self relational 69–72; water, relational account of 73–4
Airoboman, F. A. 8, 82
Ai yole abha len oria 110
Akan cultures 22; triad understanding 22; Wiredu's/Kaphagawani's analyses 45
Akan language 44
Anglo-American approach 63
Anglo-Saxon tradition 7
Ani, Emmanuel 11
Anyanwu, K. C. 5, 7
Anyanwu's analysis 8
Appiah, Kwame Anthony 9
Aristotelian-Thomistic subject-object tradition 84
Aristotle 43, 67, 108–10
Asekhauno, A. A. 9, 82

Bartle, P. F. W. 22, 23
beliefs: African belief system 1, 20; belief-forming mechanism 27; Christian beliefs 120; justification, belief, and truth (JTB) 131; universe-of-harmony 20, 22–8; Yoruba belief system 5
Bengston, Jan O. 161
Bewaji, J. A. I. 118, 123–5
biocognition 49–51
Brown, Lee 41–2

Carothers, John 115
Chewa cultures, Wiredu's/Kaphagawani's analyses 45
Chewa linguistic scheme 44
Christian beliefs 120
City of God 152
clairvoyance 4
cloning 168
co-dependency 53, 58
cogito ergo sum 48
cognitive sciences: philosophy and philosophers of 49; Western philosophy of 49
colonization, impact of 52
communalism 63

communo-cognition theory 50–6; rehumanisation 54–6; relational cognition, humanness of 57–8; study/analysis of 48; two charges 56–7; Ubuntu/relational minds 50–4; Western episteme 49
Companion to Metaphysics (Blackwell) 65
contemporary version 70, 71
Coram-deo-equality 151
Coulet, Jean-Michel 107
Curry, Tommy J. 178, 179

Dancak, Pavol 162
Declaration of Independence 155
Dennehy, R. 79, 81, 84
Descartes, Rene 48, 80, 111, 131, 152
Devisch, R. 176
Dewey, John 80, 81
Durante, Daniel 26
Dzobo, N. K. 94, 98, 100, 102

Edozien, Ndidi 40
Ehusani, George 167–8
embryonic stem cell research 168
empiricists, active 83
English-speaking works 66
epistemic communalism 99–100
epistemic ideal, representation of truth as 108–9, 112
epistemological relativity 7
Epistle to the Romans 150
Esan thought system, truth-speaking/truth-telling 111
ethno-epistemology 11
European thinking 178
euro-western Enlightenment 155
Evans-Pritchard, E. E. 115
Eze, Chielonoza 164

Friedenberg, J. 48
Fubah, M. A. 23

Gainotti, Sabina 161
Garvey, M. 117, 122
Gettier, Edmund 37–8, 131–2
global North 172, 176, 179
Gordon, L. R. 17, 124, 127
Grzegorz, K. S. 161
Gyekye, K. 2, 39, 94, 98, 101

Hallen, B. 133
Hamminga, B. 134
Hateta, anthropological idea of 149
Hegel, Georg Wilhelm Friedrich 91, 115, 160

Index **185**

Heidegger, Martin 109
Henry, P. 117, 118, 124
human emotions 4, 6
human knowledge, objectivism 80
Hume, David 91, 115
Hunter, A. 39
Husserl, Edmund 36

Igbo, of West Africa 21, 40, 44, 86–7, 89, 163–7, 169
Ike, Obiora 40
Ikuenobe, Polycarp 10, 99
immaterial world: Cartesian conception of 80; Descartes conception of 80; of gods and ancestors 27; human beings' relationships with 95; knowledge, role of 102; mode of acquiring knowledge about 20; Plato conception of 80
Irikheife, Paul 10–11
Ivory Tower 174

Johansson, J. 139
Johnson, M. 80
Judeo-Christians traditions 95
justification: justification, belief, and truth (JTB) 131; for knowledge claims 132

Kantian revolution 85
Kantian transcendentalism 85
Kant, Immanuel 36–7, 83, 85, 91, 109
Kaphagawani, Didier 2, 9, 44, 45, 133, 162, 163
Kaplan, Mark 37, 38
knowledge: acquisition of 141; for Africa 92; African and Western conceptions of 7; African cultural practices 11; African epistemology and 19n2, 20, 29; African theories of 50; alien cultures 175; attitudes of Africans 19; claims 2, 4, 9, 42, 51–2, 56, 122–3, 126, 131–3, 137, 140–1, 163, 172, 175, 176; conceptions of 174; epistemological dislocation 175; family of 180; global discourse of 10, 11; 'grounding' 139; nodes and mode of 176; objectivism 80; ontologised 19–31; Plato's analysis of 36; 'real' knowledge claims 123; Senghor's analysis of 6; of spiritual existence 95; transcultural 172; *see also* knowledge acquisition in Afro-Caribbean
knowledge acquisition in Afro-Caribbean: Afro-Caribbean philosophy 116–22; history 116–22; Ogoko 86; overview of 115–16; perspectival epistemology

125–8; socio-cultural epistemology 122–5
Knowledge, Belief and Witchcraft: *Analytic Experiment in African Philosophy* (Hallen and Sodipo) 133
'knowledge first' project 37
knowledge object, in African spaces: 'being,' in African spaces 86–8; nature of object 80–1; overview of 79; philosophy 82–6
knowledge/truth, in African epistemology: African communitarian epistemology (ACE) 35; communitarian epistemology 38–45; knowledge derivation 37–8; theorising 36–7
kpele rite 23
Kripke, Saul 72–3
Kuhn, Thomas 38

Lakoff, G. 80
Lauer, Helen 10
Levy-Bruhl, L. 115
linguistic community 76
literature, African epistemology 19
Lockean/ Parfitian appeal 72
Lutz, David 40

Määttänen, P. 80–1
MacIntyre, Alasdair 97
male pregnancy 168
Malherbe, Jeanette 2, 162–3
Malherbe, J. G. 2, 133, 162–3
Marley, Bob 117, 122
Martinez, Mario E. 51
Marx, Karl 115
Masolo, D. A. 115, 119
Mbira dzavadzimu's space 23
Mbiti, John 39, 67, 94, 98, 139
Melina, Livio 169
memory, collective relational of 53
Menkiti, I. A. 39–40, 96–8, 100, 101
Metaphysics 43
moderate communitarianism (MC) 39, 57, 100
Molefe, Motsamai 57
Mondin, Battista 160
Mpofu, Elias 70

Nagel, Thomas 72
Negritude project 5–6
neo-Kantians 83
Nietzsche, F. 55, 116, 126
Niger-Congo language 107
Nixon, Richard 65
Njoku, C. A. 4, 176

Nkulu-N'Sengha, M. 3–4
non-African traditions 92, 96–7
non-artefactual objects 69, 74
non-European cultures 175
non-human being 87, 92, 102–3
Ntu (Kagame) 87

Obama, Barack 65
Oduwole, Ebunoluwa 167
Ogungbure, Adebayo O. 4
Okere, T. 176
Olu-Owolabi, K. 8, 9
ontological foundation, of African knowledge: African communitarian knowledge 91–3; communitarian ontology 97–102; individual 100–2; metaphysical questions 93–5; spiritual (immaterial) existence 95–7
ontologised knowledge 20n3, 28, 30; African belief system(s) 20; African epistemology 28–30; preliminary considerations 20–4; universe-of-harmony belief 24–8
Ontologised knowledge 20, 20n3, 28–30, 31n1
onto-normative monism, of Zera Yaqob 148; *äḥättism* 148–9; ambivalence/love/ superiorism 154–6; autobiography 146; cognitive dissonance 153–4; existential exhaustion 146–8; Gregorian calendar 145; *ḥasäwäism* 149–50; häteta, inquiry 151–2; human nature 150–1; Western philosophy 145; the will 152–3
Onuoha, C. 163, 166–7
Onwuategwu, I. N. 164
Onyewuenyi, I. 94
Orangun, Adegboyega 44
Osborn, James 85
ought-to-be-reality 155

personalism, idea of 159, 160–2
personalistic tradition 161
personhood: African 162–4; discourse of 164; dualistic conception of 164; epistemology of 159, 162–9; idea of personalism 160–2; Igbo perception 165; overview of 159–60; Western notion of 166; Western perspectival understanding 57
Petrini, Carlo 161
Philosophy and an African Culture 9
Poli, Roberto 93
Popper, Karl R. 111
predecessors 150, 153
Putnam, Hilary 73–4, 76

qua money 75
Quine, Orman 25–6, 38

racial therapy 178
Rastafarianism 121, 122
reality, African ontological notion of 94
relational account, of the self 69–72; contemporary version 70; historical version of 70–1; origination version of 70
revivalism 121
Rorty, Richard 38, 69, 74, 80
Roy, P. K. 9
Russell, Bertrand 43, 109

Sahara Desert 67; African cultures of 29; pre-colonial life-forms of 21
Sandel, Michael 97
Sanders, Peirce 80–1
self-conscious 91, 155, 166
self-recognition, Afro-communitarianism 57
self, relational account of 69–72
self-understanding 155, 172–5, 177, 179–80
Senghor, Léopold 5–9, 41, 98
sex change 168
Shona cosmology 23
Shutte, Augustine 54
Silverman, G. 48
smartphone applications 51
social epistemology 29–30, 37–8, 42
social interactions 29, 38, 41
social reality 109
societal practices 41
socio-cultural milieu 123
Sodipo, J. O. 133
Spiritual Baptists 121
spiritual beings 92–3, 95, 97, 102–3, 162
spiritual knowledge, ontological argument 96
spiritual realm 95–6
Stanford Encyclopedia of Philosophy 65
sub-Saharan African communities 93
Sumner, C. 149, 151, 152, 154
Supreme Deity 140
Svensson, F. 139

Taylor, Charles 97
telepathy 4
Tempels, Placide 86–7, 94, 96, 163
Thomas, J. 19
Tractatus Logico-Philosophicus (1921) 111
transcultural knowledge 172
Trans-Sahara (Arabic) Slave Trade 117
truth, in African/Esan philosophy: epistemic ideal 108–9; Esan philosophy 111–12;

human person, in Esan metaphysics 110–11; moral ideal 109–10; overview of 107–8
truth, in Akan 137

Ubuntu 50, 53, 54, 57

Vest, J. L. 175
virtue ethics, in African culture: epistemic tyranny 137–9; justification phenomenon 131, 139–40; objections 137; virtuous person 135–7; Yorùbá *Weltanschauung* 132–5
Vital Force 22, 86, 87, 89, 110, 164

Walzer, Michael 97
water, relational account of 73–4

Westermann, Diederich 115
Western cognitive sciences 51
Western culture, fundamental teaching of 97
Western-oriented epistemology 12
Western society society 160
Williamson, Timothy 37, 38
Williams, Thomas D. 161, 162
Wiredu, Kwasi 8, 9
womb, commercialization of 168
Wright, Bankole Oluwaseun 135

Yaqob, Zera 145–8, 152, 154, 155
Yoruba belief system 5, 44, 121, 141, 167

Zezuru, progeny-progenitor relationship 23

Taylor & Francis eBooks

www.taylorfrancis.com

A single destination for eBooks from Taylor & Francis with increased functionality and an improved user experience to meet the needs of our customers.

90,000+ eBooks of award-winning academic content in Humanities, Social Science, Science, Technology, Engineering, and Medical written by a global network of editors and authors.

TAYLOR & FRANCIS EBOOKS OFFERS:

- A streamlined experience for our library customers
- A single point of discovery for all of our eBook content
- Improved search and discovery of content at both book and chapter level

REQUEST A FREE TRIAL
support@taylorfrancis.com